VERMONT CO
MONTPELIER, VE   ONT

W9-CDS-835

WITHDRAWN

WITHDRAWN

**American Thought in Transition:
The Impact of Evolutionary Naturalism,
1865-1900**

The Rand McNally Series on the History of American Thought and Culture

American Thought in Transition: The Impact of Evolutionary Naturalism, 1865-1900

Paul F. Boller, Jr.
University of Massachusetts, Boston

Rand McNally & Company · Chicago

The Rand McNally Series on The History of American Thought and Culture

David D. Van Tassel, Series Editor

EUROPEAN ORIGINS OF AMERICAN THOUGHT. Ed. David D. Van Tassel and Robert W. McAhren

AMERICAN THOUGHT IN TRANSITION: THE IMPACT OF EVOLUTIONARY NATURALISM, 1865–1900. Paul F. Boller, Jr.

THE GREAT AWAKENING AND THE REVOLUTION. Cedric Cowing

THE PROGRESSIVE MIND, 1890–1917. David Noble

THE NERVOUS GENERATION: AMERICAN THOUGHT, 1917–1930. Roderick Nash

NATIONALISM IN AMERICAN THOUGHT, 1930–1945. Charles C. Alexander

Second Printing, 1970

Copyright © 1969 by Rand McNally & Company
All Rights Reserved
Printed in U.S.A. by Rand McNally & Company
Library of Congress Catalog Card Number 69:17205

917.3
B691 a

For Marilee, Mike, and Paul

26444

Editor's Preface

Lincoln's assassination dampened but failed to extinguish America's elation over the ending of the Civil War and gave no pause to those oracles who predicted with more optimism than accuracy a period of tranquillity, orderly reunion, reconstruction, and a return to the regularity of normal life spiced with a modicum of predictable progress. The murder of the President, however, was more than the closing act of a great schismatic war; it was the opening event of the most violent, bloody, and turbulent peacetime era in the history of the country. Reunion and reconstruction there were; and if change be progress, then there was plenty of that too, though scarcely of the predictable variety. Tranquillity, however, entirely eluded the America of the Gilded Age.

The decades between the end of the Civil War and the closing of the Spanish-American War saw the building of all the transcontinental rail lines and the completion of the country's railroad network. Telegraph lines crisscrossed the continent, controlled mainly by one giant corporation, Western Union. Other huge corporations, known generically as trusts, grew along with the development of the national transportation and communications system and constituted the organizational structure of a burgeoning national industrial complex, which in turn attracted ever increasing numbers of Europe's poor to

Columbia's shores. America's restless, growing population spilled into the West and the Great Plains, subduing the remaining Indian tribes and closing the era of the frontier. Other Americans, drawn by the wealth and glitter of the cities, added their mite to the urban explosion. The rapid fluctuations in the economy, from boom to bust, helped to focus mounting political and social discontent, manifested by such outbursts of violence as accompanied the general railroad strike of 1877, the Haymarket Riot of 1886, and the Homestead and Pullman strikes of the 1890's. Political insurgency took shape in the Grange, Alliance, and Populist movements, as well as the developing socialist movement. In short, it is in the Gilded Age that America makes the transition from a rural-agrarian federation to an industrial, urban nation-state, from a pastoral adjunct of the British Empire to an independent power in the world.

Underlying many of these changes, as important as most of them, and in its fashion just as violent, was the revolution in the ideas and outlook of Americans. This revolution involved the secularization of society, reflected in part by the growth of the great universities and graduate schools—secular cathedrals of an emerging faith in science. As Mr. Boller points out, it also involved a transition from a static, formalistic world view to a dynamic vision that conceived of everything in a perpetual process of evolution—a transition, in fact, from the security of an orderly and stable universe to one in constant flux and process of creation. Mr. Boller ably organizes and relates the events in American thought and culture around the concept of evolutionary naturalism. Although the idea of evolution had been around for a long time in many fields, including history, geology, and even biology, it was the synthesis of Charles Darwin in his *Origin of Species* that did most to hasten the revolution in thinking. Mr. Boller traces in depth the struggle that took place among American scientists before Darwin's theories were fully accepted by the scientific community. Then he follows the controversy as it erupted in the field of religion, dividing churches, ministers, and congregations as nothing since the slavery controversy. Nor were the problems simplified for that part of the American intellectual community that accepted Darwinism and the ideas of Herbert Spencer, for even more difficult dilemmas appeared as the ideas seemed to conflict with valued American ideals. Concepts of naturalism implied determinism, which negated the traditional American faith in individual free will. Mr. Boller ably analyzes the thought and examines the means by which leading thinkers in different fields adapted the new naturalism to their special needs and to American values. Each one differed in the process, for evolutionary naturalism was neutral, amoral, and open to many interpretations. William James or Oliver Wendell Holmes, Jr., equipped with a widely shared faith in inevitable moral progress, could look with hope toward an open universe, which to an aging Mark Twain yielded no hope for the "Future of Man." On the other hand, the naturalism of Henry and Brooks Adams led them to view evolution as a progressive decline in human and social energy, rather than as an upward development toward a better society.

This book is an intensive study of ideas; yet Mr. Boller gives to the history of this transition in thought in the Gilded Age every bit of the narrative movement, the zest, action, and human agony expected of the best social or political histories. In so doing, *American Thought in Transition* fulfills a major objective of this series, which is to help the general student synthesize the intellectual and cultural developments of a period and summarize meaningful segments of an expanding knowledge of this vast area of American experience.

The History of American Thought aims to fill the need for synthesis through a series of short, readable volumes covering broad chronological periods. No such synthesis now exists in spite of the fact that the history of American thought and culture, although a relatively new area for scholarly inquiry, has had an enormous and rapid growth. The written histories are legion, and every college and university has a course or two in social, intellectual, or cultural history. An increasing number have a plethora of courses embraced by programs of American studies or "American civilization." Despite this flourishing condition, there are no new general surveys that cover the whole history, and only a few such works even by pioneers in the field. The cause lies in the fact that a particularly strong variety of viral specialization afflicted intellectual history before it ever established any boundaries as a field. Consequently, it developed neither orthodox approach, traditional organization, nor core of accepted subject matter "to be covered." The "generalists" opened up the field, but now only specialists are cultivating isolated segments of it. Thus, most of the recent work even of a survey nature has been either topical, as defined by social institutions, or conceptual, limited by period, subject, or sources. These approaches have proved very effective means for scholars to organize and extract meaning from such a vast range of human endeavor. But the general student is in need of a synthesis, a means of tying together developments in religion, education, philosophy, or science, and relating significant portions of the growing literature in the field. *The History of American Thought* is designed to help bridge the gap between topical surveys and monographic studies by giving some conceptual framework to significant periods and thus drawing together the burgeoning knowledge of this vast area of the American past. Each volume embraces a chronological period that is characterized by a dominant theme, coherent pattern of ideas, or major intellectual movement. The authors are experts in their fields, but they do not represent any one "school" of intellectual history. Each author has chosen his own approach or emphasis, but the general aim is to present ideas in depth and to point out the significant relationships between developments in all areas of intellectual and cultural expression within the period.

Mr. Boller, through close analysis of the secondary and primary literature of the period and the thought of representative intellectuals, has managed to sum up and add to the recent scholarly literature about the thought of the period. This is a volume that should quickly win a place as a standard work in the field.

David D. Van Tassel

Foreword

This is a book about American ideas in the Gilded Age, that is, in the period roughly from the end of the Civil War to the end of the Spanish-American War. In their satirical novel, *The Gilded Age* (1873), from which the late nineteenth century in the United States takes its name, Mark Twain and Charles Dudley Warner confined their descriptive title to the 1860's and 1870's, but they recognized that the repercussions of the events of those years were to be long continuing. "The eight years in America from 1860 to 1868," they declared,

> uprooted institutions that were centuries old, changed the politics of a people, transformed the social life of half the country, and wrought so profoundly upon the entire national character that the influence cannot be measured short of two or three generations.

The transformation of American ideas was also profound and it continues to affect our thinking today.

The intellectual transformation went far deeper than a simple response to economic development, though industrialization and urbanization inevitably wrought great changes in American thinking. At a deeper level, however, what was involved, essentially, was a decline in the static, formalistic way of thinking about things and the rise of what John Fiske called "the dynamical conception of a world in a perpetual process of evolution from one state into another." Charles Darwin's *Origin of Species* played a major role in touching off the revolution in thought, and revealed religion was the first to feel the impact of the evolutionary naturalism underpinning Darwin's book. But Darwin's rejection of the notion of fixed species designed by God was only the first step in the challenge to ancient certainties. The notion of fixed forms and supernatural design was gradually undermined in science as a whole and in philosophy (William James), as well as in religion; and also in law (Oliver Wendell Holmes), social analysis (William Graham Sumner), economics (Thorstein Veblen), and other fields of thought. The revolt against formalism was far from complete; natural-law concepts continued to be important in the Gilded Age, and they have indeed persisted far into the twentieth century. But the groundwork was laid in the Gilded Age for a dynamic view of the universe (and of the categories designed by man for comprehending it), as well as for the anxiety (Henry Adams) and the sense of release (James) that the loss of old certainties entails.

"All subject matter," according to Thomas Mann, "is boring if no ideas shine through it." But ideas are also boring if not grounded at some point in experience. Both the "enormous emptiness" of abstract propositions (to use James's phrase) and the enormous congestion of unrelated facts are wearisome; facts must be meaningful and meaning factual if our interest is to be engaged. This book emphasizes ideas—scientific, religious, social, economic, legal, and philosophical —but it also tries to place them in the context of the period and to relate them to the individual thinkers with whom they are most prominently identified. But the interest is primarily in the ideas themselves rather than in the cultural, institutional, and biographical setting. I take it for granted that what men like James, Holmes, Veblen, and others had to say deserves serious attention, speaks to our own times as well as to their own, and is worth examining on its own terms.

Paul Samuelson finds it a cause for mirth among economists that the name of David Ricardo appears nowhere in the index of a well-known history of Western thought. But every writer of historical surveys faces space limitations and he must pick and choose among the many things he would like to say. Ricardo's name does appear here; and so do the names of Smith, Darwin, Malthus, and other Europeans who influenced American thought in the Gilded Age. I trust, too, that no American name important for the thought of the period has been omitted from consideration in this book. But there have been some obvious omissions: scientists whose work was of a highly mathematical nature, artistic and literary figures who belong more properly to histories of American art and literature, and philosophers who are of primary interest to professionals. There are doubtless other names missing that could have been mentioned, at least in passing; but, if the book was to breathe at all, it was necessary to avoid jumping from one name to another in quick succession. I have, to be sure, in discussing some of the ideas of the period—laissez-faire, imperialism, end-of-century "prognostics"—sometimes quoted people who are not very well known any more; but my interest has been in an exposition of the ideas themselves, not in overwhelming the reader with unfamiliar names. With men discussed at length here whose work continued into the twentieth century, I have stressed their thinking during the Gilded Age; but I have also indicated the direction of their later thought, which in any case was an elaboration of their earlier ideas. Throughout, accuracy and fairness (to the best of my ability), not novelty or idiosyncrasy of presentation, have been my main consideration in describing the thought of the period.

A Frenchman visiting the United States in the 1890's had this to say:

> The word "enough" is the loneliest, and the least often employed, word in the American vocabulary. There is not diversity of striving; all are striving for money, money, money. This makes the race fast and furious; and competition and rivalry bitter, and not always honorable. Money here is tyrant, as it is tyrant nowhere else.

Preoccupation with money was surely a major feature of the Gilded Age (and lurks behind many of its ideas); but it was by no means the whole story. Some Americans were less interested in pursuing wealth than in pondering the big questions of existence that face all men at all times. The intellectual achievements of the age were considerable; those of our own seem modest by comparison. It should, in fact, be a matter of pride for Americans to know that there were people in the Gilded Age who were able to transcend the pecuniary environment of their day and formulate broad-ranging ideas on perennial human problems that would be creditable in any age and in any country.

PAUL F. BOLLER, JR.

Contents

Chapter 1

The Scientific Reception of Darwinism

In March, 1860, a superb review of a revolutionary new book appeared in the *American Journal of Science and Arts*. The book was Charles Darwin's *Origin of Species*, which had appeared in England the previous November, and the reviewer was Asa Gray, professor of natural history and director of the herbarium at Harvard University. Gray's review essay was thorough, informed, perceptive, lucid, sympathetic, thoughtful, suggestive, and witty; and Darwin regarded it as one of the ablest notices that his book received. In it the Harvard botanist predicted a "spirited conflict among opinions" about the book similar to the "conflict in nature among races in the struggle for life which Mr. Darwin describes." He was quite right; the controversy over Darwin's views was spirited indeed.

The Darwinian World View

In the *Origin of Species,* Darwin rejected the notion, commonly held when his book appeared, that species of plants and animals (including man) originated in a special act of creation which fixed their forms for all time. Evolutionary change, he insisted, not immutability, is the law of life; living organisms are the products of gradual, minute

1

changes taking place over vast periods of time, and their origins can be traced back to ancient species that are quite different in form from those prevailing in modern times.

To explain how organic development took place, Darwin proposed the concept of natural selection. In formulating this concept, he found a clue in the writings of Thomas Malthus, who stated that the human population, because of its natural fecundity, tends to outrun the food supply and is kept in check only by war, pestilence, and famine. Darwin broadened Malthus' law of population to apply to all forms of life, and he came to the conclusion that because of the tendency of living organisms to multiply far beyond the means of subsistence, there is a ceaseless struggle for existence taking place in the animal and vegetable world. Some organisms, however, are better prepared for the struggle than others because they are born with chance variations that enable them to adapt more efficiently to the environment than other organisms. Those organisms possessing variations that are useful in the struggle for existence live to reproduce their kind and transmit these variations to their offspring. Those lacking the beneficial variations tend to be weeded out in the struggle for survival and hence leave no descendants. In this fashion species evolve slowly and gradually in the direction of the variations that are most useful in the struggle for life. Darwin used the term "natural selection" to describe the process by which organisms with unfavorable variations are eliminated in the struggle for life and those with favorable variations survive to hand on these variations to their descendants. In later editions of *Origin,* he also used the expression "survival of the fittest," suggested by Herbert Spencer, the English philosopher, to convey the same idea. "Fittest" in this context, of course, refers to organisms possessing the most useful adaptive variations, and it may involve color, size, and shape, as well as strength. For significant structural modifications to occur in a species, it is clear, billions of random variations for natural selection to operate on must have appeared and immense periods of time are required.

The concept of natural selection was the most original feature of Darwin's work and it was a tremendous contribution to the advance of scientific understanding. The idea of evolutionary change itself, however, was not original with Darwin. It was being discussed in European intellectual circles in the late eighteenth century. The French naturalist Buffon (George Louis Leclerc, Comte de Buffon) believed that species were changing, not fixed, and he explained organic development as a response to climatic and other changes in the physical environment. Externally caused changes in organisms, he thought, were inherited by the offspring. Jean Baptiste Lamarck, another pre-Darwinian evolutionist, also believed in the inheritance of acquired characteristics, but he had a somewhat different explanation for organic development, which he called the "law of use and disuse." According to this law, great changes in the physical environment bring about changes in the needs of living organisms; these changes in needs, in turn, produce changes in behavior by which the organism, in an effort to adjust to its environment, utilizes (and thus develops) some of its parts more than others; and the structural changes caused by the use or disuse of various organs become fixed in the adult organism and are passed on to its descendants. Lamarck's ideas were rejected by scientists during his lifetime in favor of the doctrine of species immutability. But Herbert Spencer made the Lamarckian doctrine of acquired characteristics a part of his evolutionary philosophy in the 1850's, and Darwin himself accepted Lamarckian factors—inheritance of acquired characteristics and the agency of use and disuse—along with fortuitous variations and natural selection as explanations for evolutionary development. He also proposed the concept of sexual selection—according to which the strongest or most attractive males are most successful in attracting the females and produce offspring that inherit their "sexy" characteristics—as in additional explanation for organic development. In the 1880's, however, the German zoologist August Weismann succeeded in purging Darwinism of all Lamarckian and other factors and resolved it into the doctrine of natural selection pure and simple. He succeeded in doing so by making a distinction between germ cells (which are passed along unchanged from generation to generation, unaffected by environmental influences) and somatic cells (which can be modified by the environment but are not inherited). With Weismann's discoveries, Lamarckianism went into a decline and the stage was set for modern genetics.

Darwin and Asa Gray

In his long review of *Origin of Species* in 1860, Asa Gray did not concern himself with Buffon or Lamarck. He concentrated on Darwin's main point—evolutionary development by means of natural selection—and he was disposed to accept much of what Darwin was proposing. Gray began his review by contrasting the views of his Harvard colleague Louis Agassiz on the supernatural origin and distribution of species (which Gray called "theistic to excess") with those of Darwin ("a legitimate attempt to expand the domain of natural or physical science"), and he then declared:

> Having no prepossession in favor of naturalistic theories, but struck with the eminent ability of Mr. Darwin's work, and charmed with its fairness, our humbler duty will be performed if, laying aside prejudice as much as we can, we shall succeed in giving a fair account of its methods and argument. . . .

Gray was eminently fair. With copious quotations from Darwin's work, he discussed the concepts of struggle for existence (which he accepted as undeniable), variation (the actual causes of which, he noted, were unknown), and natural selection (the applicability of which he was not yet prepared to extend to as wide a range of cases as was Darwin). While acknowledging that the new theory was "perfectly compatible with an atheistic view of the universe," he singled out Darwin's incidental references to a Creator as an indication that Darwin "implies that all was done wisely, in the largest sense designedly, and by an intelligent first cause." He also insisted that Darwin could not be charged with "the atheism of fortuity," since *Origin* assigned "real causes for harmonious and systematic results," and he concluded by stating his own "profound conviction that there is order in the universe; that order presupposes mind; design, will; and mind or will, personality."

The ideas contained in *Origin of Species* were by no means new to Gray. For some years he and Darwin had been exchanging letters on the subject of species. It was Darwin who initiated the exchange. A letter that Gray wrote to the English botanist Joseph D. Hooker in February, 1854, first fired Darwin's interest in Gray and led him to begin a correspondence that continued until Darwin's death in 1882. In this letter, which Hooker forwarded to Darwin, Gray discussed the "species-question" at some length. Gray's masterly grasp, in this letter, of the perplexities involved in trying to define species, given the assumption of their immutability, "pleased and surprised" Darwin, as he told Hooker, and in April, 1855, after consulting Gray's *Manual of the Botany of the Northern United States* (1848), he wrote to ask Gray for additional information regarding the Alpine flora of

North America. ". . . I have," he explained, "for several years been collecting facts on 'variation,' and when I find that any general remark seems to hold good amongst animals, I try to test it in plants." Then, apologizing for being so presumptuous as to make "even the most trifling suggestion to such a botanist as yourself," he went on to propose a plan of publication on the subject.

Darwin was highly gratified by Gray's response. Not only did Gray promptly supply him with the desired data; in addition, stimulated by the searching questions that Darwin continued to send him, he prepared a statistical analysis of floristic units in North America (regarded as a landmark in the history of American botany and of basic importance for the science of plant geography), the first part of which appeared in the *American Journal of Science* in September, 1856. To be *"simply* mentioned" in such an article, Darwin exclaimed, "I consider a very great honour." Declaring that Gray's conclusions were "of great importance to my notions," he added: "You cannot appreciate your own work in the generalising line—Good Heavens if I had written a paper half as good as yours, how conceited I should have been!" As his exchanges with Darwin continued, Gray began to sense that his English friend was deeply involved in a study of the species problem along entirely new lines. He told Yale geologist James Dwight Dana late in 1856 that the settlement of "a series of pretty interesting general questions" about species "is perhaps at hand."

Gray did not have to wait long to learn what Darwin was up to. On July 20, 1857, Darwin wrote, somewhat apologetically, to explain "how I view my work." Then, after stating that he had been accumulating facts bearing on the question of the origin of species for the past nineteen years, he went straight to the point: "I must tell you that I have come to the heterodox conclusion that there are no such things as independently created species—that species are only strongly defined varieties." He added ruefully: "I know that this will make you despise me." But Gray, acutely aware by this time of the inadequacies of the prevailing view of species, was by no means shocked by Darwin's heterodox conclusion. He did, indeed, emphasize the grave difficulties confronting the derivative thesis, but he discussed Darwin's ideas with such friendliness and understanding that Darwin decided to send him a detailed outline of his theory of the origin of species. "As you seem interested in the subject," Darwin wrote on September 7, 1857, "and as it is an *immense* advantage to me to write to you and to hear, ever so briefly, what you think, I will enclose . . . the briefest extract of my notion on the means by which Nature makes her species." He enclosed a summary, in six long paragraphs, of his explanation of the evolution of species by means of variation, struggle for existence, and natural selection. Thus Gray became one of three men (Hooker and Charles Lyell, the English geologist, had already seen an abstract of Darwin's theory prepared in 1844) to have advance knowledge of the Darwinian theory. Anxious not to publish until he had overcome every objection to his hypothesis, Darwin asked Gray not to mention his doctrine publicly. Gray respected his confidence, although he could not resist telling Dana a few weeks later that "you may be sure that before long there must be one more resurrection of the development theory in a new form, obviating many of the arguments against it, and presenting a more respectable and more formidable appearance than it ever has before. . . ."

But the cat was soon out of the bag. On July 4, 1858, Darwin wrote to tell Gray of his receipt of Alfred Russel Wallace's essay on species, containing views "most curiously coincident even in expressions" with his own. Lyell and Hooker, he explained, had decided to submit Wallace's paper to the Linnaean Society, together with his own abstract of 1844 and his brief explanation of natural selection for Gray, and he wished to ascertain the exact date of his letter to Gray the previous year. In this fashion, Darwin's letter to Gray in September, 1857, helped establish Darwin's priority over Wallace in conceiving the idea of natural selection. The presentation of the Darwin-Wallace papers to the Linnaean Society in July, 1858, attracted astonishingly little attention in the scientific world. Later that month Darwin began working on a fuller exposition of his views in *Origin of Species*.

Meanwhile, Gray began his gradual introduction of Darwinian concepts into scientific circles in the United States. At a meeting of the Cambridge Scientific Club in December, 1858, and before the American Academy of Arts and Sciences in Boston in January and February, 1859, he outlined a theory of the relation between the plant life of eastern North America and eastern Asia that gave unmistakable support to the evolutionary theory. And in a footnote to his paper, published in the Academy *Memoirs* in April, Gray declared that Darwin's theory was the only noteworthy attempt at a scientific solution of the "fundamental and most difficult question remaining in natural history" and that it would play "a prominent part in all future investigations into the distribution and probable origin of species. It will hardly be doubted that the tendencies and causes indicated are really operative; the question is as to the extent of their operation." In May, Gray explained Darwin's theory to the Cambridge Scientific Club in some detail, "to see how it would strike a dozen people of varied minds and habits of thought." His chief target at all of these meetings was Louis Agassiz, distinguished Harvard scientist, whose philosophical idealism he regarded as a threat to the empirical tradition in natural science. ("Gray," said Agassiz after the May meeting, "we must stop all this.") As a devout Christian, however, Gray was already concerned, he confessed to Hooker, about the implications of natural selection for religious philosophy.

On November 24, *Origin of Species* was published in England. It contained four references to Gray's work: on American trees, on naturalized plants in the United States, on the rarity of intermediate forms, and on Alpine plants. Gray read the copy he received from Darwin between Christmas and New Year's. Again he was troubled by the bearing of Darwin's ideas on religion. Nevertheless, he wrote Hooker that the book "is done in a masterly manner. . . . It is crammed full of most interesting matter, well expressed, close, cogent; and taken as a system makes out a better case that I had supposed possible."

"I am free to say," he told Darwin, "that I never learnt so much from one book as I have from yours." Since Agassiz was beginning to denounce it publicly as atheistic, Gray determined that Darwin "shall have fair play" in the United States. To that end, he prepared his long essay on *Origin* for the *Journal of Science* and made arrangements for an American edition of the book containing additions and corrections sent him by Darwin.

Darwin was delighted by Gray's review. Though Gray assured him that what he had written did not "exhibit anything like the full force of the impression the book has made on me," Darwin declared: "Your Review seems to me *admirable;* by far the best which I have read." But this was only the beginning. As the battle over *Origin of Species* mounted in fury in England and in the United States (with Agassiz leading the American opposition), Gray quickly became Darwin's main sponsor in the United States. He resumed his debates with Agassiz before the Cambridge Scientific Club and the American Academy. He prepared for the July, August, and October issues of the *Atlantic Monthly* articles explaining Darwin's ideas to the general public which Darwin considered so well done that he arranged to have them reprinted as a pamphlet and circulated widely in England. In September he did another article on *Origin* for the *Journal of Science*. Darwin could scarcely find words of praise fine enough for Gray's efforts on his behalf. "How splendidly," he cried, "Asa Gray is fighting the battle." He "fights like a hero in defence," he wrote Wallace. He "goes on fighting like a Trojan," he told Thomas Huxley; "he is thorough master of the subject." To Lyell he declared that Gray was "one of the best reasoners and writers I ever read." "I declare," he wrote Gray, "that you know my books as well as I do myself; and bring to the question new lines of illustration and argument in a manner which excites my astonishment and almost my envy!"

> ... you never touch the subject without making it clearer. I look at it as even more extraordinary that you never say a word or use an epithet which does not express fully my meaning. Now Lyell, Hooker, and others, who perfectly understand the book, yet sometimes use expressions to which I demur. . . .

But already Darwin was beginning to draw apart from Gray over the matter of design in nature. From the very beginning, Gray's objective as an exponent of Darwinism had been twofold: (1) to uphold freedom of scientific inquiry in the United States by securing a fair and unbiased hearing for Darwin's views, and (2) to convince both scientific materialists and religious believers that natural selection was not incompatible with theism. That he succeeded in his first purpose—his labors for Darwin in the United States have been justly compared to those of Huxley (Darwin's "bulldog") in England—is not open to question. He was, however, considerably less successful in his second endeavor, to reconcile Darwinism with design.

Gray touched only briefly on the question of design in his first review of *Origin*. Thereafter, however, he came gradually to place major emphasis on this problem in his publications relating to Darwinism. When he prepared a collection of his various papers on evolution for publication in 1876 (*Darwiniana*), he added a long chapter on "Evolutionary Teleology." Four years later he published a book entitled *Natural Science and Religion*, based on lectures presented to students at the Yale Divinity School, which was devoted almost exclusively to this problem. Meanwhile, the opinions that he and Darwin were exchanging on the subject, though friendly, became increasingly irreconcilable.

As a young man Gray had been thoroughly grounded in eighteenth-century rationalism and empiricism, and he was, for a time, even something of a skeptic. In 1835, however, he experienced a moderate conversion ("the tone of my mind and the whole tendency of my education and habits of thinking," he said, "do not incline me to credulity, or subject me to the influence of fanaticism"), joined the Presbyterian church, and was a faithful church member for the rest of his life. In his introduction to *Darwiniana* he described himself as "scientifically, and in his own fashion, a Darwinian, philosophically a convinced theist, and religiously an acceptor of the 'creed commonly called the Nicene,' as the exponent of the Christian faith." But he was in no sense a "fundamentalist." He was severely critical of those who, like Agassiz, "are prompt to invoke the supernatural to cover our ignorance of natural causes." The Bible, he declared, was

not handed down to us for our instruction in scientific knowledge, and . . . it is our duty to ground our scientific beliefs upon observation and inference, unmixed with considerations of a different order . . . Its fundamental note is, the declaration of one God, maker of heaven and earth, and of all things, visible and invisible, a declaration which, if physical science is unable to establish, it is equally unable to overthrow.

But Gray did, in fact, labor to establish a foundation for theism in the principles of evolutionary science. His method was to equate the operation of natural selection with teleology, thus substituting, in effect, what might be called supernatural selection for Darwin's principle. "In Darwinism," he declared, "usefulness and purpose come to the front again as working principles of the first order; upon them, indeed, the whole system rests." Natural selection, however, accounts for usefulness and purpose in the structure of plants and animals simply as the mechanical result of the survival of undesigned but advantageous variations in the struggle of organisms to live and reproduce. It became necessary, therefore, for Gray to insist that variations (whose causes were, at the time, as he pointed out, "utterly unknown and mysterious") had been "led along certain beneficial lines." But, as Darwin pointed out with dismay,

The view that each variation has been providentially arranged seems to me to make Natural Selection entirely superfluous, and indeed takes the whole case of the appearance of new species out of the range of science. . . . It seems to me that variations in the domestic and wild conditions are due to unknown causes, and are without purpose, and in so far accidental; and that they become purposeful only when they are selected by man for his pleasure, or by what we call Natural Selection in the struggle for life, and under changing conditions.

Gray recognized the force of Darwin's objection. Adaptations in nature, he conceded, "appear as outcome rather than as motive, as final results rather than final causes." Nevertheless, he insisted: "We infer design from certain arrangements and results; and we have no other way of ascertaining it." But teleology has to do with purposeful, not accidental, design, and Gray came more and more to rest his case on faith in an orderly system of nature as a whole, rather than on evidence of design in the details of the natural world. "To us," he declared, "a fortuitous Cosmos is simply inconceivable. The alternative is a designed Cosmos."

Difficult as it may be to conceive and impossible to demonstrate design in a whole of which the series of parts appear to be contingent, the alternative may be yet more difficult and less satisfactory. If all Nature is a piece—as modern physical philosophy insists—then it seems clear that design must in some way, and in some sense pervade the system, or be wholly absent from it. Of the alternatives, the predication of design—special, general, or universal, as the case may be—is most natural to the mind.

Faith "in an *order,* which is the basis of science," he concluded, "will not—as it cannot reasonably—be dissevered from faith in an *Ordainer,* which is the basis of religion."

Darwin freely confessed that he was in an "utterly hopeless muddle" over the problem. He had difficulty, he told Gray, in reconciling misery in the world with a beneficent and omnipotent God. On the other hand, he could not bring himself to regard "this wonderful universe, and especially the nature of man," as simply the result of blind chance or brute force. "I am inclined," he wrote,

to look at everything as resulting from designed laws, with the details, whether good or bad, left to the working out of what we may call chance. Not that this notion *at all* satisfies me. I feel most deeply that the whole subject is too profound for the human intellect. A dog might as well speculate on the mind of Newton. Let each man hope and believe what he can. Certainly I agree with you that my views are not at all necessarily atheistical. The lightning kills a man, whether a good or bad one, owing to the excessively complex action of natural laws. A child (who may turn out to be an idiot) is born by the action of even more complex laws, and I can see no reason why a man, or other animal, may not have been expressly designed by an omniscient Creator, who foresaw every future event and consequence. But the more I think the more bewildered I become.

But Gray remained undisturbed by the problem of evil. Christianity, he emphasized, was fully aware of the mixture of good and evil in the world to which Darwin called attention. The Bible, he exclaimed on one occasion, did not portray an ideal world or an "elysium where imperfection and distress were never heard of!" In the end, however, Darwin and Gray came to a parting of ways. Darwin eventually adopted an undogmatic agnosticism (references to a Creator were omitted from later editions of *Origin*) as to the ultimate origins and purposes of creation, while Gray continued to see meaning and purpose, rather than chance and contingency, in the development of life in the universe.

Gray continued to give favorable notices to Darwin's later work, but he had nothing to say publicly about *The Descent of Man* (1871), in which Darwin extended his evolutionary framework to man, because he regarded the book as outside his own field of competency. Referring to *Descent*, Darwin wrote him teasingly: "I shall probably receive a few stabs from your polished stiletto of a pen," and Gray responded: "Almost thou persuadest me to have been 'a hairy quadruped, of arboreal habits, furnished with a tail and pointed ears' &c." But in his last book, *Natural Science and Religion* (1880), in which he committed himself to Darwinism more fully than ever before, Gray finally accepted man's place in the Darwinian scheme of things. "We are sharers," he declared, "not only of animal but of vegetable life, sharers with the higher brute animals in common instincts and feelings and affections." But to the very end he continued to insist that "natural variation, the struggle for life, and natural selection" were "only the order or mode in which [the] Creator, in his own perfect wisdom, sees fit to act."

Scientific Opposition to Darwinism

In essence, it is clear, Darwinism involved two major ideas: the idea of evolutionary change and the idea of natural selection. It was possible to accept the first without the second, but one could not then be regarded as a Darwinist. Darwinism itself not only meant evolutionary change; it meant evolutionary change without plan or purpose. The principle of natural selection, despite Gray's best efforts, removed all teleological elements from organic development. For the strict Darwinist, evolutionary development was a purely mechanical process in which chance (the accidental conjuncture of individual variations and certain environmental conditions) played the crucial role. In this form, evolution was hardly acceptable to most Americans, not even scientists. The number of Americans who could be considered Darwinists, pure and simple, was not large during the Gilded Age. Most American scientists—like most American laymen who familiarized themselves with the new evolutionary science— accommodated themselves to the new view of life either by minimizing the role of natural selection in evolution or by insisting, with Gray, that it was in some fashion compatible with design.

A few scientists would have nothing to do with either evolution or natural selection. The Reverend Edward Hitchcock, Massachusetts geologist, president of Amherst College, and one of the earliest students of glacial theory in the United States, had published a book in 1852 reconciling geology with the Scriptures, and he saw no reason to modify his outlook. He remained a strict creationist and charged that the doctrine of evolution rendered belief in God unnecessary, destroyed the idea of immortality, and led "inevitably to the grossest materialism." Timothy A. Conrad, Quaker conchologist and paleontologist, also bitterly opposed evolution, insisted on "the permanence of certain forms of life from the beginning," and predicted that Darwin's "wild" speculations would soon be forgotten. F. A. P. Barnard, former president of the American Association for the Advancement of Science, insisted, in his inaugural address as president of Columbia College in 1864, that the "strength of the scientific world" was enlisted against the "doctrine of progressive development." "Though repeatedly revived," he added, "it has been just as often trodden out of life. And so it must be with all mere hypothesis." Matthew F. Maury, naval officer and oceanographer, firmly rejected Darwinism as being irreconcilable with the Bible:

The Bible, they say, was not written for scientific purposes and is therefore no authority in matters of science. I beg pardon. The Bible is authority for everything it touches. The agents concerned in the physical economy of our planets are ministers of Him who made it and the Bible.

The best known foe of Darwinism, of course, was the Swiss-born Louis Agassiz, professor of natural history at Harvard, whose work in ichthyology, paleontology, and glacial geology had earned him a high reputation among scientists everywhere, including Darwin himself. Agassiz was no Biblical literalist like Maury; he had, in fact, little interest in organized religion. His opposition to Darwin rested largely on an idealistic philosophy of nature which he had formulated as a young man in Europe. For Agassiz, every specific form of plant and animal represented "a thought of God" at the moment of creation; and structural affinities between living organisms were "associations of ideas in the Divine Mind," not evidences of community of descent. "The study of nature," he said, "is an intercourse with the highest mind." Within a species, Agassiz acknowledged, individuals change and vary; but species themselves remain fixed and unchanging and bear no organic relationship to one another. From time to time (as, for instance, during the glacial period), according to Agassiz, the Creator annihilated old species and created new ones. To those who objected to the notion of a series of special creations, he exclaimed: "Have those who object to repeated acts of creation ever considered that no progress can be made without repeated acts of thinking?" As for man, the "resources of the Deity," he said, "cannot be so meagre, that in order to create a human being endowed with reason, he must change a monkey into a man." Agassiz' exhibits in the Harvard Museum of Comparative Zoology were intended to reflect the permanence of species; the "great object of our museums," he wrote in 1868, "should be to exhibit the whole animal kingdom as a manifestation of the Supreme Intellect." Darwin's *Origin* he regarded as "mischievous in its tendency" (next to one passage in the book he wrote, "This is monstrous!"), and in lectures, popular articles, and books, he waged a militant campaign against any form of Darwinism and on behalf of his own version of special creationism. In the last article he wrote on the subject, shortly before his death in December, 1873, he did concede that Darwin "brought to the subject a vast amount of well-arranged information, a convincing cogency of argument, and a captivating charm of presentation," but to the very end he insisted that "there is no evidence of a direct descent of later from earlier species in the geological succession of animals."

Scientific Accommodation to Darwinism

Agassiz' Harvard colleague Jeffries Wyman, the anatomist and ethnologist, thought the "immediate creation of each species" was preposterous and he regretted that Agassiz used his immense learning and prestige to combat Darwin:

> He was just the man who ought to have taken up the evolution theory and worked it into good shape, which his knowledge of embryology and palaeontology would have enabled him to do. He has lost a golden opportunity, but there is no use in talking of that.

For his own part, Wyman (under whom young William James studied comparative anatomy) defended Darwin's ideas in lectures and in the classroom; though devoutly religious, he believed, as his friend Gray did, that Darwinism could be reconciled with religion. Long before Gray, however, he came to apply evolution to man and to insist that man "must have gone through a period when he was passing out of the animal into the human state, when he was not yet provided with tools of any sort, and when he lived simply the life of a brute."

More common among American scientists than Agassiz' implacable hostility and Gray's and Wyman's receptivity to Darwinism from the very beginning was a gradual accommodation to some limited form of evolutionism. Arnold Guyot, the Princeton geographer, who, like Agassiz, looked upon nature as a manifestation of God and natural laws as essentially divine, at first clung tenaciously to his belief in the fixity of species; in time, however, he came to accept, with reservations, the idea of evolution through natural causes, though he excepted man and some of the animals from the process. James Dwight Dana, Yale geologist who led the way in transforming American geology from a collection of isolated facts into a historical science, was similarly slow to accept the new view of species. His somewhat metaphysical doctrine that "a species corresponds to a specific amount or condition of concentered force defined in the act or law of creation," as well as his profound Christian faith, predisposed him against Darwin's dynamic views. He did not get around to reading *Origin* until 1863 and he then told Darwin that in his own field of geology there were still not enough facts to convince him that life had evolved through a method of derivation from species to species. "Do not suppose," Darwin responded, "that I think that, with your strong convictions and immense knowledge, you could have been converted. The utmost that I could have hoped would have been that you might have been here or there staggered." Dana refused to be staggered at first. In the second edition of *Manual of Geology* (1871), he insisted that geology "has brought to light no facts sustaining a theory that derives species from others." In 1874, however, he conceded that the "evolution of the system of life went forward through the derivation of species from species," though he insisted there had been "abrupt transitions between species" and that for man "there was required . . . the special act of a Being above nature." Toward the end of his life he told a clergyman: "While admitting the derivation of man from an inferior species, I believe that there was a Divine creative act at the origin of men; that the event was as truly a creation as if it had been from earth or inorganic matter to man." Gray once wrote Dana that he wondered "if you quite get hold just right of Darwinian natural selection." Gray's doubts were probably justified; Dana seems never to have grasped Darwin's basic point fully. Still, the Yale geologist, a strict creationist in the beginning, had come farther along the evolutionary path by the end of his life than Darwin had ever thought possible. "To change," Dana once wrote, "is always seeming fickleness." Then he added: "But not to change with the advance of science is worse; it is persistence in error."

Joseph Le Conte, Georgia-born geologist teaching at the University of California, was another gradual convert. Le Conte had studied under Agassiz, and he confessed that as late as 1872 he was still a reluctant evolutionist. Within a few years he had become "an evolutionist, thorough and enthusiastic," but it is doubtful whether he ever entirely freed himself from Agassiz' influence. Though he came to believe that the "law of derivation of forms from previous forms was *absolutely certain*," he stressed "paroxysmal" rather than uniform changes in nature, and he thought that Lamarckian factors involving the transmission of acquired characteristics were just as important as Darwinian factors in accounting for evolutionary change. In *Evolution and Its Relation to Religious Thought* (1888), Le Conte explained adaptive modification in living organisms in four ways. The first two were Lamarckian: (1) changes in organisms resulting from the effect of the physical environment (heat and cold, dryness and moisture) and inherited by the offspring; (2) structural changes (also passed on to the offspring) in living beings brought about by the increased use or disuse of organs. The second two factors were Darwinian: (3) natural selection or survival of the fittest; and (4) sexual selection. Le Conte pointed out that Darwin, while regarding all four factors as relevant, considered the latter two, especially natural selection, the most potent. He also noted that neo-Darwinists, like August Weismann, "out-Darwin Darwin himself" in rejecting Lamarckian explanations and stressing natural selection. Le Conte did not entirely discount Weismann's distinction between germ cells and somatic cells; but he suggested that Lamarckian factors may have been operative when a species was first formed and that natural selection came into play later on when the struggle for life became intensified. In the end, however, he concluded that neither Lamarckian nor Darwinian factors were sufficient explanations for evolutionary development; such factors "may produce *varieties,* but not species," he said, and "the great factor of change and the real cause of evolution is still unknown." But of one thing Le Conte was absolutely certain: evolution, however carried out, was the expression of a divine plan. There is, he insisted,

> a God *immanent,* a God resident *in* Nature, at all times and in all places directing every event and determining every phenomenon. . . . According to this view the phenomena of Nature are naught else than the different forms of one omnipresent divine energy or will . . . [and] the law of evolution naught else than the mode of operation of the same divine energy in originating and developing the cosmos—the divine method of creation; and Science is the systematic knowledge of these divine thoughts and ways. . . .

Like Le Conte, Alexander Winchell, professor of geology at the University of Michigan, made a religious adjustment to evolution based on the immanence of God in the world. But George F. Wright, the Oberlin geologist-clergyman who was an expert in glaciation, followed the lead of Asa Gray in making his peace with evolution. The two men were friends, in fact, and Wright, who wrote extensively on the subject of religion and evolution, drew heavily on Gray's knowledge of Darwinism in preparing his material, and in turn had some influence on Henry Ward Beecher, the famous Brooklyn preacher, in the latter's thinking about evolution. Wright admitted frankly that "Pure Darwinism leaves no place for the gospel," but both he and Gray were willing to settle for something less than pure Darwinism. In *Studies in Science and Religion* (1882), dedicated to Gray, Wright insisted that belief in a supreme designer and a final cause for creation was left untouched by Darwin; natural selection, he said, was a secondary cause only and it "necessarily leaves the whole question of ultimate causation just where it was before . . ." Wright did not think that it was possible for large numbers of individual organisms within a species to vary at the same time and in the same direction by sheer chance; there must be causes, he said, for such synchronized variations, on which natural selection operates, which Darwin left unexplained. Wright's own explanation: ". . . there must be a divinity shaping the ends of organic life, let natural selection rough hew them as it will." William Keith Brooks, professor of morphology at Johns Hopkins University and a specialist in marine zoology, agreed with Wright and Gray that natural selection did not rule out the existence of a supreme designer. Though a former student of Agassiz, Brooks was an early convert to Darwin and accepted a wide application of the principle of natural selection. But he did not think evolution ruled out religion. Science, he said, tells us what takes place and how it takes place; it remains forever silent as to the primal cause or final purpose of the universe.

Edward D. Cope, famous for his studies in vertebrate paleontology, was America's leading Lamarckian. Quaker in background, though Unitarian in his outlook as an adult, Cope was brought up a special creationist, accepting the first chapter of Genesis as a literal description of creation. As a young man he read Darwin with some eagerness but decided that natural selection was not an adequate explanation for evolutionary change. In an early essay of 1871, entitled "The Method of Creation of Organic Forms," Cope pointed out that natural selection is "only restrictive, directive, conservative or destructive of something already created," and that it does not explain "the causes of the origin of the fittest," i.e., of variations. Cope revived the Lamarckian principle of the effect of use and disuse to explain variations, but he went beyond Lamarck in insisting that effort or use exerted by the living being on its own body produced variations for the environment to play on. Writing to his father in

1874, Cope declared: "There are three forms of evolution doctrines: (1) that non-vital force evolves life; (2) that internal consciousness is the source of non-vital force and life; (3) that external or supernatural force, applied from without, maintains development." The first position, he said, was that of the materialists, and the third of Protestant theists. Cope's own position was the second and he spent the rest of his life explaining what he meant by it. All organisms, he believed, were impelled by an inherent growth force (which he called "bathmism") to vary in certain definite directions which facilitated adaptation to the environment, and the resulting variations were inherited by the offspring. When Weismann produced concrete evidence in 1880 (he cut off the tails of several generations of mice and found that each generation nevertheless persisted in being born with tails) to show that acquired characteristics, modifications, or adaptations could not be inherited, Cope refused to accept Weismann's demonstrations as conclusive. By the time he published *The Origin of the Fittest* (1882), a collection of twenty-one essays that had previously appeared on the subject, Cope had become the leader of the neo-Lamarckian school in the United States, and he was supported in his views by leading paleontologists like Alpheus Hyatt and William Herle Dall, by A. S. Packard, his colleague on the *Naturalist*, and by several other scientists.

Cope never abandoned the losing cause of neo-Lamarckianism, and his final paper on the subject, presented to the American Society of Naturalists in 1896, bore the title "Inheritance of Acquired Characters." By this time he had piled hypothesis upon hypothesis and coined scores of clumsy new words—catagenesis, bathmogenesis, ergogenesis, emphytogenesis, statogenesis, mnemogenesis—in an effort to bolster his position. Evolutionary speculation was one thing; paleontology was another. If his evolutionary views received much criticism, his work as a paleontologist won high respect. In the early part of his career he devoted most of his energies to collecting and classifying fossils in the "boneyards" of the western United States. Before he became absorbed in Lamarckianism, he had discovered and described hundreds of links between ancient quadruped and modern types, especially horses, camels, dogs, and cats, and he thus contributed enormously to the advance of evolutionary science. Of a fossil that destroyed one of his theories Cope once said jokingly: "I wish you would throw that bone out of the window." But Cope never threw fossils—or theories—out of the window.

American Contributions to Evolutionary Science

Not all American scientists got involved in the conflict over evolution which followed publication of Darwin's *Origin*. There were many who stayed aloof from public controversy and, by quietly pursuing their researches in botany, geology, and paleontology, accumulated data providing indispensable evidence for the validity of Darwin's theory. Joseph Leidy, for one, declared that he was "too busy to theorize or make money." Leidy, usually regarded as the founder of vertebrate paleontology in the United States, has been called "a John the Baptist for Charles Darwin." One of the first to exploit the rich fossil beds in the West, Leidy, even before Darwin announced his views publicly, had been gathering a mass of information about the ancestral lineage of the horse, camel, rhinoceros, and other vertebrates long extinct in the United States, which pointed unmistakably to evolutionary development. With Gray, Leidy was one of the first to accept Darwin, and upon publication of *Origin* he helped get Darwin elected a member of the Academy of Natural Sciences of Philadelphia. Leidy once expressed admiration for John Fiske's reconciliation of evolution and religion in his *Cosmic Philosophy*, but he refused to engage in the evolutionary controversy himself, and confined himself to collecting as many facts in his field as possible.

Like Leidy, Othniel C. Marsh, Yale paleontologist, avoided the evolutionary controversy for the most part. But he was a firm exponent of natural selection and he made significant contributions to the advance of evolutionary science. In 1870 Marsh launched a series of expeditions to hunt for ancient fossils in the West which yielded invaluable evidence for the evolutionary theory. His discovery of birds possessing teeth and other reptilian characteristics established a genetic link between reptiles and birds which, according to Thomas Huxley, removed Darwin's theory "from the region of hypothesis to that of demonstrable fact." Of Marsh's monograph on the extinct toothed birds of North America, published in 1880, Darwin wrote to say: "Your work on these old birds, and on the many fossil animals of North America, has afforded the best support to the theory of evolution, which has appeared within the last twenty years." Equally impressive was Marsh's collection of fossil horses, which traced the evolutionary changes that had occurred during the emergence of the modern horse. Huxley, who visited the United States to lecture on evolution in 1876, spent several days in New Haven examining the collection—"the most wonderful thing I ever saw"—and as Marsh brought out box after box of fossil-horse material, he cried: "I believe you are a magician. Whatever I want, you conjure it up." For Huxley, Marsh's specimens "demonstrated the evolution of the horse beyond question, and for the first time indicated the direct line of descent of an existing animal." Marsh, known as the "Big Bone Chief" among Indians in the West, regarded his discoveries as "the stepping stones by which the evolutionist of to-day leads the doubting brother across the shallow remnant of the gulf once thought impassable." Marsh was an ardent Darwinist. "To doubt evolution today," he told the American Association for the Advancement of Science in 1877, "is to doubt science, and science is only another name for truth."

Writing in December, 1876, John Fiske, Harvard philosopher and popular historian, declared that the victory of Darwinism in the United States was thorough and complete:

> . . . though greeted at the beginning with ridicule and opprobrium, the theory of natural selection has already won a complete and overwhelming victory. One could count on one's fingers the number of eminent naturalists who still decline to adopt it, and the hesitancy of these appears to be determined in the main by theological or metaphysical, and therefore not strictly relevant objections. But it is not simply that the great body of naturalists have accepted the Darwinian theory; it has become part and parcel of their daily thoughts, an element in every investigation which cannot be got rid of. . . . The sway of natural selection in biology is hardly less complete than that of gravitation in astronomy; and thus it is probably true that no other scientific discoverer has within his own lifetime obtained so manifest a triumph as Mr. Darwin.

Fiske claimed too much. While there is no question that the concept of evolutionary change had won almost complete acceptance among American scientists by the time Fiske was writing, it was quite otherwise with the concept of natural selection. Until the end of the century, Lamarckianism was still popular with many American scientists, and natural selection itself was rarely accepted without being wedded to a teleological point of view. Pure Darwinism—that is, natural selection without plan or purpose—was unacceptable to most American scientists in the Gilded Age. It was also unthinkable for American religious thinkers. For religiously oriented Americans, scientists and laymen alike, the substitution of flux for fixity and of chance for constancy, involved in the viewpoint of evolutionary naturalism, threatened to replace design with disorder and the absolute with the absurd. And they were determined not to give teleological ground without a vigorous struggle.

Chapter 2

The Warfare of Science and Religion

Speaking at the fiftieth anniversary of his professorship at Princeton Theological Seminary in 1872, Charles Hodge, leading American Presbyterian theologian, boasted that no new ideas had originated in the seminary while he was affiliated with it. "The Bible is the word of God," he explained simply. ". . . If granted, then it follows, that what the Bible says, God says. That ends the matter." That ended evolution for Hodge, too. In his three-volume *Systematic Theology,* published the same year, Hodge insisted that Darwin's theory held that

> hundreds or thousands of millions of years ago God called a living germ, or living germs, into existence, and that since that time God has no more to do with the universe than if He did not exist. This is atheism to all intents and purposes, because it leaves the soul as entirely without God, without a Father, Helper, or Ruler, as the doctrine of Epicurus or of Comte.

In *What Is Darwinism?,* published two years later, Hodge was even blunter. By ignoring design in creation, he declared, Darwin had "dethroned God." Hodge refused to take seriously the vague references to a Creator in *Origin;* the fact was, he noted, nowhere in the book did Darwin look upon existing species of plants and animals as products of divine intelligence. For Hodge there was only one possible answer to the question "What is Darwinism?" "It is," he concluded, "Atheism."

Orthodox Resistance to Darwinism

Hodge was not the only Protestant minister who thought that Darwin's version of evolution was ungoding the universe. *The Religious Magazine and Monthly Review* thought that atheists were eagerly seizing upon Darwinism "as a no-godsend to them"; a writer in the *Southern Presbyterian Review* spoke sorrowfully of a "tormenting theophobia" animating evolutionists; and the Reverend Enoch Burr exclaimed in 1873:

Founded by atheism, claimed by atheism, supported by atheism, used exclusively in the interest of atheism, suppressing without mercy every jot of evidence for the Divine existence, and so making a positive rational faith in God wholly impossible, the Doctrine of Evolution may well be set down as not only a foe to Theism, but a foe of the most thorough-going sort.

For Dr. Henry A. Dubois, Darwinism was a "monstrous assumption." The Darwinian outlook, he wrote in the *American Church Review* in January, 1872, "having no hope, because it is without God in the world, looks upon nature as the play of blind forces,—dark, meaningless, fantastic; and upon the end of all things as a return to choas. . . ." In an article on "The New Gospel" for *Zion's Herald* on January 31, 1878, Borden P. Bowne, professor of philosophy at Boston University, spelled out the implications of Darwinism even more starkly for his readers: "Life without meaning; death without meaning; and the universe without meaning. A race tortured to no purpose, and with no hope but annihilation. The dead only blessed; the living standing like beasts at bay, and shrieking half in defiance and half in fright."

For orthodox Protestants, reared in Biblical literalism and Scriptural infallibility, Darwinism shattered the Christian cosmos. It destroyed the idea of a personal God, intervening in His creation as He saw fit, demolished the Biblical account of the origin of life, and consigned Biblical chronology (whereby James Ussher, Archbishop of Armagh in the seventeenth century, had calculated that creation began in 4004 B.C.) to the dustbin. It also ruled out the classic Christian doctrines: the fall of man, the Virgin Birth, the divinity of Christ, immortality, and the Christian scheme of redemption. At best, evolution substituted a remote First Cause for the Christian God; at worst, it was completely silent as to ultimate causes and purposes. "If this hypothesis be true," said the *American Quarterly Church Review* of Darwin's theory in July, 1865, "then is the Bible '*an unbearable fiction,*' fabricated during successive ages," and Christians have been "duped by a monstrous lie" for nearly two thousand years.

Orthodox Protestants (or fundamentalists, as they came to be called in the twentieth century) preferred to believe that Darwinism, not Christianity, was a fiction and a lie. And they resorted to ridicule and sarcasm, as well as to anger, horror, and indignation, in discussing the subject. "As near as I can tell," said the Reverend De Witt Talmage, popular Presbyterian preacher in Brooklyn, New York, "evolutionists seem to think that God at the start had not made up His mind as to exactly what He would make, and so He has been changing it all through the ages." There were numerous attempts by orthodox believers to reduce Darwinism to absurdity. "Give us time enough," wrote Dr. Daniel R. Goodwin, president of Trinity College, in the *American Theological Review* for May, 1860, ". . . and anything may be made out of anything, or made into anything: light may be made out of darkness, order out of chaos, conscience out of a cucumber, mind out of matter . . . and man out of a tadpole or a bramble bush." In an editorial in December, 1861, the conservative Unitarian *Monthly Religious Magazine* tried to laugh off a theory that turned dogs into monkeys, who in turn "rubbed off their tails, learned to speak plain," and became "rude" and "uncultivated" men. Professor Randolph S. Foster, future bishop in the Methodist Episcopal Church, drew the following contemptuous conclusions from Darwinism: "Some future pup, Newfoundland or terrier, in the infinite ages, may write the *Paradise Lost* . . . a pig is an incipient mathematician."

Some religionists simply did not understand Darwin's basic point about natural selection. The Reverend Enoch Burr thought that unguided evolution turned nature into a kind of sideshow of freaks in which "the head of one animal would be set on the body of another, the wings of a bird on the body of a quadruped." If Darwin is correct, he wrote in *Pater Mundi* (1873), then there should be "species of animals with more or less legs than they can use; or with necks too short for conveniently reaching the pasture; or with eyes in their feet instead of the head; or with stomachs fit only for grass, while the teeth are carnivorous." Another writer, discussing *Origin* for the *American Quarterly Church Review* in July, 1865, thought that natural selection took the place of divine intelligence in Darwin's scheme. Natural selection, he wrote, was "an omnipotent, beneficial, discriminating 'Power,' which accomplishes all the changes and explains the mysteries of Creation." Darwin, he continued, "invests this power with the attributes of a controlling, intelligent Creator, constantly at work." Having misrepresented Darwin in this fashion, the writer went on to express astonishment that anyone could seriously believe that "blind, accidental concatenation of physical causes, occurring in the struggle for life among animals," could result in the "production of an *intelligent* and *beneficent* power" like natural selection.

In criticizing the concept of evolution, orthodox Protestants liked to cite the views of distinguished scientists who were critical of the Darwin formulation. Louis Agassiz (despite his heretical theory of a plural origin for man) was a favorite authority, and his passing in 1873 was much lamented in orthodox circles. Charles Lyell, the great British geologist, who was slow in coming around to a full acceptance of Darwinism, was also admired for a time, and so was James Dwight Dana because of his initial objections to the theory. Anti-evolutionists were delighted when Professor J. Lawrence Smith, a chemist, attacked evolution in his presidential address before the American Association for the Advancement of Science in 1873; they were pleased, too, when President George Mercer Dawson of McGill University, a geologist, marshaled arguments from his own field against Darwin and upheld the account in Genesis of the creation of man. The orthodox also made frequent references to Sir William Thompson's new estimate of the age of the sun to show that the demands on time necessitated by Darwin's theory were inordinate; they quoted the British Catholic scientist St. George Mivart, who had reservations about natural selection; and they spoke approvingly of Alfred Wallace for having demurred at applying natural selection to man. Even Thomas Huxley, that *bête noire* of the orthodox, was gleefully quoted as having acknowledged that certain facts militated against the theory of natural selection.

Huxley expected increasing evidence in favor of Darwinism, but orthodox Protestants had no such expectation. They made much of factual gaps in Darwin's theory. Frederick Gardiner, professor at the Berkeley Divinity School in Middletown, Connecticut, insisted that "Mr. Darwin's theories are simply theories" which did not rest upon "positive evidence," and Francis Bowen, Harvard philosopher, pointed out that Darwin did "not pretend to have any *direct evidence* that a species, or even a variety, ever *did* originate by a process of natural selection. . . ." In the *Baptist Quarterly*, Heman Lincoln, professor of ecclesiastical history at Newton Theological Institution, announced that the theory of development was "supported by no facts, pertinent and well established." Elaborating, he said: "Not one decisive fact is found in the whole geologic record; no fossil relics of any species assuming new organs, or changing its internal structure,—no connecting links to prove that such changes were ever in progress." Even Thomas Hill, a Unitarian with a strong predisposition to accept the evolutionary hypothesis, thought there was strong presumptive evidence against "the possibility of an evolution passing over certain gaps,—such, for example, as from inorganic to organic, from vegetable to animal, from brute to man." Less restrained critics made persistent and scornful demands for eyewitness accounts to the fact of evolution. Scoffing at the notion that a geranium, oak, mole, and elephant had been produced by gradual changes from a common ancestor, the Reverend Thomas A. Eliot insisted, "We must witness the process; we must see one animal turn into another." The reviewer of *Origin* for the *New Englander* in May, 1861, made the same point. "But do we find any fossil records of these intermediate varieties through which our present existing races must have been developed from the primeval forms or form?" he asked. "Certainly not." Then he added scornfully: "Unfortunately, they have all perished; but if they had not perished, analogy teaches that we ought to find them, and therefore we may believe that they did exist." He went on to compare the method of the evolutionists with that of a fake artist who, asked to depict the Israelites and the Egyptians crossing the Red Sea, splashed red paint all over a wall and explained that the Israelites had crossed the sea and the Egyptians were all drowned in it.

Reactions to Darwin's later book, *The Descent of Man* (1871), among orthodox believers were, if anything, more violent than to *Origin of Species*. The *American Church Review* regarded it as shocking to think that "man should be thus born of the monkey by a natural process of stock breeding, of the same kind as that which produces the race-horse and the prize ox." Darwin, continued the *Review*, "would degrade mankind to the level of the brute, and stamp out the image of God from the soulless clay." In the *Mercersburg Review*, one writer accused Darwin of transforming man into a "magnified ascidian" and an "unfolding catarrhine ape." There were the usual demands for eyewitness accounts. For Professor William Rice, "it will be time to believe in Darwinism when we see an ape turning into a man." One preacher was reported to have pulled himself up to his full height during a sermon and cried out: "If they believe that man descended from an ape, let them take a monkey from the zoo-logical gardens, and by a process of natural selection and cultivation, make a man of him. Surely this is not unreasonable to ask!" In his Brooklyn pulpit, De Witt Talmage poured out all the scorn and contempt he could muster for Darwin's view of man. "Go away back," he said sarcastically, by way of summarizing Darwin for his congregation,

> and there you will find a vegetable stuff that might be called a mushroom. This mushroom by innate force develops a tadpole, the tadpole by innate force develops a polywog, the polywog develops a fish, the fish by natural force develops into a reptile, the reptile develops into a quadruped, the quadruped develops into a baboon, the baboon develops into a man. . . .

Evolution is *"brutalizing in its tendencies . . ."* he proclaimed. "Why, according to the idea of these evolutionists, we are only a superior kind of cattle, a sort of Alderney among other herds."

Not all of Darwin's critics used as extravagant language as Talmage. Dwight L. Moody, the popular lay evangelist (sometimes called the "original fundamentalist"), in his single recorded allusion to evolution said simply: "It is a great deal easier to believe that man was made after the image of God than to believe, as some young men and women are being taught now, that he is the offspring of a monkey." But to orthodox Protestants, Darwinism as applied to man seemed so preposterous that it was difficult for them to respond with moderation. "Some may ask," wrote John T. Duffield in the *Princeton Review* in January, 1878, "—suppose science should eventually prove that man was descended from the ape, what then becomes of the Bible and evangelical religion? This question," he continued, "may be answered by asking another. Suppose that, hereafter, it should be discovered that two and two make five, what then becomes of our mathematics?"

Since Herbert Spencer eventually became identified more prominently with evolution in the American mind during the Gilded Age than Darwin himself, many of the gibes at Darwin's doctrine were directed against Spencer himself. Adoniram J. Frost suggested that the bachelor Britisher get married, and he proposed the following for the occasion: "Do you, Herbert Spencer, take this anthropoid to be your co-ordinate, to love with your cellular tissues, until a final molecular disturbance shall resolve its organism into primeval atoms?" When Spencer, visiting the United States in 1882, was honored by a banquet at Delmonico's in New York City, De Witt Talmage made this scornful comment: "There the banqueters sat around the table in honor of Herbert Spencer, chewing beef, turkey, and roast pig, which, according to their doctrine of evolution, made them eating their own relations!"

Despite the frequency of enraged outbursts against Darwinism by men like Talmage, much of the discussion of *Descent of Man* among religious conservatives was, in fact, fair-minded and restrained in nature. Frederick Gardiner, for example, in an essay on "Darwinism" for the *Bibliotheca Sacra and Theological Eclectic* in April, 1872, explored with the utmost seriousness Darwin's theory of man and explained why he thought it totally inadequate to account for man's mental faculties and his moral sense. But there was enough of the Talmage kind of polemics against evolution in the Gilded Age to lead John William Draper, professor of chemistry at the College of the City of New York (*History of the Conflict between Religion and Science*, 1874), and Andrew D. White, president of Cornell University (*The Warfare of Science with Theology in Christendom*, 1895), to conclude that organized religion had been a foe of intellectual progress through the ages. White was struck by the number of heresy cases involving evolution and by the stifling of intellectual freedom in denominational colleges and seminaries: the dismissal of geologist Alexander Winchell from Methodist-controlled Vanderbilt for upholding evolutionary ideas; the expulsion of Orientalist Crawford H. Toy from Southern Baptist Seminary in Louisville, Kentucky, because of his efforts to reinterpret the Old Testament in the light of modern science; the forcing of Dr. James Woodrow (Woodrow Wilson's uncle) from his post at Presbyterian Theological Seminary in Columbia, South Carolina, for avowing his belief in the truth of evolution; and the driving out of young professors from the American College in Beirut for accepting evolution as probable. *"In all modern history,"* White warned,

> *interference with science in the supposed interest of religion, no matter how conscientious such interference may have been, has resulted in the direst evils both to religion and to science, and invariably; and, on the other hand, all untrammelled scientific investigation, no matter how dangerous to religion some of its stages may have seemed for the time to be, has invariably resulted in the highest good both of religion and of science.*

There were religionists who heartily agreed with White's sentiments. Professor William North Rice of Wesleyan University, a devout Methodist, pronounced himself in favor of special creationism but warned against the spirit of the Inquisition in dealing with Darwin; and Unitarian minister Samuel R. Calthrop, in a paper read before a religious conference in Saratoga, New York, in 1874, warned that there was no surer way of "driving the bright young intelligence of our time into blank Atheism" than by insisting on an "ignorant Theism." But the attitude of James McCosh, leading Presbyterian theologian and president of Princeton University, was crucial for many Protestants. In a speech before the Sixth World Christian Alliance in New York in October, 1873, McCosh insisted that evolution was a scientific, not a religious, question, and he complained that too much energy was being wasted on conflicts between evolution and religion and not enough on showing the possible harmonies. In McCosh's opinion, no greater harm could be done to Christianity than to issue solemn declarations from the pulpit week after week to the effect that if evolution were true, the Scriptures were false.

James McCosh's *Modus Vivendi*

McCosh was the first prominent Protestant leader to come to terms with Darwinism. In a series of lectures at Union Theological Seminary, later published in book form as *Christianity and Positivism* (1871), and in a number of articles and pamphlets on the religious aspects of evolution, McCosh worked out a *modus vivendi* with Darwinian evolution that helped other Protestants to accept the new science. The fact of evolution, or "development" (as he preferred to call it), he was prepared to accept without hesitation. "There is nothing irreligious in the idea of development, properly understood," he declared. "We have constant experience of development,—of the development of individual plants and animals from parent plants and animals. And why, if proof be produced, should we not be allowed to believe in the development of a new species from the crossing of two species in favorable circumstances?" The question, McCosh insisted, was to be decided by scientists, not by theologians, who, "so far as I can see, have no authority from the Word of God to say that every species of tiny moths has been created independent of all species of moths which have gone before." As far as the Bible was concerned, McCosh saw a general correspondence between the Scriptural and the evolutionary accounts of creation. "In both," he said, "the inanimate comes before the animate; in both, the grass and herb and tree, before the animal; in both, fishes and fowls, before creeping things and cattle. In both, we have, as the last of the train, man standing upright and facing the sky. . . ." In McCosh's opinion, when a law had been established "so as to stand the tests of scientific induction, the theologians may reverently use it, in expounding the traces of design discoverable in the universe." McCosh saw abundant evidence of design in the developmental view of the universe; there were proofs of design, he thought, not only in the structure of individual plants and animals, but also in the "whole structure of the Cosmos" and in the way in which it "makes progress" from age to age. He also was willing to accept natural selection as one of the means by which development takes place. "That this principle is exhibited in nature," he said, "and working to the advancement of the plants and animals from age to age, I have no doubt. We see it operating before our eyes every spring, when we find the weak plant killed by the frosts of winter, and the strong surviving and producing a progeny as strong as itself."

But McCosh did not think that natural selection was the only principle at work in nature; he thought it accounted for some of the phenomena of nature, but left others unexplained. And he drew a firm line against applying it to man. The "power of God," he insisted, "whether acting directly or by secondary agency, which produced life at first and endowed the lower animals with psychical properties, has also been employed in creating man and furnishing him with his lofty attributes." McCosh was friendlier to the concept of struggle for existence than to natural selection. The view that struggle is at the heart of life he regarded as closer to the truth than the idea of universal harmony emphasized by eighteenth-century deists. McCosh thought that champions of natural religion, in their eagerness to stress the benevolence of God, had drawn too pretty a picture of the world and had ignored the vast amount of suffering and evil in creation. Darwinism had at least this much in common with Calvinism: it showed that the world was not like what "the sentimental believer in theism represents it." For McCosh, there was severity, as well as goodness, in God's creation; it appeared to be meant as "a probation, a battlefield." At the same time McCosh saw dangers in the Darwinian stress on struggle. According to Darwinism, he noted, "there are essentially inferior races, which are doomed to give way 'in the struggle for existence'" in order that "a few favored races are enabled to advance on 'the principle of natural selection.'" McCosh warned against the brutal implications of such a view of things. "The law of the weak being made to give way before the strong is very apt to be abused," he said,

and will certainly be perverted by those who do not take into account the other and higher laws which limit it, and are expected to subordinate it. If they look to it alone, they will understand it as meaning that the poor and helpless need not be protected or defended, but may be allowed to perish. . . . If the tenet which I am denouncing comes to be the prevailing belief in this country, it will issue in the weak races on this continent, the Indian and the Negro, being consigned to a slow but certain dissolution. . . .

Only the Christian religion, he concluded, with its faith in the spiritual equality of all men before God, could prevent the law of the jungle from governing interpersonal relations.

Henry Ward Beecher's Christian Evolutionism

McCosh's reconciliation of Darwinism with religion (though not his warnings against what came to be known as Social Darwinism) had considerable effect in Protestant circles in the 1870's. Reconciliation became the order of the day after McCosh, and in 1875 E. L. Youmans, editor of the fervently pro-Darwinian *Popular Science Monthly*, announced jubilantly that he could run his magazine alone on articles received "from the theological side, aiming to harmonize present religious thought with the present condition of science." Another big boost to evolution among Protestants was given by Henry Ward Beecher, perhaps the most famous preacher of his day. Beecher, who attracted huge audiences for his sermons at Plymouth Church in Brooklyn, went much further than McCosh in departing from the Calvinism of his Congregational background. In an article on "Progress of Thought in the Church" for the *North American Review* in August, 1882, which created a storm in evangelical circles, Beecher called evolution "the most revolutionary tenet ever preached" and predicted that it would be to Calvinist theology what "Newton's discoveries were to the old astronomy." Beecher, who called himself "a cordial Christian evolutionist," was fully prepared to de-Calvinize his own theology in the interest of evolution. In January, 1883, he lectured on "Evolution and Revelation" to a huge audience at Cooper Union in Manhattan, and in May, 1885, when he commenced a series of sermons on evolution at Plymouth Church, hundreds of people were turned away because of the crowds. Beecher's sermons on evolution were telegraphed to Boston and Chicago and at least two newspapers published full reports, covering most of their front pages, every Monday. The sermons were also published as a book later in the year entitled *Evolution and Religion.*

Beecher's *Evolution and Religion,* consisting of eight sermons discussing the bearing of evolution on fundamental doctrines of evangelical Christianity and eighteen sermons applying evolutionary principles to the practical aspects of religious life, hailed the "evolutionary philosophy with joy." In another generation, Beecher predicted, evolution would be regarded "as uncontradictable as the Copernican system of astronomy, or the Newtonian doctrine of gravitation." Beecher had no problem with the matter of design. "Evolution," he said, "instead of obliterating the evidence of divine Design, has lifted it to a higher plane, and made it more sublime than it ever was contemplated to be under the old reasonings." But Beecher rejected the idea of special design as being inconsistent with natural selection and applied design to the structure and process of creation as a whole. "Design by wholesale," he insisted, "is grander than design by retail." With his macroteleological view, then, Beecher was able to interpret evolution as "God's thought in the evolution of matter," "the deciphering of God's thought as revealed in the structure of the world," "the history of the divine process in the building of this world," and "a view of God as revealed in the history of the unfolding creation." The Bible itself Beecher saw as "the record of the gradual and progressive unfolding of human knowledge in respect to social and spiritual things through vast periods of time." Beecher cheerfully admitted that, in the light of evolution, theology would have to abandon Calvinistic doctrines like original sin, the fall of man, foreordination, and divine election, and that the nature and destiny of man would have to undergo drastic reinterpretation. Regarding man, Beecher was not willing to trace his origin "below the line of mammals," though he had no doubts that the human race began at a very low point. For the fall of man he substituted the ascent of man; evolution, he thought, showed an "ascending scale" according to which men moved steadily up from an animal condition to the social, moral, intellectual, and spiritual states. "Man was born at the bottom on purpose," he declared. "It was the creative and organic decree that he should begin at the bottom and work his way up steadily until he reached the very top, until, as it were, his life was mingled with the divine life." Redemption and regeneration for Beecher involved the progress of man from lower to higher stages of spirituality, and the kingdom of God itself was a growth. Beecher acknowledged that there was tremendous waste, as well as destruction and death, in the evolutionary process, but he insisted that through it all there was "an unfolding process that is carrying creation up to higher planes and upon higher lines, reaching more complicated conditions in structure, in function, in adaptation, with systematic and harmonious results, so that the whole physical creation is organizing itself for a sublime march toward perfectness." Theology and the church were themselves part of this process toward perfection, "changing upwards and for the better."

Lyman Abbott's New Theology

Under Beecher's influence, Lyman Abbott, Congregational minister who was associated with Beecher in editing the *Christian Union* from 1876 to 1881 and who took over Plymouth Church at Beecher's death in 1887, became an enthusiastic theistic evolutionist and in sermons, books, and editorials presented a religious version of Darwinism that found favor with many Protestants. Abbott became editor in chief of the *Christian Union* (renamed the *Outlook* in 1893) on Beecher's retirement in 1881, and he carried a sympathetic editorial on Darwin's death in 1882. Praising Darwin for his "acute, careful, and absolutely unprejudiced observations, and the influence which he has exerted in liberating and shaping theological thought," the *Christian Union,* somewhat prematurely, announced that "the time when ministers scoffed and derided Darwin and his disciples has forever passed." Abbott outlined his view of evolution—called the New Theology or Progressive Orthodoxy—in a series of lectures at the Lowell Institute in Boston, later published as *The Evolution of Christianity* (1892). In his lectures, Abbott insisted that when Christianity was restated in terms of evolution, it was "so cleansed of pagan thought and feeling" that it became "purer and more powerful." Abbott's point of departure was Joseph Le Conte's definition of evolution as "continuous progressive change, according to certain laws, and by means of resident forces." For Abbott, the laws were evolutionary and the resident forces were divine. God, in short, was immanent in the universe and He revealed Himself progressively in nature, in society, in the church, in the individual soul, and in Christianity itself. Abbott reinterpreted every facet of the Christian religion in the light of continuous progressive change: the Bible became a record of man's moral and spiritual growth, revelation was the gradual and progressive "unveiling in human consciousness" of divine truth, sin was a relapse into a lower stage of spiritual development, redemption was the entire process of intellectual and spiritual development by which man passes into "the condition of virtue," and Christ was "the Infinite entering into human life and taking on the finite" in order to "evolve the latent divinity" in man and bring men "to know and be at one with God." Summarizing his "evolutionary theology," Abbott closed his book by affirming that

> God is in his world. Nature is not a machine which a mechanic has made, wound up, and set going, and with which he must from time to time interfere, as a watch-maker interferes to regulate a somewhat imperfect time-keeper. Nature is the expression of God's thought, the outward utterance of himself. He dwells in it and works through it. Amid all the mysteries by which we are surrounded . . . nothing is more certain than this, that we are ever in the presence of an Infinite and Eternal Energy from which all things proceed. This Infinite and Eternal Energy from which all things proceed is an intelligent Energy. It is an Energy that thinks, and creation is the expression of the thought of this Infinite and Eternal Energy. . . . There is a God in history, as there is a God in

nature—a God who is working out some great design among men, as there is a God who is working out great designs through all material and mechanical phenomena.

The ultimate goal of evolutionary development was the kingdom of God on earth, a co-operative society based upon Christian love rather than pagan selfishness.

Abbott's New Theology was both praised and blamed. The *Boston Herald* thought it the most "reverent statement of the new way of looking at Christianity which has yet been made in this country." The Reverend Edward M. Gushee, however, thought Abbott was too radical; according to Christian evolutionism, he said, Luther would be considered superior to Christ because he came later. But the Reverend Minot J. Savage, prominent Boston and New York Unitarian with a keen interest in evolution, thought Abbott was too conservative, and he criticized him for clinging to a belief in miracles and in the supernatural birth and resurrection of Christ. Savage, like Abbott, believed in divine immanence; "God," he said, "is a power whose center is everywhere and his circumference nowhere." But Savage was considered a radical among his Unitarian brethren. He discarded all specifically Christian doctrines, which he called "relics of barbarism," and insisted that religious beliefs, and the human conscience itself, were products of evolution.

Comparative Religion and Biblical Criticism

In developing his own views, Minot Savage made use of comparative religion and of the "higher criticism" of the Bible, both of which were anathema, like evolution, to the orthodox. Comparative religion, which attracted wide interest with the publication of James Freeman Clarke's *Ten Great Religions* in 1871 (it went through twenty-one editions in fifteen years), became part of the intellectual equipment of liberal Protestants in the Gilded Age. During the Columbian Exposition of 1893, a World's Parliament of Religions, attended by representatives of ten religions, was held in Chicago and its motto was: "Have we not all one Father? Hath not one God created us?" Dr. John Henry Barrows, organizer of the Parliament, which was attended by more than 150,000 people, asked this rhetorical (he thought) question: "Why should not Christians be glad to learn what God has wrought through Buddha and Zoroaster?" Orthodox Protestants had an answer to that one; non-Christian religions, according to James S. Dennis, were "gross caricatures and fragmentary semblances of the true religion."

The orthodox had a similar animus against textual criticism of the Bible, imported from Germany, because it undermined belief in the infallibility of the Scriptures. According to the "higher criticism," the Bible was not the word of God; it was the creation of man, consisting of sixty-six books containing poetry and history, folklore and morality, developed over the period of a thousand years. To the orthodox, Biblical scholarship was a "lower," not a "higher criticism." De Witt Talmage said he preferred the "out-and-out opposition of infidelity" to the work of "these hybrid theologians, these mongrel ecclesiastics, these half-and-half evolved pulpiteers who believe the Bible and do not believe it. . . ." Confronted by contradictions and inconsistencies in the Bible, Dwight L. Moody exclaimed: "The Bible was not made to understand!" In 1895, the Niagara Bible Conference, which had been meeting regularly since 1876 to condemn Biblical criticism and to encourage Biblical orthodoxy, announced the five points that it considered indispensable for Christian faith: inerrancy of the Scriptures, the divinity of Christ, the Virgin Birth, the substitutionary atonement of Christ, and His resurrection and second coming. The five points or fundamentals became the basis for the twentieth-century fundamentalist movement, which attempted to purge American Protestantism of all the new tendencies; and in its efforts to ban the teaching of evolution from the public schools, fundamentalism reached a climax at the Scopes trial in Tennessee in 1925.

Despite the best efforts of the orthodox, "modernism"—a concern for bringing religious thought into accord with modern knowledge and for solving problems posed by modern culture—spread rapidly among Protestant clergy and laymen in the late nineteenth century. In the 1880's, a group of British and American scholars (including conservatives) prepared a revised version of the King James Bible which won popular acclaim in the United States, and in the 1890's liberal Protestant writers publicized the findings of the higher critics in books and articles that reached a wide audience. In *Who Wrote the Bible?* (1891), a widely circulating exposition of Biblical criticism, which was used as a manual for Bible classes and YMCA's, the Reverend Washington Gladden declared that the Bible was not infallible, historically, scientifically, or even morally, since "portions of this revelation involve an imperfect morality"; nevertheless, he said, it was "a book of righteousness" and a "record of the development of the kingdom of righteousness in the world."

It would be wrong to say that "modernism" came to dominate American Protestantism by the 1890's. Still, an increasing number of clergymen, influenced by McCosh, Beecher, Abbott, and Savage, and by articles and editorials in the *Christian Union* and, later, the *Outlook*, came to accept evolution as God's way (through either design or immanence) of working in the world. Even Noah Porter, that sturdy defender of orthodoxy as president of Yale, ultimately acknowledged, though without much enthusiasm, that "Darwinism is perfectly consistent with theism." But some Protestants thought that evolution had elevated the Christian outlook. It is "far grander work," said the Reverend Samuel Calthrop,

> to create Bees who shall gradually think out a Beehive, and at last, after endless experiments, shall so improve their building capacity as to work after strict geometric law, than to create Bee-machines who shall mindlessly construct a Beehive, because they are wound up to do so, as it were, and so cannot help themselves.

Even Darwin's doctrine of man eventually met with considerable acceptance among liberal-minded Protestants, and in the 1880's Mark Twain proposed erecting a monument to Adam before he was totally forgotten by the American people. In 1893 the New York Chautauqua engaged the well-known Scottish evolutionist Henry Drummond to give a series of lectures on evolution for its audiences. "It is a sign of the times," commented the *Nation*, "which no observer can neglect."

Catholicism, Judaism, and Evolution

Among American Catholics, evolution was never the great issue that it was for the Protestants. The Catholic church stressed the teachings of the church fathers as much as it did the Bible, and, unlike orthodox Protestantism, it had never been tied to a rigid Biblical literalism. During the Gilded Age, moreover, Catholic leaders were absorbed with the task of helping Catholic immigrants from Europe to adjust to American life and had little time or energy for scientific controversy. In 1877 Pope Pius IX expressed displeasure with "the aberrations of Darwinism" as to the origin of man, but the eminent British Catholic zoologist St. George Mivart, despite his initial hostility, came to feel there was nothing hostile to religion in the theory of evolution. Pointing out that such great church authorities as Augustine, Aquinas, and Suárez had been friendly to evolution, Mivart accepted natural selection as a partial explanation of evolution, and admitted that man, physically, had evolved from the animals, though his soul was created by a special act of God.

In the United States, Catholic writers used "the shillelah with a vengeance" on Darwinism (as one Catholic writer put it) at first. Insisting that if evolution "is true, Christianity is false," Orestes Brownson charged that Darwin and his fellow evolutionists who publish theories

> which unsettle men's minds, bewilder the half-learned, mislead the ignorant, undermine the very bases of society, and assail the whole moral order of the universe, are fearfully guilty, and a thousand times more dangerous to society and greater criminals even than your most noted thieves, robbers, burglars, swindlers, murderers, or midnight assassins.

The *American Catholic Quarterly Review* made fun of what it called "that unknown god yclept Evolution" and the *Catholic World* warned Darwin that he would be called to strict account for his iniquities when he was finally "summoned before the God he had insulted." Like the Protestants, Catholics were especially incensed by the application of evolution to man, and the *Catholic World,* pouring ridicule on Darwin's "strange partiality for apelike animals," wondered whether the British scientist would enjoy being introduced at the court of London "as the brother of the long-tailed and widely known orangoutang." During the 1880's there was some diminution of Catholic hostility toward Darwinism, and in the 1890's Catholic leaders like Cardinal Gibbons, Archbishop Ireland, and Bishop John Lancaster Spalding attempted to minimize the conflict between religion and science. In 1895 Father John A. Zahm published *Evolution and Dogma,* in which he argued that

> not only is Evolution a theory which is in perfect accordance with science and Scripture, with Patristic and Scholastic theology; it

is likewise a theory which promises soon to be the generally accepted view; the view which will specially commend itself not only to Christian philosophy, but also to Christian apologetics as well. . . .

Zahm's book came under heavy attack from churchmen, and in 1899, learning that the Holy See objected to it, Zahm withdrew it from circulation. Nevertheless, he expressed his conviction that "every eminent man of science throughout Europe is in perfect sympathy with my views" and that in the twentieth century "nine out of every ten thinkers will be evolutionists as opposed to believers in special creation."

American Judaism had as much trouble with Darwinism in the beginning as American Catholicism. "The idea of gradual development," according to Rabbi Kaufman Kohler, "is precluded by its conception of divine revelation, by its doctrine that both the oral and the written Torah were given at Sinai complete and unchangeable for all time." In *Cosmic God* (1875), Rabbi Isaac Mayer Wise condemned Darwinism as a "Homo-Brutalism" that robs man of his dignity, destroys morality, assumes that might makes right, and converts nature into a battleground on which "war to the knife" is the rule. Though he was no foe of scientific progress, Wise could bring himself to accept evolution only in a drastically modified form. His preference was for a kind of "mystical vitalism" in which the basic cause of development lay in "the internality and not in the externality of nature, in the vital force itself, and not in the morphic structure it produces, in the psychical substances and not in matter." Wise saw design, purpose, and final cause both in the totality of nature and in all its minutest parts, and he pointed out that where there was purpose there was God. In November, 1885, Rabbi Wise joined other reform-minded rabbis at a conference in Pittsburgh to discuss "the present state of American Judaism, its pending issues, and its requirements," and to agree on "such plans and practical measures as seem demanded by the hour." The Pittsburgh Platform, which became the basis for Reform Judaism, was the result. In point two of the platform, the Reform rabbis, while clinging to the Bible as "the most potent instrument of religious and moral instruction," insisted that "the modern discoveries of scientific researchers in the domains of nature and history are not antagonistic to the doctrines of Judaism. . . ." The Pittsburgh Platform, which Wise called a "Jewish Declaration of

Independence," paved the way for the gradual acceptance of Darwinism among Jewish believers in the United States.

John Fiske's Cosmic Philosophy

Perhaps no one did more to popularize evolution in the Gilded Age and harmonize it with religion than John Fiske. Philosopher, historian, and popularizer of science, Fiske worked out a reconciliation between religion and evolution which was thoroughly in accord with the optimistic doctrine of progress which had dominated American thought since the eighteenth century. Fiske was influenced more by Herbert Spencer than by Darwin himself (he discovered both of them, to his great delight, as an undergraduate at Harvard in 1860) and, like Spencer, he viewed evolution as an all-embracing law explaining human as well as natural history. In thirty-five lectures on evolution in 1871, later expanded into *Outlines of Cosmic Philosophy* (1874), and in numerous articles, lectures, and books, Fiske formulated an ambitious philosophy based on evolution in which the concept of God "as immanent in the world of phenomena and manifested in every throb of its mighty rhythmical life" was dominant. Fiske's God was infinite power, stripped of all anthropomorphic attributes, and though he could be known only by his manifestations in nature, he was, for Fiske, a proper object for religious feelings. The doctrine of evolution, according to Fiske,

> brings before us with vividness the conception of an ever present God,—not an absentee God who once manufactured a cosmic machine capable of running itself. . . . The doctrine of evolution destroys the conception of the world as a machine. It makes God our constant refuge and support, and Nature his true revelation; and when all its religious implications shall have been set forth, it will be seen to be the most potent ally that Christianity has ever had in elevating mankind.

Fiske thought that the perfecting of man was the primary objective of God's evolutionary process and that mankind could look forward to the day when strife and sorrow would give way to peace and love and the spirit of Christ would reign supreme.

Fiske had only one original suggestion to make in applying evolution to all phases of human existence. Briefly in *Cosmic Philosophy* and at more length in an essay on "The Meaning of Infancy" (1883), he explored the significance of prolonged human infancy for social development. The "steady increase of intelligence, as our forefathers began to become human," said Fiske,

> carried with it a steady prolongation of infancy. As mental life became more complex and various, as the things to be learned kept ever multiplying, less and less could be done before birth, more and more must be left to be done in the earlier years of life. So instead of being born with a few simple capacities thoroughly organized, man came at last to be born with the germs of many complex capacities which were reserved to be unfolded and enhanced or checked and stifled by the incidents of personal experience in each individual. In this simple yet wonderful way there has been provided for man a long period during which his mind is plastic and malleable, and the length of this period has increased with civilization until it now covers nearly one third of our lives.

The newborn babe, despite his tremendous capacities for development, is almost completely helpless; he is utterly dependent on his parents for survival at first, and during the first few years of his life he needs to learn a wide range of behavior patterns under their "tender care and wise counsel." Those members of the prehuman stock whose parents took good care of them would be the most likely to survive, and they would tend to pass on to their offspring the kind of solicitude they had received from their own parents. By a process of natural selection, then, there was a gradual growth in parental concern for the young. Fiske traced the origin of the family, the clan, and civil society itself to this impulse to help the human young through their prolonged infancy. He explained the development of morality in a similar fashion: the offspring of parents in whom sympathetic virtues were present would be most likely to survive and transmit these virtues to their own offspring. Thus altruism came gradually to replace selfish jungle traits in the human species.

Chauncey Wright's Evolutionary Naturalism

Chauncey Wright, brilliant young Cambridge mathematician and philosopher of science, had nothing to say about Fiske's theory of infancy, but he was severely critical of Fiske's cosmic evolutionism.

"All that the transmutation hypothesis presupposes," he said, "is continuity and uniformity in the temporal order of nature." To introduce design, destiny, and deity into the evolutionary process was to make flagrant misuse of a scientific concept. Wright insisted on the "metaphysical neutrality" of science and he strenuously opposed all efforts to draw metaphysical and theological conclusions from Darwinism. Science, he thought, should be freed from all ethical, religious, metaphysical, and teleological considerations and concentrate on advancing knowledge by means of careful and painstaking empirical observations and experiments. Of Wright's attitude William James once wrote: "when the mere actuality of phenomena will suffice to describe them, he held it pure excess and superstition to speak of a metaphysical whence or whither, of a substance, a meaning, or an end." Wright accepted Auguste Comte's classification of human thought into theological, metaphysical, and scientific (or positivistic) stages, and he emphasized the third, the scientific method, as the only valid way to factual knowledge.

Wright was an ardent Darwinian. He read *Origin of Species* shortly after its publication, accepted natural selection at once, wrote articles for the *North American Review* by way of "definition and defense of Darwinism," and made original applications of the principle of natural selection to explain the building instincts of bees and the arrangement of leaves around a stem or plant axis (phyllotaxis). In *The Descent of Man* (1871) Darwin made three references to Wright's work, and he liked Wright's essay replying to Mivart's criticisms of natural selection so much that he reprinted it as a pamphlet in England at his own expense. Wright visited Darwin in 1872, had a long, absorbing conversation with him, and, like everyone else who ever encountered Darwin, was impressed by the great man's "wide, suggestive, and apt observation and criticism, with judgments so painstakingly and conscientiously accurate. . . ." Wright's most important article, "The Evolution of Self-Consciousness" (1873), grew out of queries that Darwin directed his way. In it Wright proposed a naturalistic account of the development of human self-consciousness (i.e., the ability to reflect or think about thoughts) from psychological antecedents in animal life. Consciousness, Wright insisted, is not confined to man; animals also possess it in elementary forms. The reflective use of consciousness—which metaphysical idealists and theologians in Wright's day insisted was, like the human soul, unique to man and explainable only as a divine creation—evolved naturally out of the mental faculties of animals. For Wright, human self-consciousness was simply an extension of the animal powers of sensation and memory; it was learned and functional in nature and in no sense intuitive or metaphysical.

Wright's thoroughgoing evolutionary naturalism led him, despite his Unitarian background, to become a religious skeptic. If he rejected Fiske's reconciliation of evolution and religion by means of divine immanence, he also rejected Gray's efforts to harmonize the two by the argument from design. Wright thought that the argument from design added nothing to the faith of one who already believed in a benevolent God; as for the unbeliever, the design argument was unconvincing since disorder, as well as design, can be found in the universe. Wright, though an agnostic, did not regard himself as irreligious. He accepted religion on the ethical level. Action from pure love of duty, right, and principle (as contrasted with action out of fear of legal or moral sanctions) he regarded as religious; he also suggested that since whatever is the object of man's highest concern might be called a religious object, agnostics, like himself, have a religious object: society and its welfare.

American Free Thought

Wright was not the only freethinker in Gilded Age America; nor was he the only American who wished to detheologize religion and make of it a humanistic body of thought. In varying degrees, members of the Free Religious Association, the National Liberal League, and the Society for Ethical Culture shared his anti-metaphysical outlook. The Free Religious Association was founded in Boston by Unitarian ministers in 1867 to encourage the scientific study of religion and to further what it called a "Religion of Humanity." Though not all of the members of the FRA were agnostics (Francis E. Abbot, for example, advocated what he called "scientific theism"), they were all devout evolutionists (O. B. Frothingham, first president, insisted on evolution as a point of departure for all religious thought) and extremely critical of the Christian religion. According to Francis E. Abbot, editor of *The Index*, official organ for many years of the FRA, Christianity was a great organized superstition, "perpetuating in modern times the false belief, degrading fears, and benumbing influence of the Dark Ages." The FRA, which was open to men of all faiths or none, had as its objectives the advocacy of a rational religion without a priesthood; a moral code without a theology; a God without a dogmatic system; a religion of liberty, recognizing no limits of thought; a religion of reason, submitting all things to its decision; a religion of action, holding the chief good to be man's humanity to man; a religion of equality, acknowledging in its most comprehensive sense human brotherhood; a religion of love, yielding obedience to it as the great fundamental law of moral agency.

The National Liberal League, founded in 1876 to promote secularism in American public life, was an outgrowth of the FRA. Its object was to secure complete separation of church and state in the United States "to the end that equal rights in religion, genuine morality in politics, and freedom, virtue and brotherhood in all human life, may be established, protected, and perpetuated." Among other things, the National Liberal League (later known as the American Secular Union) sought the exclusion of religious teaching from the public schools and the taxation of church property. The Society for Ethical Culture, founded in New York City in 1876 by Felix Adler, held that moral law, not God, should be the object of religion; the essence of religion, according to Adler, was "fervent devotion to the highest moral ends."

Most Americans never heard of the FRA, the National Liberal League, or the Society for Ethical Culture; and names like Frothingham, Abbot, and Adler were not widely known. One freethinker, however, received wide popular fame during the Gilded Age: Robert Green Ingersoll. Though only temporarily associated with the National Liberal League (Ingersoll was essentially a free-lancer), Ingersoll probably did more for the freethinking movement than any other American in the latter part of the nineteenth century. As a young man in Illinois, Ingersoll showed great talents as a lawyer, and he could have had a great career in law or in politics if he had so chosen. But, reacting against the harsh Calvinist atmosphere of his childhood (his father, a Presbyterian minister, he once said, had a "Presbyterian pair of eyes set in Calvinist sockets"), Ingersoll decided to devote his life to a crusade against religious ignorance and superstition. An eloquent and witty speaker in an age that admired oratory, Ingersoll spent three decades traveling around the country preaching the gospel of science and attacking organized religion as an obstacle to progress. To orthodox believers Ingersoll was the "devil's ambassador," the "Pagan Prophet," and "Robert Godless Injuresoul," but for many Americans he took his place beside Paine and Voltaire in the pantheon of freethinkers.

For Darwin Ingersoll had a respect approaching reverence. "This century," he predicted, "will be called Darwin's century. He was one of the greatest men who ever touched this globe." Darwin, in Ingersoll's opinion, had destroyed the foundations of orthodox Christianity.

> He shows that man has for thousands of years steadily advanced; that the Garden of Eden is an ignorant myth; that the doctrine of original sin has no foundation in fact; that the atonement is an absurdity; that the serpent did not tempt; and that man did not "fall."

For Ingersoll there was "no possible way by which Darwin and Moses can be harmonized." But if Ingersoll rejected orthodoxy, he also rejected the reconciliation made by liberal Protestants with Darwinism. For him the design argument was not compelling. When a woman, hoping to get him to admit the existence of a benevolent Deity, presented him with a bouquet of flowers and asked "who made these beautiful flowers," Ingersoll replied: "The same, my dear young lady, that made the poison of the ivy and the asp." Ingersoll would have agreed with Presbyterian theologian Charles Hodge's statement of the issue: "What is Darwinism? It is Atheism." But Ingersoll was himself a "genial atheist"; he preferred, in fact, the term "agnostic," which Thomas Huxley coined in 1869 to describe his own willing suspension of belief. Ingersoll respected Christ as a courageous ethical teacher, stressed the Christian virtues of peace and good will in his own thinking, and counted as his friends such believers as Henry Ward Beecher and James Garfield; nonetheless, he spent most of his life, as a freethinking lecturer, urging the American people to rid themselves of all vestiges of supernaturalism. Human happiness, not the glory of God, he insisted, was the chief end of life, and the highest values were human. The instruments of man should be scientific, not religious, and with science as a tool Ingersoll believed man could improve his life on earth in marvelous ways. He thought the Trinity of Calvinism should be replaced by a "Trinity of Science," and he once formulated his own creed as follows:

I believe in Liberty, Fraternity, and Equality—
the blessed Trinity of Humanity
I believe in Observation, Reason, and Experience—
the blessed Trinity of Science
I believe in Man, Woman, and Child—
the blessed Trinity of Life and Joy.

"The religion of the future," he said in 1881,

> is humanity. The religion of the future will say to every man, you
> have the right to think and investigate for yourself. Liberty is my
> religion. Everything that is true, every good thought, every beau-
> tiful thing, every self-denying action—all these make my Bible.
> . . . Every violet, every blade of grass, every tree, every mountain
> crowned with snow, every star that shines, every throb of love,
> every honest act, all that is good and true combined, make my
> Bible, and upon that book I stand.

For all his paeans to Darwinism, however, Ingersoll shrank from
the harsher aspects of the Darwinian world view. The picture of
nature as a jungle in which life feeds relentlessly upon life was horrible to him; "nothing can be more terrible," he once said, "than the
tusk and the tooth, the beak and claw plan of this poor world." He
was also repelled by the idea that Darwinian concepts—struggle for
existence and survival of the fittest—could justify poverty and oppression. Though a firm Darwinist intellectually, he was at heart an
idealistic humanist who hated the exploitation of man by man. Unlike many of his countrymen, Ingersoll never became a Social Darwinist. If he agreed with Charles Hodge in thinking Darwinism and
Christianity were antithetical, he also agreed with James McCosh in
preferring Christian ethics to the brutal application of the struggle-
for-existence outlook to human relations.

Chapter 3

An Evolutionary View
of Society

In 1882, Herbert Spencer came to the United States for a seven-week visit. He was welcomed in New York City by Edward L. Youmans, editor of the *Popular Science Monthly*, did some sight-seeing in New York State, attended a scientific meeting in Montreal, went down to see Washington, and then made his way up to New England to examine Othniel P. Marsh's fossil collection at Yale and to meet Asa Gray and visit his friend John Fiske in Cambridge. It was an exhausting trip and Spencer, who was ailing at the time, regretted having made it; still, he was touched by the warmth and hospitality that greeted him everywhere he went. He later dedicated one of his books to his American admirers.

The climax of Spencer's well-publicized American tour was a banquet in his honor at Delmonico's in Manhattan on the eve of his return to England. The guest list was impressive; on hand for the occasion were, among others, lawyers David Dudley Field (with his brother, Cyrus, of Atlantic cable fame) and Chauncey Depew; publishers William H. Appleton, Henry Holt, Edwin L. Godkin, and Charles A. Dana; statesmen Carl Schurz and William M. Evarts; clergymen Lyman Abbott, Henry Ward Beecher, and Minot J. Savage; steel king Andrew Carnegie; paleontologist Othniel Marsh;

sociologists William Graham Sumner and Lester Frank Ward; astron-
omer Henry Draper; and cosmic evolutionist John Fiske. William
Evarts introduced Spencer to the guests, and in an effort to lighten
the solemnity of the occasion he announced that natural selection
had culled out those present from the host of Spencer's admirers in
America who would have liked to do honor to Spencer that evening.
When Spencer came to speak, he unexpectedly lectured the American people on their "high-pressure life" and recommended a "gospel of relaxation" to his listeners. But the tributes following his address were by no means relaxed. Sumner hailed Spencer's work in
sociology as a grand step forward in the history of science; Schurz
recalled reading Spencer's *Social Statics* after the battle of Missionary
Ridge and realizing that if the South had known the book it would
never have fought a war to preserve slavery; Marsh announced that,
partly because of Spencer, evolution was "no longer a theory, but a
demonstrated truth"; Fiske compared Spencer to Aristotle and Newton and said that his contributions to religion were as great as his
contributions to science; and Beecher, announcing that he owed
more to Spencer than to his own parents, concluded, amid great ap-
plause, by informing Spencer: "You wear an invisible crown on your
heart that will carry comfort to death—and I will greet you beyond!"

The Popularity of Spencer in the United States

The acclaim that Spencer received at Delmonico's was hardly surprising. Even before the Civil War, Spencer's books had attracted
attention in the United States; and after 1860, when he launched his
ambitious *Synthetic Philosophy*, a series of ten volumes uniting all
fields of human knowledge under the aegis of universal evolution, he
had been winning an increasing number of fervent disciples in America from many walks of life. Spencer's American followers subscribed
to his *Synthetic Philosophy*, published articles by and about him in
popular as well as serious journals, took his ideas as points of departure for philosophical excursions of their own, and utilized his
books on ethics, psychology, and sociology in the college classroom.
For middle-class Americans Spencer was the greatest thinker of the
age. His reputation was far greater in the United States than in his
own country, and men like Henry Ward Beecher regarded him as
the "ablest thinker of them all, and the ablest man that has appeared
for centuries."

Spencer's popularity is not difficult to understand. His uncompromising individualism was appealing to Americans; so was his seeming optimism and faith in progress. His insistence that science and religion could co-exist was reassuring, and his use of evolution to construct a philosophy that was not too technical for laymen to grasp was bound to be popular in a period in which the reading public was fascinated by science, particularly evolutionary science, and curious about its implications for life and thought. But it was Spencer's sociology that attracted the greatest interest in the United States. The utilization of evolutionary concepts to explain social development was of particular interest to thoughtful Americans living in an age of rapid change. The United States produced able social evolutionists of its own: William Graham Sumner, Lewis Henry Morgan, and Lester Frank Ward. But for a long time Spencer was more celebrated in America than these men, partly because he was a pioneer in the field, partly because he ranged so freely and self-confidently in all fields of knowledge, and partly because his "Social Darwinism" harmonized so readily with the American faith in the free individual. Only gradually did Americans discover that Sumner, Morgan, and Ward were making important contributions of their own to an understanding of historical and social change and deserved a respectful hearing.

The Spencerian Philosophy

Spencer was a pre-Darwinian evolutionist. As a young man in the early 1840's he encountered Lamarckianism in Charles Lyell's *Principles of Geology* and was promptly converted to the idea of evolutionary development, even though Lyell was trying to refute it. In 1851 he came across German biologist Karl Ernst von Baer's formula (presented in 1827) for the development of an egg from homogeneity to heterogeneity through a series of differentiations, and he decided that it could be extended to cover the evolution of plants, animals, society, and the solar system itself. The law of progress, he came to believe, was the same everywhere: the evolution of the simple into the complex by successive differentiations. By uniting the principle of the persistence of energy (according to which matter and energy continually change in form but are never destroyed) with the principle of evolution (by which natural objects develop from an unstable homogeneity to a more stable heterogeneity), he thought he had a scientific generalization that explained everything that happens in the universe. By the time *Origin* appeared, then, Spencer had developed all of his main evolutionary ideas, including "survival of the fittest" (the full significance of which, however, he did not grasp at the time); and though he accepted Darwin's natural selection as one of the explanations for evolution, he remained Lamarckian in his belief in the inheritance of acquired characteristics to the end of his life. In 1860 he issued the prospectus for his *Synthetic Philosophy*, announcing his plan for a series of studies of biology, psychology, sociology, and ethics from the evolutionary point of view. Between 1862, when *First Principles* appeared, and 1896, when the third volume of *Principles of Sociology* was completed, Spencer spent most of his time on his task of interpreting the universe in terms of evolutionary science.

In *First Principles*, Spencer disposed of religion at the outset. Both science and religion, he said, recognize that there is an ultimate reality, a basic cause, an inscrutable power that works through myriad agencies in shaping the structure of the universe and its phenomena. This "Ultimate Being," Spencer said, "known with absolute certainty as existing, but of whose nature we are in ignorance, is the sphere for religious feelings." As an agnostic, Spencer hastened to reject theological and metaphysical investigations into the nature of this Ultimate Being as fruitless; it was "our highest wisdom and our highest duty," he said, "to regard that through which all things exist as the Unknowable." But Spencer knew plenty about the Unknowable: he said it was infinite, absolute, impersonal, inscrutable, unconditional, and indestructible, and by the time he was finished many of his readers felt quite at home with it. John Fiske, for one, transformed it into a divine power shaping all creation, and other American Spencerians found no difficulty in transforming Spencer's Unknowable into a knowable of some kind. Spencer was bothered at first by the American tendency to make more of his section on religion in *First Principles* than he had intended; but in later years, though he never abandoned his agnosticism, he became friendlier to religion, having been persuaded by his American disciples that he was an important religious thinker.

To explain transmutation in both nature and society Spencer utilized an overarching formula that he had elaborated from the clue given him by von Baer: "Evolution is a change from an indefinite, incoherent homogeneity to a definite, coherent heterogeneity, through continuous differentiations and integrations." Some people were impressed by Spencer's effort to explain the entire universe by this evolutionary principle. One admirer put it this way: "the fluctuations of the Exchange are thus subject to the same law as the passage of a comet; while the victories of Alexander and the works of Shakespeare are reducible to the same factors as the Falls of Niagara and the spots on the sun." Others were impressed only by the vagueness of Spencer's proposition. Harvard philosopher Josiah Royce ridiculed Spencer's "beautiful logical naïveté" in believing that "if you found a bag big enough to hold all the facts, that was a unification of science." And British mathematician Thomas P. Kirkman parodied Spencer's definition of evolution as follows: "Evolution is a change from a nohowish, untalkaboutable, all-alikeness, to a somehowish and in-general-talk-aboutable not-all-alikeness, by continuous something-elseifications and sticktogetherations." But most Americans took Spencer's definition seriously. Andrew Carnegie, for example, applied Spencer's great law to American cities; the growth of cities, he said, is a "stupendous change" that marks "the development of the Republic from the first stage of homogeneity of pastoral pursuits into the heterogeneous occupations of a more highly civilized state."

Spencer was a laissez-faire individualist as well as an evolutionist, and his hostility to all forms of government intervention fitted admirably with the American tradition of individual initiative and self-help. Spencer summarized his social principles in two major laws: (1) the "law of equal freedom," which he regarded as man's most basic natural right: "Every man has freedom to do all that he wills, provided he infringes not the equal freedom of any other man"; and (2) "the law of conduct and consequence," which was essentially the survival of the fittest applied to society: "Each individual ought to receive the benefits and evils of his own nature and consequent conduct, neither being prevented from having whatever good his actions normally bring to him, nor allowed to shoulder off on to other persons whatever ill is brought to him by his actions." Spencer divided society into two types: the militant and the industrial. The militant society, which originated in war, was authoritarian, regimented, and rigidly disciplined, and it subordinated the individual to the community. The industrial society, toward which Spencer believed mankind was evolving (it was a more definite, coherent heterogeneity), was just the opposite: organized for peace and voluntary co-operation, it placed the individual above the community and freed him from unnecessary rules and regulations.

Though he believed social evolution was automatic and mechanical, Spencer did what he could to give history a push toward more individual freedom by writing books about it. In *Social Statics* (1851) and in other books and essays, he confined government to administering justice, enforcing contracts, and defending the country. In Spencer's ideal society there was to be no regulation of industry, no social-welfare legislation, no public education, and no state postal system. Spencer's reasoning was that state aid of any kind interferes with the natural processes of adaptation by which the fit succeed in society and the unfit fail and are pushed aside. Health, education, and welfare measures, he thought, tend to preserve the weaker types and thus retard social progress. Of the poor he said: "If they are not sufficiently complete to live, they die; and it is best they should die." The whole effort of nature, he thought, "is to get rid of such, to clear the world of them, and make room for better." The severity of Spencer's social philosophy, which came to be called Social Darwinism, was mitigated somewhat by his concession that a person may help his fellows if he can do so without inconveniencing himself (the "law of positive beneficence").

Until late in life (when he become quite gloomy about the trend away from laissez-faire) Spencer was optimistic about the future. Evolutionary forces, he thought, if allowed free play, would carry mankind slowly but surely toward a state of perfect adaptation. "Progress," he said, "is not an accident but a necessity. What we call evil and immorality must disappear. It is certain that man must become perfect. . . . Always towards perfection is the mighty movement —towards a complete development and a more unified good." In the end, there was to be maximum freedom and happiness for all individuals and the state itself would disappear.

Spencer and American Thought

Among Spencer's many admirers in the United States, John Fiske was one of the most indefatigable in his efforts to Americanize Spencerism and to Spencerize American thought. Fiske shared Spencer's vision; his *Outlines of Cosmic Philosophy* borrowed heavily from Spencer and was filled with evolutionary optimism. Fiske discovered

Spencer in his first year at Harvard and by reading Spencer's books he made the transition from the Calvinistic Congregationalism of his Connecticut boyhood to evolutionary theism with a minimum of painfulness. "The influence of your writings," he later told Spencer, "is apparent alike in every line of my writings and every sentence of my conversation. . . ." Fiske had an "intellectual drunk" over Spencer's *Principles of Psychology;* he took *First Principles* with him when courting his wife and rejoiced to see her eyes sparkle at a tough passage in it. Some years later, when Spencer wrote to praise Fiske's work in applying the law of evolution to the development of language, he insisted that Spencer's letter be handled "as carefully as if it were a scroll of Al Korân, just tumbled from the prophet's pen . . ." In 1873, after meeting Spencer for the first time, Fiske wrote a friend: "I first saw our God the 9th Oct." Fiske, known as a "prince of the art" of popularizing, did much in his public lectures and in such books as *Darwinism and Other Essays* (1879) and *Excursions of an Evolutionist* (1883) to further the dissemination of Spencer's ideas in America. Though more interested in religion than in sociology, he followed Spencer in insisting on laissez-faire and on the automatic nature of social evolution.

Edward L. Youmans, popular lecturer and writer on science, was as devoted to Spencer as Fiske was. His interest in Spencer was kindled in 1856 when he read Spencer's *Principles of Psychology;* and when, in 1860, he saw the famous prospectus for *Synthetic Philosophy,* he wrote at once to Spencer offering assistance in securing American subscribers and in furthering the project by every means in his power. Spencer's gratified response initiated a lifelong friendship. Youmans eventually became an adviser on publications to William Henry Appleton and he encouraged the Appletons to publish books by Spencer, Darwin, Huxley, and other evolutionists. In 1871 Youmans initiated the International Scientific Series and persuaded Spencer to take time off from *Synthetic Philosophy* to do a volume for him on sociology. When Youmans learned that because of debts Spencer would be unable to go on issuing his books, he joined Fiske and other American Spencerians in raising $7,000 for Spencer. To spread the "gospel of evolution" he wrote notices and reviews of Spencer's books as fast as they appeared and pressed other writers into doing the same. "I can tell you one thing—" William Appleton told a critic of Spencer, "Spencer won't die as long as Youmans lives!" In 1872 the Appletons founded the *Popular Science Monthly* and made Youmans editor. Under his management the magazine's major emphasis was on evolution. It published Spencer's books serially and also presented articles by Huxley, Gray, Fiske, Wallace, John Tyndall, and Ernst Haeckel. In the matter of social evolution Youmans was a faithful Spencerian. Once when he was denouncing political corruption in New York City and criticizing wealthy people for tolerating and even furthering it, the reformer Henry George asked: "What do you propose to do about it?" "Nothing!" exclaimed Youmans. "You and I can do nothing at all. It's all a matter of evolution. We can only wait for evolution. Perhaps in four or five thousand years evolution may have carried men beyond this state of things."

Andrew Carnegie joined Fiske and Youmans in looking to Spencer for light and guidance. In his autobiography Carnegie confessed that "Few men have wished to know another man more strongly than I to know Herbert Spencer." Troubled, like Fiske, with religious doubts, Carnegie came upon Darwin's and Spencer's works and "light came in a flood and all was clear." Unlike most American Spencerians, Carnegie became an agnostic rather than an evolutionary theist; but he was at one with his fellow Spencerians in his evolutionary optimism. After reading Spencer, he wrote,

> "All is well since all grows better" became my motto, my true source of comfort. Man was not created with an instinct for his own degradation, but from the lower he had risen to the higher forms. Nor is there any conceivable end to this march to perfection. His face is turned to the light; he stands in the sun and looks upward.

Carnegie also found confirmation in Spencer for his conviction that individualism, private property, the "Law of the Accumulation of Wealth" (whereby wealth accumulates in the hands of those with the greatest ability and energy), and competition were "the highest results of human experience, the soil in which society, so far, has produced the best fruits." For Carnegie, as for all Social Darwinists, the "law of competition" was the social equivalent of the struggle for existence in nature, and the wealthy man represented the "survival of the fittest" and could thus claim scientific sanction. "The price which society pays for the law of competition . . ." he said,

> is . . . great; but the advantages of this law are also greater still than its cost—for it is to this law that we owe our wonderful material development, which brings improved conditions in its

train. But, whether the law be benign or not, we must say of it . . . : It is here; we cannot evade it; no substitutes for it have been found; and while the law may be sometimes hard for the individual, it is best for the race, because it insures the survival of the fittest in every department. We accept and welcome, therefore, as conditions to which we must accommodate ourselves, great inequality of environment; the concentration of business, industrial and commercial, in the hands of a few; and the law of competition between these, as being not only beneficial, but essential to the future progress of the race.

But the progress of the race, Carnegie thought, depended on philanthropy as well as on competition. In a famous essay on "The Gospel of Wealth" for the *North American Review* in June, 1889, he insisted that men of wealth have a duty to return some of their money to the community from which they had earned it. The millionaire, according to Carnegie, must look upon his wealth as a "sacred trust" to be administered for the common good during his lifetime. According to the doctrine of stewardship put forth by Carnegie, the wealthy man has an obligation

to set an example of modest, unostentatious living, shunning display or extravagance; to provide moderately for the legitimate wants of those dependent upon him; and, after doing so, to consider all surplus revenues which come to him simply as trust funds, which he is called upon to administer, and strictly bound as a matter of duty to administer in the manner which, in his judgment, is best calculated to produce the most beneficial results for the community—the man of wealth thus becoming the mere trustee and agent for his poorer brethren, bringing to their service his superior wisdom, experience, and ability to administer, doing for them better than they would or could do for themselves.

Carnegie recommended that men of wealth spend their "surplus wealth" on universities, libraries, hospitals, medical and scientific research, art galleries, museums, and churches; and during his later years he set an example in his own giving. But to be a good philanthropist, one must of course make plenty of money; the gospel of wealth "advocates leaving free the operation of laws of accumulation." It also made the quest for gain an ethical imperative. It was the millionaire's duty, said Carnegie, "to increase his revenues. The struggle for more is completely freed from selfish or ambitious taint and becomes a noble pursuit. Then he labors not for self, but for others; not to hoard, but to spend. The more he makes the more the public gets." John D. Rockefeller expressed the same idea in religious terms. "I believe the power to make money is a gift of God," he declared. "It is my duty to make money and still more money, and to use the money I make for the good of my fellow man according to the dictates of my conscience."

Carnegie was the only prominent American businessman who could accurately be described as a Spencerian, and even he diluted his Social Darwinism with a heavy dose of philanthropic stewardship. Outside of Carnegie there was little or no awareness of Spencer in the business world, though an occasional businessman utilized the catch phrases of Social Darwinism. It was social scientists, economists, and journalists, not businessmen, who familiarized themselves with Spencer and who spoke Social Darwinese when analyzing the American system of acquisition and enjoyment. Most businessmen talked like Rockefeller rather than Carnegie; they explained themselves to the world in terms of hard work and Christian stewardship, not in terms of Social Darwinist concepts.

William Graham Sumner

The most influential Social Darwinist in the United States was Yale's political economist and sociologist William Graham Sumner. Sumner was much more than a Social Darwinist and he by no means saw eye to eye with Spencer on all issues. Nevertheless, he was a firm supporter of that union of laissez-faire individualism and organic evolution known as Social Darwinism, and by his influence on countless students at Yale, where he was an exacting but popular teacher, and through his vigorously written articles in popular magazines and books, he probably did as much as any one man to ensure the ubiquity of Social Darwinist ideas in America in the Gilded Age and after.

Social evolution for Sumner, as for Spencer, was automatic; man's task is to discover the laws of society, as he does the laws of nature, and then conform his behavior to them. One of the principal social laws is the struggle for existence. This struggle, according to Sumner, takes two forms: first, the struggle of individuals to win the means of subsistence from nature; and, second, the struggle of men with each other for the prizes of life. Sumner called the first the "law of the survival of the fittest"; nature is harsh and niggardly, and only the ablest and most energetic people succeed in wresting a satisfactory living from her. Sumner insisted there was no way in which man could soften the struggle against nature in order to make it easier for the less competent without injuring society grievously. "The law of the survival of the fittest," he said, "was not made by man and cannot be abrogated by man.. We can only, by interfering with it, produce the survival of the unfittest." The second law Sumner referred to as "the competition of life," and he once conceded that if a man "comes forward with any grievances against the order of society so far as this is shaped by human agency, he must have a patient hearing and full redress. . . ." But Sumner was not patient with most proposals to interfere with either law. He did, unlike Spencer, favor public education (he served on the Connecticut State Board of Education for twenty-five years), and he also favored efforts to improve the conditions of women and children at work, for he did not think they could look out for themselves. Further than this, though, he would not go. All schemes for government intervention, including the protective tariff (which he called "legalized robbery"), he regarded as socialistic; and socialism he defined as "any device whose aim is to save individuals from any of the difficulties or hardships of the struggle for existence and the competition of life, by the intervention of the state."

Poverty, in Sumner's philosophy, "belongs to the struggle for existence and we are all born into that struggle." Moreover: "This is a world in which the rule is, 'Root, hog, or die,' and it is also a world in which 'the longest pole knocks down the most persimmons.' " To take poles away from the fit, who had obtained them by their honest efforts, and give them to the unfit, who do not know how to use them properly, is to wreck society; it deprives deserving individuals of their liberty and property and destroys their incentive. We must reconcile ourselves to a situation in which some people, because of superior ability, have better poles than others, and some people, because of inherent inferiority, have no poles at all. "Such is the system of nature," said Sumner.

If we do not like it, and if we try to amend it, there is only one way in which we can do it. We can take from the better and give to the worse. We can deflect the penalties of those who have done ill and

throw them on those who have done better. We can take the re-
wards from those who have done better and give them to those
who have done worse. We shall thus lessen the inequalities. We
shall favor the survival of the unfittest, and we shall accomplish
this by destroying liberty. Let it be understood that we cannot
get outside this alternative: liberty, inequality, survival of the
fittest; non-liberty, equality, survival of the unfittest. The former
carries society forward and favors all its best members; the latter
carries society downwards and favors all its worst members.

Sumner shed no tears over the lot of the poor and underprivileged;
they were where they were because of what they were. Leave the
drunkard in the gutter, he advised. "A drunkard in the gutter is just
where he ought to be. Nature is working away at him to get him out
of the way, just as she sets up her processes of dissolution to remove
whatever is a failure in its line." Sumner's sympathies were for the
middle-class American who, like himself, was inspired by the gospel
of hard work (which in 1904 the German sociologist Max Weber
called the "Protestant ethic"). Honest, thrifty, temperate, sober, and
frugal, the average American worked hard to support himself and
his family and asked no favors from anyone else, but he was unfairly
taxed to support society's ne'er-do-wells. Sumner called him the "forgotten man" because humanitarian reformers never took him into
account. A and B (social reformers), he said, were always putting
their heads together and coming up with some scheme whereby C
(the forgotten man) would do something to help D (the unfit). Sumner
omitted E (the wealthy man) from his famous formula; but it is important to note that he admired E almost as much as he did C. Defending the concentration of wealth in the hands of a few, Sumner
maintained that the captains of industry possess superior talents for
organizing great enterprises and handling large amounts of capital
and therefore rise to their positions by a process of natural selection.
Millionaires, he said,

are a product of natural selection, acting on the whole body of men
to pick out those who can meet the requirement of certain work to
be done. . . . It·is because they are thus selected that wealth—both
their own and that intrusted to them—aggregates under their
hands. . . . They may fairly be regarded as the naturally selected
agents of society for certain work.

Sumner did not like it when industrialists sought special favors (tariffs and subsidies) from government. He was as hostile to plutocracy as to socialism. The ideal was laissez-faire; government on the sidelines, protecting property against domestic and foreign enemies but keeping aloof from the struggle of individuals to get as far ahead in life as their talents and energies can carry them. Individual character, molded by the Protestant ethic of diligence and prudence, was the key to social advance. "Let every man," he said, "be sober, industrious, prudent, and wise, and bring up his children to be so likewise, and poverty will be abolished in a few generations."

Sumner rejected Spencer's belief in natural rights. Before nature, he said, man has "no more right to life than a rattlesnake; he has no more right to liberty than any wild beast; his right to the pursuit of happiness is nothing but a license to maintain the struggle for existence if he can find within himself the power with which to do it." Rights are civil, not natural; they are developed by man out of his historical experience and they are justified by their social advantage. Individual liberty for Sumner was a convention of man, not a gift of nature; but Sumner warmly supported it, especially in the form of economic enterprise, because he thought it contributed to society's welfare.

In addition to rejecting natural rights, Sumner also rejected Spencer's optimistic belief in inevitable progress. Sumner's outlook was a somber one. Impressed by Malthus' law of population, Sumner thought that social development was at the mercy of the man-land ratio, that is, the ratio of population to the land (and material resources) necessary to support life. When land is plentiful in proportion to population (as has been the case, generally speaking, in the world, Sumner thought, since the great geographical explorations of the fifteenth and sixteenth centuries spread the population of Europe over the globe), the struggle for existence and competition of life are not so severe and it is possible for there to be a great deal of liberty, equality, and democracy. But Sumner saw no reason for thinking that the favorable man-land ratio would continue indefinitely. With the gradual depletion of natural resources and the relentless growth of the world population, "earth hunger" was bound to result. The struggle for land and resources would become intensified, wars would become common, and nations would abandon democracy and liberty and become increasingly nationalistic, authoritarian, militaristic, and imperialistic. Sumner could not share the hopeful outlook of Spencer and his American disciples. Still, he respected Spencer for his pioneering work in sociology and he acknowledged that Spencer's *Study of Sociology* (which he used as a text at Yale in what was probably the first course in sociology in the United States) was one of the factors that led him, in 1872, to abandon the Episcopalian ministry, for which he had been trained, to devote himself to a scientific study of society.

Sumner was an indefatigable researcher in the field of social relations as well as a polemicist for Social Darwinism. He mastered a dozen languages and made painstaking investigations in a wide variety of sources into the origin and development of countless habits, customs, and traditions that have shaped mankind. He did not publish a preliminary report on his findings until *Folkways*, in 1906, but he had reached his major conclusions about social development, and presented them in lectures, long before that. Sumner, who as a sociologist abandoned most of the religious views (though not the moral fervor) of his clerical years, took a naturalistic view of man. Man was not a special creation of God; he was an animal brought forth on earth by the natural evolutionary forces that had produced other forms of life.

According to Sumner, man is controlled by four major motives: hunger, sex, vanity, and ghost fear; driven by these four impulses, he seeks to adapt himself as well as he can to his experience. The struggle against nature and competition of men with one another for survival is a tough one and man makes many errors at first in his efforts to get along. Human nature is fundamentally selfish and contentious, but man quickly learns that he has a better chance for survival if he curbs his impulses, accepts some restrictions on his freedom, and learns how to co-operate with his fellows. Society grows out of the common efforts of men for survival and maintenance; and it is held together by what Sumner called "antagonistic co-operation." According to Sumner, men suppress some of their lesser antagonisms toward one another in order to work together for group, and thus individual, survival. By a long and slow process of trial and failure, men gradually discover convenient ways of performing the tasks of living, and these are adopted by the group as folkways. Folkways are ways of doing things, developed by trial and error, which experience has proved to be expedient: ways to catch game, win a wife, cure disease, treat strangers, raise crops, and so on. They are habits of the individual and customs of society which have been found to work best. Some folkways are relatively trivial in nature; others are of such crucial importance to the survival of the group that they become mores. Mores are folkways with a moral sanction added to them because they are regarded as indispensable to society's survival and well-being; they exert moral pressure on members of society to conform to them. The mores are characterized by rigidity, inertia, persistence, and authority, according to Sumner, and they change only slowly and gradually as life conditions and interests change. Only to a small degree are they modifiable by conscious effort; and it is the classes, not the masses, who take the initiative in introducing variations in them. In most respects, Sumner was a thoroughgoing social determinist.

Sumner traced all customs, traditions, laws, institutions, ethical codes, and philosophical systems to their origin in folkways. "World philosophy," he said, "life policy, right, rights, and morality are all products of the folkways. They are reflections on, and generalizations from the experience of pleasure and pain which is won in efforts to carry on the struggle for existence under actual life conditions." Sumner insisted on ethical relativism in *Folkways;* ethical standards and moral ideals, he said, grow out of and are related to the historical experience of particular social groups and possess no universal validity. The folkways and mores and values of one community may be quite irrelevant to the folkways and mores and values of another community. "The mores," said Sumner, "can make anything right and prevent condemnation of anything." Everything in the mores of a time and place, he insisted, "must be regarded as justified with regard to that time and place. 'Good' mores are those which are well adapted to the situation. 'Bad' mores are those which are not so adapted." Elsewhere he wrote: "Goodness or badness of the mores is always relative only. Their purpose is to serve needs, and their quality is to be defined by the degree to which they do it." As a matter of plain fact, however, Sumner, like most men, tended to be a relativist about matters that did not concern him much personally and an absolutist about things that engaged his deepest feelings. Thus it is not difficult to demonstrate that Sumner, though a professed relativist, was an absolutist at heart when it came to the economic principles of Social Darwinism. But Sumner was a dedicated scholar as well as a Social Darwinist and, like his hero Charles Darwin (whose picture he kept always over his desk), he labored hard to accumulate information that would advance human knowledge; and Ralph H. Gabriel, in his analysis of Sumner in *The Course of American Democratic Thought,* is undoubtedly right in suggesting that for all of his ethical relativism, Sumner had private ethical absolutisms of his own: "He believed that freedom and honesty of thought, of investigation, and of expression are eternally good."

Lewis Henry Morgan

Long before Sumner began gathering material for *Folkways*, Lewis Henry Morgan, sometimes called the "father of American anthropology," was collecting information about the American Indians. Morgan's interest in Indians came naturally enough. Reared near a settlement of Iroquois Indians in west-central New York, Morgan had been interested in Indians since early childhood. As a young man he and some of his friends organized a secret society, modeled after the Iroquois Confederacy, which was devoted to studying Indian lore, performing Indian ceremonies, and wearing Indian regalia—feathers and all—on stated occasions. Morgan wrote the society's constitution and he made frequent visits to Indian camps to get ideas for rites and ceremonies. What began as recreation developed into serious research into Iroquois customs and institutions and then into investigations of primitive institutions as a whole. Morgan was struck by the kinship terminology (whereby a father's brother was called "father," a mother's sister called "mother," and their children "brother" and "sister," etc.) which he discovered among the Iroquois, and he concluded that it had something to do with tracing relationships. He was even more impressed when he learned, while in Michigan, that the method of tracing relationships among the Ojibwa Indians closely resembled that of the Iroquois. He went on in his researches to show that the kinship system he had found among the Iroquois and Ojibwas was common to Indians throughout America and that, further, it was also found among the Tamil people of southern India. Convinced that he had established the Asian origin of American Indians in this fashion, he published his findings in *Systems of Consanguinity and Affinity of the Human Family* in 1871. By now Morgan was convinced of the common origin and psychic unity of all races of men, and he was anxious to demonstrate that the development of human institutions from primitive to civilized forms had been the same everywhere. His remarkable *Ancient Society* (1877), which was based mainly on an analysis of Greek and Roman and American Indian cultures, was the result.

In *Ancient Society* Morgan showed himself to be a thoroughgoing evolutionist. Man, for Morgan as for Sumner, was an animal, and he had evolved physically, as well as mentally and morally, from a brute condition that "could scarcely be distinguished from the mute animals by whom he was surrounded." In tracing the evolution of man, Morgan stressed both ideas and external facts. His concern was with the growth of intelligence as seen in inventions and discoveries, and with the growth of ideas of government, family, and property. In the first part of the book Morgan presented his basic thesis (an extremely influential one) that human institutions evolve through similar stages—savagery, barbarism, civilization—all over the world. He divided savagery into a "lower status," in which men didn't know how to use fire and lived on fruits and nuts; a "middle status," in which man discovered fire and acquired a fish subsistence; and an "upper status," which began with the invention of the bow and arrow. The period of barbarism was similarly divided into three stages: a lower one, commencing with the manufacture of pottery; a middle stage, characterized by the use of domesticated animals in the eastern hemisphere and by irrigation and the use of adobe and stone in architecture in the western hemisphere; and an upper stage, which began with the manufacture of iron. The invention of the phonetic alphabet and the use of writing marked the beginning of civilization.

Morgan's second evolutionary scheme, in his section on government, distinguished between a primitive society *(societas)*, based on ties of kinship, and a political society or state *(civitas)*, founded on territory and property (the precursor of the modern nation-state), and it has been as influential as his theory of ethnological periods. His theory of the evolution of the family (treated in the third section of *Ancient Society*) from a promiscuous horde through successive stages culminating in the "pre-eminent institution" of monogamy is no longer taken seriously (monogamy is found among the most primitive peoples); but his section (in the last part of the book) on the evolution of property relations continues to evoke great interest. In discussing the idea of property (which "commenced in feebleness and ended in becoming [a] master passion"), Morgan emphasized four main points: the importance of technology in determining property relations; the development of property from primitive communism to private ownership; the democratic nature of primitive communities, with slavery not appearing until the upper status of barbarism; and the role of property in initiating changes in society as a whole. Morgan's emphasis on the part played by technology in shaping social evolution and on the importance of property relations for culture as a whole led both Karl Marx and Friedrich Engels to praise *Ancient Society* highly. Engels, in fact, placed Morgan's contribution to "primeval history" on an equality with Darwin's theory of evolution and Marx's theory of surplus value, and he utilized *Ancient Society* as a basis for his own study of *The Origin of the Family, Private Property and the State* (1884). Engels particularly liked a passage toward the end of *Ancient Society* in which Morgan, though no socialist, appeared to look forward to a classless society:

> Since the advent of civilization, the outgrowth of property has been so immense, its forms so diversified, its uses so expanding and its management so intelligent in the interests of its owners, that it has become, on the part of the people, an unmanageable power. The human mind stands bewildered in the presence of its own creation. The time will come, nevertheless, when human intelligence will rise to the mastery over property, and define the relations of the state to the property it protects, as well as the obligations and the limits of the rights of its owner. The interests of society are paramount to individual interests, and the two must be brought into just and harmonious relations. A mere property career is not the final destiny of mankind, if progress is to be the law of the future as it has been of the past. The time which has passed away since civilization began is but a fragment of the ages yet to come. The dissolution of society bids fair to become the termination of a career of which property is the end and aim; because such a career contains the elements of self-destruction. Democracy in government, brotherhood in society, equality in rights and privileges, and universal education, foreshadow the next higher plane of society to which experience, intelligence, and knowledge are steadily tending. It will be a revival, in a higher form, of the liberty, equality and fraternity of the ancient gentes.

Lester Frank Ward

Morgan's social evolutionism took him into the distant past and made him necessarily vague about the future. Lester Frank Ward, another distinguished social evolutionist of the Gilded Age, was more interested in the present than in the past, and he had definite ideas about the future. Like Sumner, he was a sociologist with a zeal for grounding his discipline in the methods and achievements of natural science. He shared Morgan's faith in progress but he insisted that man must take active measures to direct the course of social evolution in the direction of the democratic ideals invoked in the final pages of *Ancient Society*. Laissez-faire he regarded as "social Nirvana," and he preferred *"faire marcher."* He was a "Reform Darwinist." Though he believed in evolution as firmly as Spencer and Sumner, he regarded the Social Darwinism they advocated as superficial, illogical, unrealistic, and contradictory.

Ward disliked the elitism of Social Darwinism. His own youth was one of poverty and hardship and he was largely self-educated; all of his life he felt a kinship with the lower classes (he called himself a "true pleb") and insisted that, given equal opportunities, the poor and humble would display as much talent and energy as the privileged classes. Ward's first important positions were with the federal government: the Division of Immigration, the Bureau of Statistics, and the U.S. Geological Survey. He liked civil service work and saw nothing frightening in the idea of government action for the welfare of society. Ward was one of the most learned men of his day; indeed, he has been called a "Yankee Aristotle." He was proficient in geology, botany, and paleobotany, and he could have had a distinguished career in any of those fields. But his major interest was in the social sciences. He wanted to work out a system of sociology that, like Spencer's, would be a synthesis of all knowledge and based upon natural science, but which, in contrast to Spencer's, would be harmonious with social reform. In 1883 he published his first major work, *Dynamic Sociology,* on which he had been working since 1869. It was a major challenge to Social Darwinism. In it Ward took a dynamic and utilitarian rather than a static and passive view of social evolution. The purpose of sociology, he said, was not only to study what men are and what they do; it was also to search out ways of modifying and improving society so as to reduce misery and increase human happiness. The book was not much noticed at the time, except by a few Spencerians, and in his disappointment Ward almost forsook sociology for botany and geology. A second edition of the book in 1897, however, attracted more attention, and Ward was soon recognized as a major figure in sociology.

Ward's major criticism of Social Darwinism was that it confused social evolution with organic evolution. Nature and history, he insisted, are two quite different processes. Nature proceeds blindly and haphazardly; man has plans and purposes. Natural selection is not particularly admirable; it is a slipshod, hit-and-miss, and tremendously uneconomical process. The waste of reproductive powers in nature, Ward pointed out, borders on insanity. Some of the lower organisms produce billions of offspring, but only a few survive the struggle for existence and develop into maturity. The octopus has to lay 50,000 eggs to maintain itself; a codfish must hatch 1,000,000 young fish a year in order that two may survive. It would be absurd for man to copy nature in his social policies. But man, in fact, has never done this. He has always preferred artificial selection to natural selection. Civilization has been built on his success in interfering with the natural processes of organic evolution. There has been nothing automatic and mechanical about the progress of civilization.

Ward thought that Spencer and Sumner had failed to appreciate the role of the human mind in evolution. "Psychic factors," he said, were more important than natural factors in building civilization. Man, it is true, is an animal, produced by evolution. But he differs from other animals because of his mental powers; he possesses reason, memory, imagination, and foresight that make him unique in the natural world. "The advent with man," said Ward, "of the thinking, knowing, foreseeing, calculating, designing, inventing, and constructing faculty, which is wanting in lower creatures—repealed the law of nature, and enacted in its stead the psychologic law, or law of mind." With his intellectual capacities, it has been possible for man to interfere with natural evolutionary forces in order to utilize them for his own benefit. "We are told to let things alone, and allow nature to take its course," said Ward. "But has intelligent man ever done this? Is not civilization, with all it has accomplished, the result of man's *not* letting things alone, and of his *not* letting nature take its course?"

Nature's method, said Ward, is "genetic," that is, it is unplanned, involuntary, automatic, and mechanical. Man's method is "telic": planned, voluntary, rational, and dynamic. Where nature develops aimlessly and wastefully, man engages in "telesis," that is, conscious, creative planning. He carefully cultivates the soil and drastically modifies the struggle for existence in nature and by so doing produces cereals and fruit trees that are far superior to those resulting from blind competition in nature. Domesticated animals are similarly much "fitter" than those produced in wild nature by the genetic method.

"Whenever competition is removed, as through the agency of man in the interest of any one form," Ward pointed out, "great strides are immediately made by the form thus protected, and it soon outstrips all those that depend on competition for their motive to advancement." All of man's progress has been achieved by triumphing over nature in this fashion.

Every implement or utensil, every mechanical device, every object of design, skill, and labor, every artificial thing that serves a human purpose, is a triumph of mind over the physical forces of nature in ceaseless and aimless competition. The cultivation and improvement of economic plants and the domestication of useful animals involve the direct control of biologic forces and the exemption of these forms of life from the operation of the great organic law which dwarfs their native powers of development. All human institutions—religion, government, law, marriage, custom—together with innumerable other modes of regulating social, industrial, and commercial life, are, broadly viewed, only so many ways of meeting and checkmating the principle of competition as it manifests itself in society. And finally, the ethical code and the moral law of enlightened man are nothing else than the means adopted by reason, intelligence, and refined sensibility for suppressing and crushing out the animal nature of man—for chaining the competitive egoism that all men have inherited from their animal ancestors.

Ward thought that man had achieved tremendous results by means of telesis or anthropoteleology (he loved to coin neologisms), but he also thought much remained to be accomplished. Man had used the telic method thus far mainly to control nature, he said, and he had applied it largely on an individual basis. It still remained to apply telesis to society as a whole. If further progress were to be made, telesis could no longer be left to individual effort; it must be socially planned and utilized and it must concentrate on controlling social as well as natural forces. What Ward called collective or social telesis was to be as superior to individual telesis as the latter was to nature's genetic method. Social telesis would not only involve making the benefits of science and invention available to all citizens; it would also mean focusing social energies on the task of improving social conditions in the same way that individual telesis, through the invention of labor-saving devices, had improved the physical conditions of man. A new kind of society, obviously, was required for Ward's social telesis. He called it a "sociocracy": government of society, by society, and for society. Though there was to be no socialization of the industrial resources of a nation, as in socialism, there would be an emphasis upon social planning in the interest of society as a whole. "The individual has reigned long enough," said Ward.

> The day has come for society to take its affairs into its own hands and shape its own destinies. . . . It should imagine itself an individual, with all the interests of an individual, and becoming fully *conscious* of these interests it should pursue them with the same indomitable *will* with which the individual pursues his interests. Not only this, it must be guided, as he is guided, by the social *intellect*, armed with all the knowledge that all individuals combined, with so great labor, zeal, and talent, have placed in its possession, constituting the social intelligence.

How was social intelligence to be developed? And how was the social intellect to be instructed and informed so that the social will could choose wisely? Ward's answer: by means of social scientists trained in the aims and methods of dynamic sociology. In Ward's sociocracy, legislators were to be proficient in scientific sociology and legislatures themselves were to become sociological experimental laboratories in which social problems would be analyzed scientifically and tentative solutions proposed for trial by society. The sociocratic state, in short, would go in for social engineering. It would concentrate on formulating "attractive legislation" (laws satisfying human needs and advancing human happiness) and "attractive labor" (ways of making labor pleasant rather than irksome for all citizens). A central national university, staffed by the ablest social scientists in the land, would be established to advise legislators on social questions. But education was not to be confined to a privileged few in Ward's ideal society; it was to be made available to all members of society. "The great demand of the world is knowledge," said Ward. "The great problem is the equalization of intelligence, to put all knowledge in the possession of every human being." Ward believed that the differences in native capacities among individuals were infinitesimal compared to differences in the extent of their knowledge. The "denizens of the slums," he said, are potentially the intellectual equals of the graduates of Harvard; they lack only the opportunities for education which would bring their natural talents to the fore. In his sociocracy, knowledge was to be distributed to all citizens; he had no doubt that as a result tremendous creative energies, lying dormant in the masses of people, would be released and that society would move swiftly forward.

William Graham Sumner took a sardonic view of all plans, like Ward's, to make the world over. Social reformers, he thought, were meddlers, social magicians, quacks, and charlatans hoping to repeal the laws of nature by making water run uphill. But, Sumner to the contrary, natural law can be interpreted variously; who is to decide what is natural and what is unnatural? Reviewing Sumner's *What the Social Classes Owe Each Other* in 1884, Ward could not resist writing facetiously:

> *Laissez faire* is "translated" into "blunt English" as meaning "mind your own business," and this injunction he drives home to almost everyone who has ever done anything except to write about "what social classes owe to each other".... Again in his severe condemnation of the "friends of humanity," as he sneeringly calls all who believe in the attainment through human effort of a higher social state, he seems to forget that these very troublesome persons are merely products of society and *natural.* To hear him, remembering his premises, one would suppose that these men either had invaded the world from some outer planet or had artificially created themselves. But they belong to society as much as the hated paupers and worthless invalids whom he would turn over to nature. Why then not let them alone? Why meddle with the natural course of things? In fact what is the *raison d'être* of this earnest book that wants to have so much done? On his own theory, the author should let his deluded victims alone, should *laissez faire....*

But it would take more than a *reductio ad absurdum* by Ward to weaken the force of natural economic law in a nation whose basic political faith, proclaimed in the Declaration of Independence, rested on the "laws of nature and nature's God."

Chapter 4

The Old Political Economy
and the New

In 1876, the American people celebrated the centennial anniversary
of their national independence. There were speeches, parades, songs,
essays, poems, and Fourth of July orations hailing the Declaration of
Independence; and in Philadelphia an exposition consisting of nearly
two hundred buildings exhibiting the natural resources of the country was held from May until November to commemorate the great
event. But some Americans believed there was another document
worthy to be placed alongside the Declaration of Independence in
that festive year: Adam Smith's *An Inquiry into the Nature and Causes
of the Wealth of Nations.* It was no mere coincidence, they thought,
that Jefferson's Declaration, an immortal charter of political liberty,
appeared in the same year as Smith's *Wealth of Nations,* a great
charter of economic liberty. For many Americans the ideas contained
in the two documents were inextricably intertwined. On December
12, one hundred people attended a dinner at Delmonico's in New
York City to celebrate the hundredth anniversary of the publication
of Smith's book. The journalist Parke Godwin presided and there
were speeches by Edward Atkinson, David A. Wells, William Graham Sumner, and other well-known political economists of the
period. In an editorial on "Honor to Adam Smith" afterward, the

Popular Science Monthly said that *Wealth of Nations* was "probably the most important book in its influence upon the politics of states and the economical welfare of mankind that was ever written. . . ." And the *Banker's Magazine* declared that "its usefulness is now as great as ever."

Few Americans versed in economic matters would have disagreed with these appraisals. The classical school of political economy, of which Adam Smith was the fountainhead, had dominated American thinking about economic matters since the first part of the nineteenth century. Professional economists, popular writers on economics, and the writers of textbooks for use in colleges were generally agreed that the basic principles set forth by Smith and developed by David Ricardo, Thomas Malthus, and James and John Stuart Mill were not only applicable to the United States and Great Britain, but were also valid for all nations. Most American economic writers, however, rejected the pessimistic elements in Malthus (the law of population) and in Ricardo (whose "iron" law of wages held that wages in the long run could never rise above the subsistence level). They preferred the French economist Frédéric Bastiat, whose *Harmonies of Political Economy* (1850) demonstrated that a system of free enterprise would produce a harmony of interests. But all of them looked to Adam Smith as the great founder of economic science. Classical economics, beginning with Smith, was based squarely on the eighteenth-century concept of natural law. It is not surprising that the American people, whose nation had been founded on "the laws of nature and nature's God," should have looked to fundamental law in the economic as in the political realm for inspiration.

The Natural Laws of Political Economy

In 1884 Henry Wood, a Bostonian who wrote extensively on economic and religious subjects, published a little book called *Natural Law in the Business World,* explaining "the sure, continuous, and unerring operations of certain fixed principles" at work in society. Natural law in the business world, he said, is similar to the law that "runs through physics or morals, mechanics or chemistry. It is but one of the many subdivisions of Universal Natural Law, or the grand Unity of Truth." Efforts to suspend or abolish it were fruitless; it is "bad policy to pick a quarrel with established truths." Wood reminded those who thought they could transgress "natural principles with

impunity" so long as they didn't violate statute law that the penalty
for violating natural law was even more severe than that for violating
man-made law. But who in his right mind would wish to violate
natural law? It was beneficent in its operations, in the business world
as elsewhere, and it was to man's advantage to study the "eternal
principles of economic science" and behave accordingly. Wood proceeded to expound these principles with clarity, precision, and loving
care.

The first principle, according to Wood and other exponents of conventional economics during the Gilded Age, was that self-interest was
the mainspring of human action. "It is a natural law," said Wood,
"than any unusual opportunities for gain will call out seekers and
competitors." But man was not blindly selfish; the quest for gain
sharpened his wits. According to Simon Newcomb, distinguished
atronomer and amateur economist who shared Wood's views, "nothing sharpens the faculties and dispels prejudice as effectively as self-
interest"; in his opinion, "no one will judge so well of an enterprise
as he whose pecuniary interests are staked upon it." The "economic
man," as economists liked to call the self-seeker, was motivated by the
desire to gain pleasure and avoid pain. His behavior was predictable:
he always bought in the cheapest market and sold in the dearest.
Economists acknowledged that human nature had non-economic as
well as pecuniary motives and that the economic man was an abstrac-
tion made for the purposes of analysis. But they insisted that the
concept was absolutely necessary for economic science. E. L. Godkin,
editor of the *Nation* and the *New York Evening Post,* and perhaps the
most influential writer on economics of the period, compared Ricardo's economic man to the first law of motion. No moving body
actually continues for an indefinite period in rectilinear and uniform
motion, he pointed out; but if scientists had not assumed that a body
set in motion in a vacuum behaved that way, there would have been
no progress in astronomy or mechanics. Similarly with economic man;
all theories of production, value, and exchange rested upon the assumption that man "desires above all things . . . to get as much of the
world's goods as he can with the least possible expenditure of effort
or energy on his own part." To remove economic man from political
economy would be to reduce it to "empty logomachy." In all economic investigations, Godkin insisted, the first inquiry is: "What
will the economic man do when brought in contact with certain
selected phenomena of the physical or social world?" Godkin thought

that the more complicated the facts of the industrial and social world were, the more essential economic man was to the economist to help steer him through the maze.

The second essential for classical economists was competition in what Wood called the "free and untrammelled market." Adam Smith was frequently quoted on this point. He favored an "obvious and simple system of natural liberty" in which "every man, as long as he does not violate the laws of justice, is left perfectly free to pursue his own interest in his own way, and to bring both his industry and his capital into competition with those of any other man, or order of men." Competition, said the *Popular Science Monthly* in March, 1889, was as lasting as human nature. "It is simply, in the last resort, individual self-assertion; and as long as there are individuals they will assert themselves." Henry Holt, the publisher, ridiculed people who thought competition could be abolished. "They might as well attempt to do away with gravitation," he wrote in *Forum* in March, 1895. "The two began together when our cycle of evolution began and the particles of star-dust rushed to their centres. There was conscious competition as soon as there was conscious need of food." The "effort of all economic science," he wrote the following month, "is to free competition. . . ." Holt acknowledged that perfect competition was an ideal; but he described it as

an ideal toward which all civilization is progressing, which is brought nearer by every discovery that conquers time and space or friction of any kind, which every man should strive for. Every step toward it is a step toward the relief of social discontent, and increase of the social discontent attends every step away from it— every effort to prevent laborers competing for employment or employers competing for labor—every intimidation of a non-union man—every interference with an employer's control of his business.

The third point stressed by Wood and others was the law of supply and demand. According to this law, if the demand for, say, shoes exceeds the supply, the price of shoes will rise, the shoe manufacturer will gain, and the profitableness of shoes will attract capital and labor from other occupations into the shoe industry. But as the supply of shoes comes to meet the demand for them, the price will fall; and if the supply comes to exceed the demand, the price might even fall below the real value of the shoes. The classical economists, however, thought that there was a tendency for the price of shoes (and other goods) to approximate their real value in a competitive system. The "natural" price of any article was the price resulting from an equilibrium between demand and supply. If economic men were permitted to compete freely for profit, as they should be, then the law of supply and demand would not only automatically regulate price levels; it would also regulate wage scales (the demand for labor in a particular industry would increase wages) and production (to satisfy consumer demands). In the most famous passage appearing in *Wealth of Nations,* Adam Smith wrote:

> When a man directs his industry so that its product will be of the greatest possible value, he intends only his own gain, and he is in this, as in many other cases, led by an invisible hand to promote an end which is not part of his intention. . . . By pursuing his own interest he frequently promotes that of society more effectually than when he really intends to promote it.

The law of supply and demand was crucial for classical economists; it was the most important of all the laws that economic men were led by the invisible hand to set in motion. It "lies at the foundation of all modern commerce, civilization, invention, and science," according to Henry Wood. "It has been the main-spring and impelling force in every transaction, trade, or exchange, back to the time when men existed under the most primitive conditions."

American political economists thought it was foolish to try to interfere with the operation of the law of supply and demand. No individual, said the *Popular Science Monthly* in September, 1890, "is wise enough to undertake to interfere with the natural laws of supply and demand, or to substitute artificial adjustments of his own devising for those naturally existing in the economic sphere." Not only should government refrain from interfering with prices; labor unions should avoid trying to influence wages. It is for the greatest good of the greatest number, Henry Holt wrote in *Forum,* "that all men should be employed at whatever prices the market will sustain"; employers seeking help, he added, "bid wages up as much as laborers seeking work bid them down," and a fair level will be the eventual result. In *Industrial Liberty* (1888), John Bonham, New York writer, declared that labor unions that seek to influence wage scales violate freedom

of contract, that is, the right of every American to enter into any contract to buy, sell, or perform work for another which he thinks will
promote his individual interest. Bonham regarded violations of the
liberty of contract of employers and employees as intolerable; he
also thought such violations hurt labor as well as capital in the long
run. Simon Newcomb agreed. In his opinion, "each individual is a
better judge of what is the most advantageous employment of his
labor or his capital than any other man or set of men can be." According to Wood, interference with personal freedom of action and contract was a defiance of natural law and thus destined to failure. If
labor unions could succeed in raising wages fifty percent, he said,
it would do no good; prices would go up in the same proportion and
workingmen would be no better off than before.

Economic man, competition, and the law of supply and demand
combined to produce a fourth major tenet of the classical school of
economics: laissez-faire on the part of government. The task of government was to preserve law and order, protect private property, and
provide for the national defense; it should scrupulously avoid med-
dling with natural law in the business world. Henry Wood took it
as a fundamental rule that government should remain aloof from all
questions of "prices, rates, wages, hours, or any others whose proper
settlement can only be found in the quotations of a free and untrammelled market." Economic man, after all, was a better judge of his
own interests than government was. The *Popular Science Monthly*
(September, 1880) thought that actions of the average individual in
economic matters were bound to be wiser than actions of Congress,
because the individual faced concrete problems within his power to
solve while Congress saw them only from a distance. In the *Nation*,
E. L. Godkin was fond of citing political corruption as evidence of the
inherent incompetence of government; government, he said, was
frequently administered by men "whom no one would make guardians
of his children or trustees of his property." According to Boston industrialist and economist Edward Atkinson, "that country will pros-
per most which requires least from its Government"; and his great
hope was that in the future the functions of government "will become less than they now are." Some Americans—though not many—
went so far in their attachment to laissez-faire as to oppose public
education. "Our own opinion," said the staunchly Spencerian *Popular Science Monthly* in March, 1887, "is that education is no part of
the functions of the state, and that it would be better, therefore, to

leave it in the hands of the family. . . ." Expanding on the subject a couple of months later, the editor declared:

> We hold that nothing would tend more to raise the spirit of the poor and enhance their sense of citizenship and of social equality than to feel that they did *not* depend on the rich for the education of their children, but that they provided for that all-important object by their own labor, and, if necessary, self-denial.

The laissez-faire or "go-as-you-please" policy, he asserted, would put education on a "natural" basis. But most American economists did not carry their laissez-faire that far. They supported public education, and also the federal postal service, government highways, and public provision for the handicapped.

Laissez-faire at home inevitably meant laissez-faire abroad. Free trade was another basic doctrine of most American political economists in the Gilded Age. Americans following the classical tradition in economics with any consistency were bound to be firm supporters of free trade among nations and implacable foes of protective tariffs. There was, to be sure, a minority of protectionists among American economists. Henry C. Carey of Philadelphia was the most prominent. But Carey was also a severe critic of the whole classical school of economic thought and, like Horace Greeley, another high-tariff man, he tended to think that free trade was a policy designed by Britain to further the interests of her own capitalists at the expense of other nations. Most American economists, however, strongly favored free trade; they could see only harm in interfering with the natural operation of the laws of trade by means of tariff barriers. Nations, like individuals, economist David A. Wells pointed out, are endowed with different natural capacities and they produce different things; freedom of exchange among them is "therefore action in accordance with the teachings of nature," while protectionism, a foolish attempt "to make things better than nature made them," was bound to promote scarcity. Wells's advice to government was that given by French merchants a century and a half earlier when asked how public officials could best promote commerce: "*Laissez nous faire!*" Simon Newcomb's views were like Wells's. He thought there was no conclusive argument "against the general law of political economy that, when things are left to take their natural course, each 'industry' and each manufacture springs up when it is wanted, and dies out only when it is no longer necessary." Newcomb enjoyed using against high-tariff advocates Bastiat's famous *reductio ad absurdum* of the protectionist argument: a petition by producers of candles, lamps, oil, and everything else connected with light for government to exclude all sunlight from French buildings on the ground that protection from the competition of the sun was absolutely essential to the thriving of their own industries.

Political Economists and Practical Issues

Free trade was more than an abstract doctrine for American economists; they became heavily involved in the political controversies over the tariff which raged during the Gilded Age. The most prominent crusaders for free trade among the economists were William Graham Sumner, Arthur Latham Perry, and David A. Wells. Sumner, having gotten into trouble with Yale alumni for using one of Spencer's books on sociology in the classroom, incurred further alumni wrath by his fulminations against protectionism, "the ism," he explained, "which teaches that waste makes wealth." When a student asked for arguments in favor of protectionism, Sumner responded: "There are none." "An Unworthy Teacher," remonstrated the *New York Tribune* in 1885. "His is not the mode of reasoning to which the father of any Yale student would wish his son to be trained." The following year Yale engaged a tried-and-true protectionist to deliver lectures on the subject.

Like Sumner, Arthur Latham Perry, who taught political economy at Williams College, also provoked the anger of alumni by his assaults on high tariffs. Perry regarded the tariff as a tax added to the "natural price" of foreign goods which produced an inevitable rise in domestic prices. The result: "natural competition equally shut off in both cases." In essence, Perry said, high tariffs meant robbing American consumers for the benefit of a privileged few, and he was so outraged by the practice—he thought it violated the law of property, the Ten Commandments, and the New Testament—that he never pronounced the word "tariff" without making it sound blasphemous. The cause of free trade came to absorb Perry's major energies. Under the auspices of the American Free Trade League he made more than two hundred speeches in various parts of the country and he also wrote extensively for free-trade magazines.

Unlike Sumner and Perry, David A. Wells, who came from protectionist New England, began as a strong supporter of high tariffs; but his experience as Special Commissioner of the Revenue in the Grant administration (in which capacity he made careful studies of the American economy and also investigated the financial policies of European countries) led him to espouse free trade (which led Grant to abolish his office). Wells's reports of 1869 and 1870 became the bible of free-trade groups in the United States for almost a generation, and Greeley charged that Wells was "bought and paid for by foreign interests." Wells, who wanted the American people to "go back to, abide by, and maintain that fundamental principle of every truly free government, namely—*noninterference to the greatest extent possible with the freedom of the individual,*" was active in the Free Trade League, published a widely circulating *Primer of Tariff Reform,* and stumped the country on behalf of free trade.

The tariff was not the only issue to engage the attention of economists in the Gilded Age. The currency question seemed just as important as the tariff to academic and popular economists. When it came to money, American economists demanded a sound national currency backed by specie (coin), fought against schemes for currency inflation, and were unalterably opposed to fiat money, that is, paper money issued and made legal tender by order of government but which could not be redeemed in specie. They were also hostile to proposals for unrestricted coinage of silver and maintained that the gold standard was the only basis for a sound monetary system. In the 1860's and 1870's they were bothered by the continued circulation of greenbacks, irredeemable paper money issued by the federal government during the Civil War, and even more alarmed by proposals by Greenbackers for increasing the amount of such money in circulation. Most economists favored the gradual resumption of specie payments and approved Congressional action in 1874 providing for specie resumption commencing in 1879. But David Wells proposed a "cremation theory" of specie resumption. He wanted the Secretary of the Treasury to burn a certain amount of greenbacks each week until they were all gone; after that the government was to stay out of the business of issuing paper money, redeemable or irredeemable. Wells, who wrote a satirical book on the money question entitled *Robinson Crusoe's Money* (1876), disliked "free silver" as much as he did greenbacks. It was his opinion that "natural laws have ordained that the use of silver, in any highly prosperous commercial community, shall be limited to its use as a subsidiary token coinage. . . ." A bimetallic standard, providing for the free and unlimited coinage of silver as well as gold, seemed preposterous to him. Pointing out that silver was too heavy and bulky for practical use as a medium of exchange, except in small amounts, he declared:

> Nature has created an abundance of both gold and silver. If man refuses to produce the metal best adapted to his wants, and persists in producing another, ill-adapted to his wants, by an artificial, bi-metallic standard, he makes warfare upon the beneficence of the Almighty. Therefore the conclusion:—that the adoption of a bi-metallic standard is a violation of the natural laws of supply and demand, and an attempt to provide for the survival of the unfittest.

The "labor question," as it was called, was another matter of grave concern to American economists. Believing that the law of supply and demand should govern wages and that liberty of contract for individual workers and employers should never be violated, economists, both in and out of the academy, were outraged by efforts of labor unions to obtain wage increases by means of collective action. In *Natural Law in the Business World,* Henry Wood, insisting that interference with "the market price of labor" by unions hurt the workingman in the long run, marshaled five arguments against trade unions. He decried, first, their antagonism toward capital ("accumulated labor"), pointing out that if there were no capitalists, there would be no factories, mills, and railroads to employ labor. He lamented, second, the dependence of workers on unions for advancement rather than upon their own "individual merit, industry, and excellence." In the third place, he pointed out that artificial advances in wages achieved by unions were inevitably followed by advances in prices, leaving the worker no better off than before. He also deplored the violent efforts of unions to prevent unorganized workers from exercising their freedom of contract by seeking employment during strikes; and he concluded with the observation that unions tended toward socialism and that socialism was not adapted to "man's constitution." Wood had no objection to labor societies formed for social and recreational purposes, but he adamantly opposed labor organizations that sought to interfere with wage scales dictated by the free market. Wood's views were typical; some economists, indeed, expressed their dislike of unions in even stronger terms. Edward Atkinson, Boston industrialist, financier, and statistician, wanted the term "scab" to become an honorable one, and he urged laborers to organize "Squires of Work" to oppose the Knights of Labor and all unions seeking to interfere with natural wage levels.

None of the economists of the Gilded Age professed indifference to the lot of the workingman in America. Wood thought that the employer should regard his workers as "men, not machines," and perhaps give them bonuses at the end of profitable years. He also thought it was only fair that if workers refrained from strikes and boycotts, employers should refrain from lockouts and use blacklisting with caution. Like other laissez-faire writers, Wood opposed laws regulating hours of labor; but he had no objections to legislation protecting children from overwork or laws setting standards of health and safety in factories. Wood thought the workingman had come a long way in the United States; the "average price of labor," he said, had been advancing for many years from "natural causes." He saw no reason why things might not continue to improve for workingmen if they worked diligently, showed utmost loyalty to their employers, and avoided labor unions like the plague.

Wood and other proponents of laissez-faire saw poverty and unemployment resulting mainly from improvidence and prodigality on the part of working people. Discussing "The Labor-Question" for *Popular Science Monthly* during the depression of 1873–79, Robert G. Eccles complained of the amount of money spent by mechanics and day laborers on tea, coffee, tobacco, beer, and whiskey, as well as on dress and ornament for their wives. Eccles thought that the only solution for unemployment was self-restraint, thrift, and frugality on the part of the individual worker. During the depression of 1893–97, a writer for *Forum* stressed "The Dangerous Absurdity of State Aid" to the poor and unemployed. "The able-bodied workman may be out of employment for several causes," he said.

> His services may not be wanted because he is drunken, lazy, and incompetent, or because he steals, or because he spoils work, or because his word cannot be trusted. Or he may refuse to give his services upon such terms as employers can afford to pay. In such cases it cannot be assumed that it is morally better for the man to become a beggar than to suffer hunger. It is morally best for those who live upon wages to save a part of them against a rainy day, in which case they will not need to beg, to starve, or to demand public

works, and it is not to be assumed that working-people are as a class improvident.

Still, there were many rainy days during the Gilded Age, and at least one laissez-faire economist, Edward Atkinson, tried to do something more for the working classes than preach sermons to them on the Protestant ethic. Atkinson was the proud inventor of the Aladdin oven. With this oven, not only was it possible to cook large amounts of food at extremely low costs for fuel; it was also possible to prepare cheaper grades of food, especially meat, so that they tasted better. Having ascertained that working people spent more than half their income on food, Atkinson estimated that the average manual laborer could keep his food costs to twenty-four cents a day if he purchased carefully and used the Aladdin oven. "How much human force is wasted in consequence of bad cooking?" Atkinson wanted to know. "How much does dyspepsia or indigestion, caused by bad cooking, impair the working capacity of the people of the United States and diminish their product? How many cooks are there who know what food to buy and how to cook it?" Atkinson arranged for his oven to be sold to workers at cost, but there were few takers. Poor people got the impression that Atkinson was trying to reduce their cost of living so that employers could reduce wages.

When it came to railroads and the trusts, laissez-faire economists were generally opposed to federal regulation. Publicity of accounts and competition (potential or actual), they thought, would ensure proper behavior on the part of the large business combinations that began appearing in the Gilded Age. Edward Atkinson denied that railroad charges were excessive, and he reminded critics of the railroads that rates had declined tremendously since the Civil War. Proposals for federal regulation he regarded as "meddlesome"; he thought competition would continue to keep railroads from abusing their power. When Congress enacted the Interstate Commerce Act in 1887, as a result of the clamor of merchants and shippers, as well as farmers, against railroad practices, Atkinson exclaimed, "Alas! Alas! with what foolishness we are said to be governed"; but he rejoiced that the ambiguous wording of the statute made it virtually inoperative. A few of the economists were willing to accept a mild form of railroad regulation but none of them wished to give the federal government the power to prescribe rates. As for trusts, laissez-faire writers, in the main, refused to be stampeded into demands for federal supervision; most of them were confident that the laws of competition would continue to operate despite the trend toward industrial consolidation. Henry Wood looked upon trusts (as he did everything else of which he approved) as the product of natural law, and he stressed efficiency, economy, and lower prices as justifications for big corporations. When a correspondent wrote the *Popular Science Monthly* in 1889, to suggest government intervention to restore competition where a trust had arrested it, the editor responded:

> To us the idea of forcing people to compete by legislative authority, whether they wish to do so or not, is a trifle extravagant. To our apprehension the best thing the State can do is to let the whole business alone. . . . The *régime* of freedom is one that will suit us best. Give us freedom, and we can take care of the trusts.

It was not the laissez-faire economists who persuaded Congress to pass the Sherman Anti-Trust Act in 1890.

Francis A. Walker

For the purveyors of economic orthodoxy in the Gilded Age, laissez-faire was not a desirability; it was a necessity. To think outside of the framework of classical economics seemed utterly outlandish to respectable economists. In the 1860's and 1870's, New England economist Francis A. Walker recalled, laissez-faire doctrine had an even stronger hold on American economists than on the British:

> . . . while "Laissez-Faire" was asserted, in great breadth, in England . . . the doctrine was carefully qualified by some economists, and was held by none with such strictness as was given to it by the United States. Here it was not made the test of economic orthodoxy, merely. I don't think I exaggerate when I say that, among those who deemed themselves the guardians of the true faith, it was considered far better that a man should know nothing about economic literature, and have no interest whatever in the subject, than that, with any amount of learning and any degree of honest purpose, he should have adopted views varying from the standard that was set up.

Walker himself did a modest amount of varying from accepted standards and he may be regarded as a transitional figure in the development of American economic thought. Walker was one of the best known economists of his day. Director of the Ninth (1870) and Tenth (1880) Census, professor of political economy in the Sheffield Scientific School at Yale, and president of Massachusetts Institute of Technology, he won a reputation as a statistician of the first rank in Europe as well as in the United States. Though the classical framework was his place of departure and though he never wandered very far from it, Walker was heretical enough to espouse international bimetallism, criticize trusts, and favor a limited amount of intervention by the state on behalf of labor. Laissez-faire purists, he contended, assumed conditions of perfect competition: workers perpetually seeking the best market for their services and employers continually adjusting wage scales to the demands of the market. But perfect competition, he said, simply did not exist. Workers were not able, in actuality, to move about freely in pursuit of good markets for their labor; nor did employers always behave toward employees as competitive theory dictated. Imperfect competition, in short, worked to the disadvantage of labor, and it was only fair for government to step in and do for labor what competition had failed to do. Walker did not go very far—he favored regulating hours and working conditions of women and children, banning labor beyond a certain age, and sanitary inspection of factories—and he regretted having to turn to the state (which he regarded as "clumsy, ignorant and brutal") at all. Nor was he ever very enthusiastic about trade-union activity. Still, he did represent something of a breach in the massive wall of laissez-faire orthodoxy that dominated the academic world after the Civil War.

Walker's chief fame among economists rested on his annihilation of the classical wages-fund doctrine. The wages-fund theory held that payments to workers depended on a ratio between the number of wage earners and the amount of capital available for wages (wages fund). The implication was clear: since the wages fund was a fixed amount, efforts by labor unions to raise wages simply meant trying to benefit some workers at the expense of others. Walker insisted that the value of the product, not a wages fund, determined the amount of wages paid by the employer. The laborer, he said, received all that he helped to produce after profits, rent, and interest had been subtracted from the value of the product. By improving production, then, workers improved their wages; and since education meant better workers (and improved production), Walker was a zealous exponent of compulsory primary education. Walker's rejection of the wages-fund theory meant some sympathy for labor. But Walker was even more sympathetic to the entrepreneur (the captain of industry who organized production and was rewarded by profit), whom he carefully distinguished from the capitalist (who furnished industrialists with capital and was rewarded by interest). In a new twist on Ricardo's theory of rent, according to which rent is determined by differences in the fertility of land, Walker suggested that profits are dependent on differences in ability among entrepreneurs. The more skillful the entrepreneur, the greater his profits; but he deserves all that he gets because of his organizing talent, administrative ability, and foresight; and the improved production which he brings about benefits labor, and society as a whole, as well as himself. Despite his eulogies of entrepreneurial activity, Walker was no admirer of trusts. When some of his friends said trusts were the product of evolution, he declared: "Some evolution is worthy of only condemnation. Some evolutionists ought to be hanged."

The New School of Political Economy

Walker's criticisms of the conventional wisdom of his colleagues were mild indeed compared to the criticisms made by a group of younger American economists which began emerging in the United States in the 1880's. These younger economists had studied in Germany and had come under the influence of Karl Knies, Adolf Wagner, and other members of the German historical school of economics who questioned just about every aspect of classical political economy. Like the German historical economists, such American economists as Henry C. Adams, Edmund J. James, Richard Ely, Simon Patten, and John Bates Clark, who had gone to Germany to study, denied that the old "automatic economics" was adequate for understanding society. In their opinion, historical and statistical methods were far more likely to yield insight into economic realities than the deductive apriorism of the old school. The "new school" of American political economy denied the validity of all the major tenets of the "old school." Above all, it rejected the notion that economic laws were immutable; influenced by Darwinism, the new economists contended that economic truth is relative to time and place and that it evolves in accordance with economic development. The new economists also questioned whether self-interest was the only motive in economic life, denied that unrestricted competition was beneficial and that individual self-satisfaction and social good were necessarily harmonious, thought that free trade was something less than sacred, and rejected the idea that government must remain severely aloof from social problems. The new school had, in fact, a strong humanitarian bent, insisted on a close relation between ethics and economics, and wanted the state to take positive action to help the laboring classes and to bring about a fairer distribution of wealth. "That is not the best government which governs least," said Henry Carter Adams, "but which governs the most wisely."

While Sumner fumed about "Dutch drivel" and E. L. Godkin was driven to despair by doubts cast on old-school truths, the young American rebels indulged themselves in a variety of major heresies. Edmund James, director of the Wharton School of Finance and Economy, supported bimetallism, studied the advantages of public ownership of natural monopolies, and suggested that the answer to communism was improving conditions of the workingman. Henry C. Adams, who taught at Cornell University and the University of Michigan and served as chief statistician for the Interstate Commerce Commission, put forth the idea that laborers have "proprietary rights" in industries to which they give their time and skill, said that both government action and private enterprise are necessary for social development, distinguished "intercorporate competition" from "interpersonal competition," and favored public ownership of natural monopolies like railroads and public utilities. Charles S. Walker of Massachusetts Agricultural College defended the use of the boycott by labor unions, sympathized with the Farmers' Alliance, and thought that proposals for free coinage of silver and government ownership of the means of communication and transportation deserved a fair hearing. John Bascom, president of the University of Wisconsin, said that social strength depended on a balance between individualism and collectivism, and Elisha Benjamin Andrews insisted that laissez-faire competition was being replaced by "laissez-faire monopoly" and that government regulation of monopolies (even to the extent of fixing prices and profits) was necessary for the "true and permanent weal of society." "The historian," wrote Andrews in 1886, "will one day be astonished at the credit our bright age has given to the theory which makes of the State a mere policeman."

In their efforts to make the state more than a policeman, the younger economists organized the American Economic Association in 1885 and issued the following statement of principles:

1. We regard the state as an agency whose positive assistance is one of the indispensable conditions of human progress.

2. We believe that political economy as a science is still in an early stage of its development [and] . . . we look, not so much to speculation, as to the historical and statistical study of actual conditions of economic life for the satisfactory accomplishment of that development.

3. We hold that the conflict of labor and capital has brought into prominence a vast number of social problems, whose solution requires the united efforts, each in its own sphere, of the church, of the state, and of science.

4. . . . We believe in a progressive development of economic conditions, which must be met by a corresponding development of legislative policy.

Francis Walker, a kind of bridge between the old and new schools of political economy, was chosen president, and Richard T. Ely, young economist at Johns Hopkins who had drafted the prospectus for the new organization, was made secretary. In 1887 the A.E.A. modified its constitution in order to attract young men of the old school and the following year the statement of principles was dropped. By 1892, when the old school's Charles F. Dunbar succeeded Walker as president, conservatives had come to dominate the organization. Still, Sumner never joined and the A.E.A. without question encouraged new directions for American political economists. When the A.E.A. was founded, Elisha Mulford had this to say: "The long controversy between the economists and human beings has ended in the conversion of the economists."

Richard T. Ely

Richard T. Ely was secretary of the A.E.A. until 1892 and one of the most active of the younger economists in seeking a wide hearing for the new views. Individual ethics, Ely asserted, must give way to social ethics; economics itself must be infused with ethical ideals. The aim of economics, he said, was "to guide and direct the forces which control the production and distribution of economic goods, that they may in the highest degree subserve the ends of humanity." In 1876 Ely had gone to Germany to study philosophy and "find the absolute truth," but he had shifted to economics and political science and learned relativism under Karl Knies. He was impressed by Knies's rejection of the absolutism of classical economic thought: the contention that its theories were valid for all times (perpetualism) and applicable to all countries (cosmopolitanism). Ely absorbed Knies's relativism regarding economic policy; he was also impressed by the idea of social solidarity and human brotherhood which the German economist emphasized. With a "yardstick of brotherhood" by which to judge policies and measures, Ely returned to the United States in 1880 determined to challenge the supremacy of the classical school. "I felt I had a mission that I must fulfill," he said of his first book, *The Labor Movement in America* (1886), which was so friendly to labor that Simon Newcomb called it the ravings of an anarchist. "Woe is me if I preach not this gospel."

What did Ely preach? That the individual was bound by innumerable ties to his fellows and could not be considered in isolation from society. That economic life is a growth and that laissez-faire, once applicable to the life of commercial England, was no longer relevant to modern life. That while natural selection and survival of the fittest may have referred to physical prowess and individual aggrandizement in savage society, they have to do with "sympathetic benevolence" in modern civilization. The pirate, Ely said, is no longer regarded as the fittest; the fittest is the individual with a strong sense of social solidarity. Competition, according to Ely, "increasingly comes to mean worthy struggle, and true progress implies that success will be secured hereafter by conformity to higher and ever higher, nobler and ever nobler ideas." Ely had no blueprint for reform; he advocated, instead, a "sort of patchwork multiplicity of reforms." The patchwork was variegated; it included socialization of natural monopolies (railroads, telephone and telegraph facilities, gas, water, and electrical utilities); factory legislation providing for safety and sanitation; abolition of sweatshops; laws limiting labor by women and children; an eight-hour law; a federal bureau of corporations to regulate big business; pure-food legislation; conservation of natural resources; public employment offices; consumers' co-operatives; the initiative, referendum, and secret ballot.

Ely was inevitably called a socialist by conservatives, but he was scarcely a Marxist. It is true that he praised *Das Kapital* as one of the "ablest politico-economic treatises ever written" and that he sympathized with many of the goals of the socialists. He was repelled, however, by the atheism and materialism of Marxism and by the doctrine of the class struggle; and he feared the threat to liberty posed by concentrating all economic power in the hands of government. Ely became, in fact, increasingly conservative with the passage of time. Once friendly to the general idea of socialism, he had become so critical by 1892 that he listed more than twenty "valid objections" to it in a series of lectures at the University of Wisconsin, where he was director of the School of Economics, Political Science and History. But he was probably something of a "Christian socialist" during his early years. He insisted that "the Spirit of Christ should be infused into the social movement," tried to persuade the churches to concentrate their energies on Christianizing the social order, and looked forward to a society based on Christian brotherhood and equality as the ultimate goal of social movement. Religion, in fact, engaged his attention almost as much as economics. He spoke frequently on social issues to church groups, worked closely with clergymen for reform, and played a major role in the development of the social gospel in American Protestantism.

John Bates Clark

Like Ely, John Bates Clark, another new-school economist who studied in Germany, emphasized ethics and religion in his early writings. Unlike Ely, he eventually moved into the realm of pure theory, and though he remained active in the church, the religious note gradually dropped out of his writings. Clark, who like Ely had been reared in a heavily religious atmosphere, had planned to go into the ministry. At Amherst, however, where he took his degree in 1872, President Julius Seelye, who taught economics as a branch of mental and moral philosophy, encouraged him to go to Germany to study economics. After three years of study under Karl Knies and other historical economists, Clark returned to the United States and began teaching at Carleton College in Minnesota, where his most unusual student was Thorstein Veblen. From Carleton he moved on to Smith and Amherst and in 1895 he joined the faculty at Columbia University. Clark began as a sharp critic of laissez-faire and American business civilization. His first book, *The Philosophy of Wealth* (1886), was extremely hostile to the basic assumptions of classical economics and quite sympathetic to Christian socialism. Orthodox critics, in fact, questioned whether the book could be considered political economy at all.

In *The Philosophy of Wealth,* which was intended for "readers and thinkers who have long been in revolt against the general spirit of the old political economy," Clark took sharp exception to the classical view of human nature. The classical economists, he thought, had a degraded conception of man; they emphasized selfish and mechanical factors to the exclusion of the better elements in man's nature. For Clark, man was not a being striving solely for personal advantage. He possessed a "sense of right" as well as self-seeking impulses, and frequently the "love of right action and aspiration for worthy character" triumphed over his lower impulses. The neglect by classical writers of altruistic motives in man, Clark said, grew out of their error in treating the individual out of his social context. Man is no isolated atom; he is "an atom in the social organism." He depends on others for survival and well-being and they upon him. The "sense of right" grows out of the interdependence of all parts in the social organism and society would disintegrate without it. Clark thought man's sense of right had grown steadily with advances in civilization. At first common ideas of right and wrong were confined to the family; then they were extended to the neighborhood, the tribe, and ever larger groups, until they finally came to embrace all mankind. Even under the competitive regime, from which Clark thought society was beginning to emerge, moral forces had modified self-seeking considerably and led man to create "numberless non-mercantile agencies for social improvement." In a chapter on "non-competitive economics," Clark called attention to the institutions that had been produced by unselfish forces in society—schools, churches, museums, libraries— and he predicted an ever widening scope for non-competitive social forces.

Clark looked forward to the day when the slogan "Every man for himself" would be replaced by "Every man for mankind." Already he saw signs that competition, once the great regulatory force in society, was dying out and being succeeded by co-operation. In the business world, small units were being gathered together into large combinations; at the same time labor was organizing unions in order to negotiate with these combinations from a position of strength. Clark did not approve of strikes and boycotts; he preferred arbitration of capital-labor disputes and he regarded the "arbitrative" method of accomplishing social and economic results as a distinct advance over individualistic competition. Even better were schemes for profit sharing, as in the whaling industry, whereby the worker becomes, in part, a capitalist, and is eager to co-operate with his employer in increasing production. Best of all was "full co-operation," under which employees own stock in the industry for which they work. Under a fully co-operative system, the worker is both capitalist and laborer and his loyalties are undivided. A society based on full co-operation would be a kind of "economic republicanism" in Clark's opinion, and he ended his book calling on the church to help foster the fraternal spirit on which it depended. He had no apologies to make for the resemblance of his ideas to the proposals of Christian socialists like Charles Kingsley in England, though he carefully disavowed what he called "political socialism," that is, Marxism.

Clark did not hold long to the views expressed in his first book. Within a few years he abandoned his belief that competition was outmoded and came to look upon it as an essential for achieving economic justice. In his second important book, *The Distribution of Wealth* (1899), which included articles he had published between 1888 and 1899, Clark insisted that "free competition tends to give labor what labor creates, to capital what capital creates, and to the *entrepreneur* what the co-ordinating function creates." By this time he had come to stress enlightened self-interest as the prime motivator of man and to argue that competition is "the source of all possible good in the economic sphere." The competitive system was "a game of give-away," not a "game of grab," he said; under it, a man makes a living by underselling his competitor and this means he offers more goods and services to society than his competitor and is thus a "better public servant." Interpreted this way, competition was "a race in which the different persons strive to excel each other in conferring benefits upon mankind." The big problem for Clark now was the trusts. He had no objections to business consolidation, which he thought made for increased production, but he did believe that government must take action when monopolistic practices obstructed the free play of competition. Clark did not favor trust-busting; but he did want government to depart from laissez-faire to the extent of regulating large corporations (perhaps through an administrative agency like the I.C.C.) to prevent them from engaging in unfair and unethical practices. Clark's later years were absorbed in developing a theory of value within the classical framework and his thought became inceasingly deductive. Eventually he won a reputation as the greatest of the American neoclassicists. From a critic of laissez-faire in the seventies and eighties he had developed into the sponsor of "a new and higher type of laissez-faire" by the end of the century.

Simon Nelson Patten

Simon Nelson Patten, an associate of Ely and Clark in the A.E.A., was what might be called an "Americanist": he wanted the American people to go in for national planning in order to develop their own unique natural resources, and he recommended protective tariffs, federal aid for internal improvements, and other forms of government intervention in order to achieve this objective. Patten's youth was spent on a farm in Illinois and he was impressed by the riches that nature stood ready to offer man if he applied science and technology to the tasks of production. In Germany, where he studied under historical economist Johannes Conrad, Patten was even more impressed by the wise and prudent use which the German people were making of their own far more limited resources. He returned to the United States in 1878, convinced that with intelligent planning the American people could put behind them forever the old static economy of scarcity on which classical economic thought had been erected and build for themselves a dynamic economy of abundance that would be a model for the rest of the world to follow.

The key to economic development, Patten thought, was in great measure man rather than nature. Where classical economists talked about objective factors (natural laws imposing their implacabilities on man's economic life everywhere in the world), Patten wrote of subjective ones: how man viewed his economic environment, man's psychological needs, wants, and consumption habits, and the efforts that man was willing to put forth in order to modify his own economic behavior as well as his social environment in the quest for material plenty. "Men complain of the niggardliness of nature," said Patten in his first book, *The Premises of Political Economy* (1885), "when really the only thing wrong is the universal disposition on the part of men to prefer those forms of wealth of which nature is least productive, instead of other commodities of which nature offers a generous supply." The economic policies of one nation may be quite beside the point for another. Each nation must discover for itself what its soil, climate, and other natural conditions make it best fitted to produce and then strive to erect a high standard of living on an effective use of these resources. Patten was a resolute pluralist. In his opinion, "a series of nations of different types, each fitted to its own environment, will make a better use of the world and reach a higher civilization as a whole than any type could if it endeavored to occupy the whole world and retain the common characteristics."

Patten was not an especially felicitous writer; the first draft of
Premises of Political Economy (which contained almost no punctua-
tion and whose first sentence ran on for fifteen pages) had to be carefully edited for publication. But his writing improved steadily; and
his major point, hammered home in articles and monographs and in
the classroom at the Wharton School of Finance and Economy, where
he began teaching in 1888, was never in doubt: nature (with God)
proposes, man disposes. Nature will be generous if man learns how to
tap her resources wisely. But the rules of the economic game are not
absolute; man must be constantly learning new things to do if he is
to make any progress. Economics itself must become dynamic. A
dynamic economics not only searches for the wisest use to be made
of local resources; it also insists on a continual modification of man's
consumption habits in the light of new techniques for developing
nature's gifts. For Patten, free trade, undoubtedly useful for Great
Britain, possessed no universal validity and it was surely not a sensi-
ble policy for the United States if she wanted to make best use of her
own natural advantages. Patten wanted the American people to be
continually developing new infant industries in the light of their national resources and in the light of new technological achievements.
The federal government was to encourage new industries by means
of protective tariffs; it was also to encourage the use of the products
of these new industries by tax policies designed to reduce demand for
old products and increase demand for new ones. Education, too, in
new consumer tastes as well as in productive skills, was to play a big
role in Patten's planned economy. "We have inherited a world much
better fitted for supplying our wants than that possessed by our ancestors," insisted Patten;

> but along with this better economic world we have also inherited
> laws, habits, and prejudices suited only to the artificial surround-
> ings of our ancestors. Only when our prejudices have been re-
> moved, and our laws and habits modified so as to harmonize with
> our present environment, can we hope to utilize all our resources,
> and to have all that variety in our consumption which a better con-
> formity to natural laws will permit. We do not need a new world
> nor a new man; but we do need a new society and a state whose
> power will be superior to that of any combination of selfish in-
> dividuals, and whose duties will be commensurate with human
> wants.

From Simon Newcomb to Simon Patten was a long step and one that the governors of America were not prepared to take. The abundance of which Patten wrote remained a dream; the scarcity he deplored continued a reality. But as time passed more and more Americans found the situation intolerable and, like Patten and the other new-school economists, they began demanding a sharp break with the doctrines of Adam Smith. Some Americans, indeed, went far beyond Patten in their proposals for reform.

Chapter 5

Complaint and Reform

There was a great deal of economic self-congratulation in the United States during the Gilded Age. Andrew Carnegie liked to boast of how productive the American steel industry was and how serviceable it had become to the nation and to the world. John D. Rockefeller was similarly proud of oil; and both he and Carnegie—and other captains of industry—heartily endorsed the American system of acquisition and enjoyment. American economists added their praise of the system to that of business leaders. In 1891, Edward Atkinson, surveying American economic development in the Gilded Age, declared with satisfaction:

> There has never been in the history of civilization, a period, or a place, or a section of the earth in which science and invention have worked such progress or have created such opportunity for material welfare as in these United States in the period which has elapsed since the end of the Civil War.

But there were rumblings of discontent as well as voices of praise. Henry George pointed out that the enormous increase in production had been accompanied by a shocking increase in poverty and that "the gulf between Dives and Lazarus" was wider than ever before and the struggle for existence fiercer. To Edward Bellamy the American system was no cause for pride; it was rather like a gigantic coach on which a privileged few rode comfortably while the masses of people, harnessed like draft animals, were forced to drag it up a hill. Ignatius Donnelly thought the nation was on the verge of "moral, political, and material ruin" and that it was being split into "two great classes— tramps and millionaires." And Henry D. Lloyd was shocked by "intolerabilities" in American life: sweatshops, slums, child labor, and widespread poverty. There were "intolerabilities" indeed, both on farm and in factory, in the Gilded Age; and both farmers and workers engaged in various kinds of collective action to solve their own immediate difficulties. But the intolerabilities also inspired reformers with plans for thoroughgoing social reconstruction. From social critics like George, Bellamy, and Lloyd and from the Populists, the Knights of Labor, the socialists, the anarchists, and the Social Gospelers came ambitious proposals for transforming American society as a whole. The Gilded Age was an age of criticism and reform as well as an age of business enterprise. Social Darwinism wasn't the only social creed proposed for the consideration of the American people.

The Populist Mind

The Populists, who attracted the fascinated but at times frightened attention of the nation during the 1890's, repudiated Social Darwinism as emphatically as Lester Ward did. Jay Burrows, writing in the *Farmers' Alliance* in May, 1891, called it "a satanic creed," and Lorenzo D. Lewelling, Populist governor of Kansas, thought it meant "the government of brutes and reptiles. . . ." "The actual state of society to-day is a state of war," lamented Burrows,

> active irreconcilable war on every side and in all things. . . . Competition is only another name for war. It means slavery to millions—it means the sale of virtue for bread—it means for thousands upon thousands starvation, misery and death. After four thousand years of life is this the best that we can achieve? If so, who cares how soon the end may come?

Ignatius Donnelly thought that the end might not be far off at the rate the nation was going. In *Caesar's Column* (1890), an angry, bloody, anti-utopian novel, Donnelly depicted in lurid detail the frightful cataclysm awaiting mankind in 1988 if the Social Darwinist philosophy persisted into the twentieth century.

The Populists did not think that the economic order resulting from Social Darwinism actually represented the survival of the fittest in any reasonable sense; it represented, rather, the survival of the trickiest, most cunning, greediest, most ruthless, and most parasitical. By an inversion of the Protestant ethic, it seemed to the Populists, those who worked hardest and had the highest moral standards ended at the bottom of the social heap in America, while the least prudent, thrifty, temperate, and industrious landed at the top. "Each person is entitled by the law of natural justice to possess and enjoy the fruits of his own skill and industry," said Thomas L. Nugent, Populist candidate for governor of Texas in 1894.

> Give to all equal opportunities, and under the operation of this law each would get his just share of the world's wealth; but give to any man the right to take not only the produce of his own labor but a portion of that which is derived from the labor of his neighbor, and you unjustly increase his opportunities for gain.

The trouble with the American system was that it did not provide equal opportunities; what is more, it permitted some people to take an unjust share of the wealth produced by others. Basing their analysis on a labor theory of value, the Populists divided American society into two classes: producers and non-producers. The producers were the farmers, workers, merchants, and small businessmen who actually added to the wealth of the nation; the non-producers were the bankers, landlords, big capitalists, and monopolists who appropriated for their own use most of what was created by the producing classes. This social dualism ran through all of Populist thought and was expressed variously: wealth producers vs. wealth owners, people vs. plutocrats, democracy vs. plutocracy, the many vs. the few. "It is a conflict between plutocracy on the one hand and the people on the other," said a writer in *Farmers' Alliance* (Lincoln, Nebraska) in March, 1891. "Between millionaires and the masses. Between the money bags of the east and the corn and wheat and beef and pork of the west. Between the insatiable greed of organized wealth and the rights of the great plain people, as vouchsafed by the constitution."

How did the non-productive groups come to control the fruits of productive effort in this fashion? By means of special privileges that they wrested from the government. Railroad companies obtained generous grants of land from government at the federal, state, and local levels for building their roads, sold their land to settlers at great profit, and milked the people by their high transportation charges. Bankers succeeded in committing the federal government to a policy of currency contraction which kept money scarce, farm prices low, and the interest on mortgages and debts difficult, if not impossible, to pay. The big industrialists flourished under protective tariffs imposed by the government and, by their monopolistic control of the market for their wares, extracted a goodly share of the earnings of the producing classes for themselves by means of high prices. The United States, in short, had ceased to be a democratic republic based on the idea of equal rights for all and special privileges for none; it had become a capitalistic plutocracy with rights and privileges reserved for a minority of wealthy people who saw to it that government did their bidding. The Populists had no doubts about the plutocratic domination of American society. In *A Call to Action* (1892), James B. Weaver, Populist candidate for president in 1892, insisted that the plutocracy

> assails the rights of man under the most seductive guise. You meet it in every walk of life. It speaks through the press, gives zeal and eloquence to the bar . . . determines who shall be our Senators, [and] how our legislatures shall be organized . . . It is imperial in political caucuses, without a rival in social circles, endows institutions of learning, disburses monthly large sums of money to an army of employes, has unlimited resources of ready cash, is expert in political intrigue and pervades every community from the center to the circumference of the Republic.

Like all people who meet continual frustration in their efforts to make reality accord with ideality, the Populists developed an exaggerated sense of causality and at times interpreted the situation in conspiratorial terms. "A vast conspiracy against mankind has been organized on two continents," wrote Ignatius Donnelly in the preamble to the Populist platform in 1892, "and it is rapidly taking possession of the world." To Populists who thought that currency inflation, especially free and unrestricted coinage of silver, would solve all their problems, the hard-money policy of bankers and big businessmen seemed deliberately and insidiously designed; and they talked about goldbugs, money kings, money power, and the "bloodhounds of money." Mary Elizabeth Lease, most fiery of all the Kansas Populists, not only told farmers to raise less corn and more hell; she also told them that "Wall Street owns the country. It is no longer a government of the people, by the people, and for the people, but a government of Wall Street, by Wall Street, and for Wall Street." Free-silver Populists charged that a secret cabal of Wall Street bankers, London financiers, and the House of Rothschild had tricked the United States into favoring the gold standard and currency contraction; and they produced books like *Seven Financial Conspiracies Which Have Enslaved the American People* (1892) to document their conspiracy thesis. Anglophobia, xenophobia, and occasional rhetorical anti-Semitism crept into the Populist discussions of the money question, but it would be wrong to exaggerate their importance for Populism as a whole. The paranoid note was not dominant in Populism; with their generous humanitarian aspirations, Populists like Donnelly were, if anything, less narrow, intolerant, bigoted, and provincial than other Americans, including their wealthy and respectable opponents in the East, who could speak quite hysterically themselves when it came to Populism. In the South, for a time, white Populists were willing to work with Negroes ("They are in the ditch just like we are") for economic justice for the poor and underprivileged of both races. Unfortunately, the injection of racial demagoguery by politicians into political contests destroyed this all too brief experiment in racial co-operation in the South.

The Populists accepted the new urban industrial order as a basic fact of life. They did not want to tear up railroads, pull down factories, and try to turn the clock back to some mythical golden age of agriculture in the past. What they wanted to do was to democratize the new industrialism, harmonize it with the ideals of the Declaration of Independence, replace privileges for a few with opportunities for everyone, and establish "an aristocracy of industry, merit, and honor" in place of "an aristocracy of wealth, arrogance, and idleness." In the Omaha platform, which the Populists announced, appropriately enough, on July 4, when they entered presidential politics in 1892 with James Weaver as their nominee, the complaints of the "plain people" were voiced and their specific demands for reform listed. In order to take government away from the plutocracy and restore it to the plain people, the Populists recommended such devices as the secret ballot, the initiative and referendum in legislation, and popular election of senators. With government safely in the hands of the people, it was then possible, they thought, to look to government as an important agent of social advance. Among others things, the Populists called for a graduated income tax and for public ownership of the railroads and of the telegraph and telephone industries, and demanded that all land held by railroads and other corporations in excess of actual needs be reclaimed by the government and made available to actual settlers. As to currency, the Populists asked the government to increase the amount of paper money in circulation until there was $50 per capita and to adopt the free and unlimited coinage of silver and gold at a ratio of sixteen to one. The Omaha platform also expressed strong sympathy for the urban workingman and declared that the "interests of rural and civic labor" were identical. The Populist movement reached its high point in 1892. Four years later the free-silverites gained control of the Populist party, despite the efforts of liberals to hold it to a broader program, and brought about fusion with Bryan and the Democrats. Bryan's defeat marked the end of Populism as an effective force in American politics; the Populist plan for an "industrial democracy" was to remain only a dream.

Labor's Discontents

During the Gilded Age the condition of the urban workingman was as deplorable as that of the farmer. It wasn't only a matter of low wages, long hours, and miserable living and working conditions brought about by the rise of the factory system. For the workingman, as for the farmer, there were problems of status, identity, and self-regard involved in adjusting to the new order of things. The transformation of skilled workers (like shoemakers) into machine tenders and the decline of the personal relations between worker and employer which had been characteristic of pre-industrial society exacerbated the economic plight in which the American worker found himself in the late nineteenth century. Even Andrew Carnegie acknowledged that in the large factories "the employees become more like human machines, as it were, to the employer, and the employer becomes almost a myth to his men." An old Yiddish sweatshop song put it even better than Carnegie:

> I work, work, work without end,
> Why and for whom I know not,
> I care not, I ask not.
> I am a machine.

In their revulsion against the depersonalization and inhumanity of the factory system, labor leaders like William H. Sylvis, Uriah Stephens, and Terence V. Powderly looked with nostalgia back to the days when the worker had been a craftsman, not a factory hand, when the distinction between worker and employer had been far less marked and it was easy for a craftsman to become an employer, and when skilled workers frequently combined the functions of both worker and employer in their own persons. For Sylvis, Stephens, and Powderly, the task of improving things for the American workingman involved nothing less than reforming industrial society as a whole in order to bring it into accord with the ideals and values of earlier times. They were, in short, "reform unionists" rather than "pure and simple trade unionists" like Samuel Gompers; and their ideals were drawn from the labor movement of the Age of Jackson. Like the Jacksonian labor leaders, the reform unionists of the Gilded Age emphasized a democratic philosophy of liberty, equality, and individualism. They also accepted the Jacksonian distinction between producing and non-producing classes (as did the Populists) and their aim was to create a society in which everyone belonged to the producing class and was both a worker and an employer. The National Labor Union (1866–72), the first national federation of labor in the United States, sponsored a long list of reforms designed to give the worker a better break, but Sylvis, who became president in 1868, made no secret of his hostility to trade unionism. "I have long since come to the conclusion," he said, "that no permanent reform can ever be established through the agency of trades-unions. . . . They are purely defensive in their character." The NLU should work, he thought, for the abolition of the wage system and for the creation of a society composed of small individual producers, that is, skilled workers owning and managing their own plants.

The Knights of Labor

Like Sylvis, the founders of the Knights of Labor were reform unionists who deprecated the use of strikes and boycotts to achieve immediate gains for the workingman. "We do not believe that the emancipation of labor will come with increased wages and a reduction in the hours of labor," explained one official of the Knights of Labor; "we must go deeper than that, and this matter will not be settled until the wage system is abolished." The Noble Order of the

Knights of Labor was organized by some tailors in Philadelphia in 1869 and, with Uriah Stephens, former Baptist preacher, as Master Workman, it was at first a secret society, with passwords, a grip, and an elaborate initiation ceremony centered around willingness to obey "the Universal Ordinance of God in gaining your bread by the sweat of your brow." The Knights grew slowly at first, and not until 1878 did it become a national organization and frankly announce its objectives. The aim of the order was to become one big union composed of all American workers, without distinction of race, sex, creed, nationality, or trade; but it also welcomed farmers, merchants, and small businessmen (as members of the "producing class") and excluded only the "non-producers": bankers, stockbrokers, professional gamblers, and the like. Like Sylvis, Terence Powderly, who succeeded Stephens as Grand Master Workman in 1879, wanted to destroy the wage system and replace it with a co-operative society based upon the small individual producer who would be at once master and workman. "The attitude of our Order to the existing system," declared the Knights in 1884, "is antagonistic, and is necessarily one of war."

The Knights, like the NLU, regarded co-operative enterprise as the major road to the promised land, and they made a number of experiments—all unsuccessful—with co-operative banks, stores, and factories. Like the NLU, the Knights also went in for piecemeal social reform, supporting public health and safety laws, equal pay for women, abolition of child labor, an income tax, the eight-hour day for wage earners, and state and federal labor bureaus. But it went beyond the NLU in supporting public ownership of railways, telegraphs, water works, gas plants, and other utilities, and in trying to form an alliance with the farmers. A farm-labor coalition, however, proved impossible to achieve. The farmers wanted high agricultural and low industrial prices, the reverse of what labor wanted, and they also took a dim view of the eight-hour movement. The harmony of interest of members of the producing class turned out to be something less complete than that assumed in the reform-unionist philosophy. But the harmony of interest of reform unionists and trade unionists within the Knights of Labor was equally shaky. Powderly regarded strikes as a "relic of barbarism," was distressed when trade-union leaders participated in strikes on the local and district level, and once described trade-union leaders as "damn gin guzzling, pot bellied, red nosed, scab faced, dirty shirted, unwashed, leather arsed, empty headed, two faced, rattle headed, itch palmed scavengers."

The anti-strike policy of Powderly and other reform unionists finally led to a defection of the trade unions in 1886 and the speedy decline of the Knights thereafter.

Samuel Gompers and the AFL

The American Federation of Labor, which was born as the Knights of Labor was dying, offered trade unionism (a philosophy that had emerged in the 1850's with the development of local and national trade unions) as an alternative to reform unionism. Organized at a convention of strong national unions meeting in Columbus, Ohio, in December, 1886, the AFL was interested primarily in collective bargaining, not social reconstruction, and its emphasis was on bread-and-butter unionism. Though it paid lip service to many of the causes championed by the reform unionists (land reform, public owner-ship of the telegraph and telephone systems, income tax, direct elec-tion of senators, etc.), it rejected the idea that the major purpose of the labor movement was to transform American society as a whole. The leaders of the AFL accepted the modern industrial order as here to stay and they regarded the objective of the reform unionists—a co-operative society centered around the small producer—as tech-nologically impossible. They also accepted the fact that the wage system was here to stay, at least as far as the foreseeable future was concerned, and that workers were likely to spend their lifetimes as wage earners. The union, in their opinion, must concentrate on im-mediate benefits for the worker—higher wages, shorter hours, better working conditions—and stop chasing idealistic will-o'-the-wisps. "We have no ultimate ends," Adolph Strasser (who with Samuel Gompers built a powerful Cigarmakers Union and helped organize the AFL) told a Senate committee in 1883. "We are going on from day to day. We are fighting only for immediate objects—objects that can be realized in a few years. . . . We want to dress better and to live better, and become better off and better citizens generally. . . ." The AFL, made up mainly of craft unions, represented the "aristocracy" of American labor; and by giving member unions considerable autonomy and building up a prosperous treasury with which to help out in time of strikes and to organize new unions, it eventually de-veloped into a major force in American life. Samuel Gompers, presi-dent of the AFL for forty years, boasted that the trade-union

movement "has evoked a spirit and a demand for reform, but has held
in check the more radical elements in society. . . ."

Gompers himself might at one time have been regarded as something of a radical. As a young cigar maker in New York City, he read
Marx, Engels, and Lassalle and for many years expressed sympathy
for socialism and interpreted the relation between capital and labor in
terms of the class struggle. (The preamble to the AFL constitution of
1886 contained Marxian language.) But Gompers came to emphasize
job- and wage-consciousness rather than class-consciousness among
workers and he became increasingly lukewarm about socialism and
finally actively hostile to it. Though he did not favor excluding
socialists from the AFL, he came to believe that socialism itself would
create "the most pernicious system for circumscribing effort and activity that has ever been invented." Under socialism, government would
become the sole employer and the workingman would lose his most
basic right—the right to strike. "Our main dependence," said Gompers, "lies in individual initiative."

In addition to opposing socialism, Gompers opposed having the
AFL involve itself in political action to any great extent. Instead of
squandering its energies on politics, labor was to concentrate on
trade-union activity, for it was the union, not the government, which
could bring real benefits to the workingman. Gompers wanted labor
to reward its friends and punish its enemies at election time and he
also favored efforts to secure legislation prohibiting child labor, making employers liable for injuries to workmen on the job, and to assure
labor of the right to organize unions and engage in strikes, picketing,
and boycotts. Beyond that, however, Gompers had little interest in
government as an instrument of reform. He opposed government regulation of trusts both because he thought that large combinations
represented "the legitimate development of natural concentration of
industry" and because he thought that strong labor unions were "the
only power capable of coping with and (if necessary) smashing" them.
He also opposed wages and hours laws (with minimum wage laws,
he said, the "minimum would become the maximum") and laws providing for unemployment insurance because he thought they would
give the government too much control over labor. The trade union,
not the government, offered a way of salvation for the worker. ". . . I
cannot and will not prove false to my conviction," he said, "that the
trade unions pure and simple are the natural organizations of the

wage-workers to secure their present material and practical improvement and to achieve their final emancipation." Emancipation not
only meant material benefits in the form of higher wages; it also
meant shorter working hours and thus more time for the workingman
to engage in cultural pursuits and become "a better citizen, a better
father, a better husband, a better man in general. . . ."

Henry George and the Single Tax

Henry George was a friend of labor; but he did not think that the
prescriptions of either the reform unionists or the trade unionists
went to the heart of the matter. In *Progress and Poverty* (1879),
George presented a diagnosis of America's ills which he regarded as
definitive. His book was astonishingly popular considering its length
(over five hundred pages) and the abstract nature of much of its discussion. But the warmth and earnestness of the book as a whole
probably compensated for the dry passages in it, and its optimistic
mood met a real need among Americans beset by the perplexities of
an age of rapid change.

George, who had known dire need as a young man in California
with a family to support, was fascinated by the great paradox of the
new industrial age: why, with all the progress in material production
brought about by the Industrial Revolution, was there such an appalling increase in the amount of deep poverty and abject misery in
industrial nations? George rejected the Malthusian explanation: that
poverty is the inevitable result of the pressure of population on the
means of subsistence and that there is very little that man can do
about it. Nature is generous, not niggardly, George declared time
and again in his book; if man makes intelligent use of the natural
resources at his disposal there will be plenty for all. George also rejected the hopeful (but exasperatingly sluggish) evolutionism of
Spencerian sociology, namely, the idea that progress does occur, but
that it comes about only by means of the automatic workings of social
evolution which man interferes with at his peril. Spencer's disciple
E. L. Youmans assured George that in five thousand years perhaps
social evolution will have solved New York City's problems, but
George was impatient. American society would succumb to revolution or anarchy long before that, he was convinced, unless steps were
taken to solve the paradox of poverty amid plenty, scarcity amid

abundance, rags amid riches. George rejected Spencer's evolutionary determinism. By taking thought, he argued, man can do something about his plight; if he takes the trouble to search out the reasons why poverty has accompanied progress in modern times, he will then be in a position to propose a remedy for the social malaise.

George thought he had found out why poverty and progress go together. The villain in the piece was the landlord. Viewing society, as the Populists and reform unionists did, as consisting of producers and non-producers, George was willing to admit every economic group, including capitalists, into the creative class of producers except one: the landlords. The landlord, in George's opinion, was the non-producer par excellence; he was the parasite who produced nothing but lived off what others produced; he was the vampire who preyed ruthlessly on everybody else in the community. George thought that landlords were getting an unearned increment out of the land they possessed. By their high rents they were extracting from the rest of the population profits that they did not earn by productive work of their own. The value of land, he pointed out, is due only in small part to the improvements made upon it; in great measure, its value is created by the community. In California, George observed that when a ship carrying supplies arrived in San Francisco, land in the vicinity doubled in price; he also noticed that when a railroad was built near Oakland, land previously worth little suddenly became enormously expensive. George concluded that the inflation of land values growing out of community development (or the expectation of such development) was the basic cause of poverty. As communities grow in size and productive endeavor, landlords keep raising rents, and they get an increasingly larger share of the wealth that other people in the community create. High rents, George believed, depress wage levels and interest rates and the landlord ends by swallowing up most of the profits that should go to capital and labor for their productive achievements. The result: poverty, periodic unemployment, and recurrent industrial depressions. Summing up his thesis, George had this to say:

> Take now . . . some hard-headed business man, who has no theories, but knows how to make money. Say to him: "Here is a little village; in ten years it will be a great city—in ten years the railroad will have taken the place of the stage coach, the electric

light of the candle; it will abound with all the machinery and improvements that so enormously multiply the effective power of labor. Will, in ten years, interest be any higher?"

He will tell you, "No!"

"Will the wages of common labor be any higher . . . ?"

He will tell you, "No, the wages of common labor will not be any higher . . ."

"What, then, will be higher?"

"Rent, the value of land. Go, get yourself a piece of ground, and hold possession." And if, under such circumstances, you take his advice, you need do nothing more. You may sit down and smoke your pipe; you may lie around like the lazzaroni of Naples or the leperos of Mexico; you may go up in a balloon or down a hole in the ground; and without doing one stroke of work, without adding one iota of wealth to the community, in ten years you will be rich! In the new city you may have a luxurious mansion; but among its public buildings will be an almshouse.

George's diagnosis contained its own prescription: take the unearned gains away from landlords and restore them to the community. George did not propose nationalizing the land. He was willing to let the landlords keep the land if the government were to impose a tax that took its socially created value away from them and returned it to society. Such a tax, he thought, could be collected easily and cheaply and it would make it possible to abolish all other taxes and imposts and thus make productive activity at home and trade with other nations completely free. Best of all, his single-tax plan would bring land monopoly and speculation in land to an end and encourage the productive use of nature's resources. "What I propose, therefore," said George of his panacea,

the simple yet sovereign remedy, which will raise wages, increase the earnings of capital, extirpate pauperism, abolish poverty, give remunerative employment to whoever wishes it, afford free scope to human powers, lessen crime, elevate morals, and taste, and intelligence, purify government, and carry civilization to yet nobler heights, is—to appropriate rent by taxation.

George was not a socialist; he thought Marx a superficial thinker and Marx regarded *Progress and Poverty* as "the capitalists' last ditch" (Spencer called it "trash"). George thought it a basic natural right that men should be able to possess and enjoy the fruits of their own exertions and he looked upon private property as one of the foundations of civilized society. But land itself was "the common property of the whole people" and he thought that private owner-ship of land (which originated in war and conquest) violated another fundamental natural right: the right of all men to share equally in the bounty of nature. Private property comes into existence only when man has put forth efforts to transform raw nature into useful com-modities; but nature's resources themselves remain forever available to all men. There were, therefore, "socialist" elements in George's philosophy despite his support of competitive endeavor, and it is no cause for wonder that the Fabian Socialists in England and land re-formers everywhere found inspiration in his ideas. Toward the end of *Progress and Poverty,* moreover, George declared that social pro-gress depends on the degree to which men stop wasting their energies conflicting with each other and come together in peaceful associa-tion for the tasks of life. The conflict and inequality that Social Darwinists thought was the only way to progress leads to social retardation, said George, not social advance. Association in equality was for George the law of progress. "Men tend to progress," he said, "just as they come closer together, and by co-operation with each other increase the mental power that may be devoted to improve-ment. . . ."

Henry D. Lloyd's New Morality

Henry George's ideal of association in equality was similar to the "new morality" preached by Henry Demarest Lloyd, but Lloyd was willing to follow out the collectivist implications of such a point of view much farther than George was. The son of a Dutch Reformed minister, Lloyd developed a social philosophy that was heavily freighted with ethical and religious imperatives. The old morality, Lloyd thought, exalted naked self-interest; the new morality, essen-tial for the survival of industrial civilization, must be built around the fatherhood of God and the brotherhood of man. Lloyd had occa-sion to study the industrial development of the United States at close range while he was financial and later general editorial writer for the *Chicago Tribune,* and he quickly came to the conclusion that the de-velopment of industrial monopoly was destroying liberty for most

Americans. The knowledge that Lloyd accumulated about railroads, trusts, and the labor movement (with which he was in hearty sympathy) was comprehensive and detailed, and the articles he wrote for the *Tribune,* and later for the *North American Review* and the *Atlantic Monthly* on various aspects of the American economy, were authoritative. Lloyd's first important article, "The Story of a Great Monopoly" (1881), a critical study of railroad practices and of the Standard Oil Trust (which William Dean Howells courageously ran in the *Atlantic* after the *North American Review* shrank from printing it), made him famous overnight, and he had a wide audience for his subsequent articles on railroads, trusts, stock-market manipulations, and on the general American business ethos. In a real sense Lloyd was the first and one of the best of the journalists of exposure who were later known as muckrakers.

In his *Atlantic* article Lloyd called Standard Oil "the greatest, wisest, meanest monopoly known to history," and his fascination with it as an illustration of the workings of monopolistic capitalism led him to assemble mountains of material (newspaper clippings, court records, legislative inquiries, personal interviews) in preparation for a more exhaustive study of the company. The result was *Wealth against Commonwealth* (1894), which Edward Everett Hale called the *Uncle Tom's Cabin* of the labor movement. Though Lloyd named no names (his strictures on corporate capitalism were rarely *ad hominen)* in his book, his factually documented revelations of the ruthlessness and dishonesty that accompanied the rise of Standard Oil were so shocking that Howell confessed it took a great deal of nervous strength to keep at the book, and naturalist John Burroughs said an hour's reading made him so mad he had to go out and kick stumps.

Lloyd wrote *Wealth against Commonwealth,* he told a friend, "with the most constructive hope of helping in the application of ethical and religious principles to the business administration of the industrial resources of our common humanity." His ethical purpose appeared most prominently in a discussion of the "Old Self-Interest and the New," in the final pages of the book. In these pages, Lloyd found Social Darwinism totally lacking as a way of life. "The prize we give the fittest," he said, "is monopoly of the necessaries of life, and we leave these winners of the powers of life and death to wield them over us by the same 'self-interest' with which they took them from us." Lloyd stated flatly that the man "who should apply in his family or his citizenship this 'survival of the fittest' theory as it is practically professed and operated in business would be a monster, and would be speedily made extinct, as we do with monsters." Co-operation, as well as competition, is found in nature, Lloyd pointed out, and the Social Darwinist erred in using evolutionary science to bolster social reaction. In society, there is the self-interest of the whole to be considered as well as the self-interest of the separate individuals composing it. Where individual self-interest is the rule, the level of everyone is forced down to that of the lowest; where the self-interest of society is the standard, the behavior of the lowest rises to at least that of the average.

Lloyd thought that individual self-interest as a master motive had produced intolerabilities for the masses in America and that it was "working decay in all our parts." He did not think that political brotherhood—democracy—could survive without industrial brotherhood ("a people half democratic and half plutocratic cannot permanently endure") and he warned that brotherhood must replace bargainhood and that the profit-seeking captain of industry must give way to the public-serving captain of industry if American civilization was to have a future. Lloyd spoke of the necessity of "honesty, love, justice in the heart of the business world," but he was not making vague exhortations to virtue. He realized that the hearts of men could be changed only if the institutions (which he called "applied beliefs") within which they live and act are modified; and that if social ideals were to become dominant it was necessary to create "the forms which will fit them." To talk of the golden rule in business was foolish, he thought, without talking about the laws, habits, forms, and institutions within which the golden rule may operate freely. Government regulation of private industry was not enough, in Lloyd's opinion; only public ownership of the major industrial monopolies was adequate for correcting injustices in American society and for developing the co-operative spirit in the American people.

Lloyd was no doctrinaire socialist; like most American reformers, he disliked the class-struggle idea and was repelled by the dogmatism of orthodox Marxists. He did not favor, moreover, prohibiting "all individual competitive effort with private capital for private gain," for he believed that individual initiative, as well as social co-operation, was indispensable for social progress. Lloyd did not want individuality swallowed up by society; he wanted to see it extended and broadened and enriched by ever widening contacts of the individual with other individuals. "The isolated man is the mere rudiment of an individual," he said. "But he who has become citizen, neighbor, friend, brother, son, husband, father, fellow-member, in one, is just by so many times individualized. Men's expanding powers of co-operation bring them to the conscious ability to unite for new benefits." Lloyd once humorously called himself a "socialist-anarchist-communist-individualist-collectivist-co-operative-aristocratic-democrat." William James put it more simply. In a letter of introduction he once prepared for the Chicago reformer, he wrote: "Introducing Henry D. Lloyd, lover of the human race."

Bellamy's Co-operative Commonwealth

Edward Bellamy was also a lover of the human race. His passion for social justice was as intense as George's and Lloyd's and his utopian novel, *Looking Backward, 2000–1887* (1888), was even more popular in reform circles for a time than *Progress and Poverty* and *Wealth against Commonwealth*. Bellamy was as much of a socialist as Lloyd was, but, well aware of the average American's distrust of socialism as something foreign, he preferred to call himself a "nationalist." The term was accurate enough where he was concerned. The co-operative commonwealth that he portrayed in *Looking Backward* and in its sequel, *Equality* (1897), was based on the ownership and control by the national government of the entire American economy.

In *Looking Backward,* Julian West, a light sleeper who resorts to hypnosis when troubled by insomnia, is put to sleep by a physician in Boston in 1887 and does not awaken until 2000. He is then discovered by Dr. Leete, who promptly takes him on a tour of (and lectures him on) the wonderful industrial utopia that has grown up in the United States during the intervening 113 years. (He also meets Edith Leete, who is just as didactic as her father, but winsome withal, and falls in love with her.) Throughout the book, Dr. Leete expatiates on the efficiency of the new co-operative order and contrasts its achievements with the shortcomings of capitalist society of a century earlier. The new society was not achieved by revolution; the transition from monopolistic capitalism to co-operative equality occurred peacefully ("the Great Bloodless Revolution") in the 1890's and was carried out in accordance with the wishes of the majority of the American people. Dr. Leete explains to Julian the organization of the new industrial order in precise and vivid detail. Under nationalism (or "public capitalism"), he tells Julian, every citizen, including women, are employees of the government and must serve in the national industrial army, which runs the country, between the ages of twenty-one and forty-five. In return for this service, the citizen receives credit tickets (money is abolished) throughout his entire lifetime, amounting to about $4,000 a year in value, and, in addition, is provided with many free health, education, and welfare benefits by the nation. The profit motive is outlawed; in its place, as an incentive for work, is the motive of prestige. There are medals and honors and prizes and promotions in the army ranks, which range all the way from the lowly workman, third grade, second class, up to division general and, beyond that, to department chief. The motives of public service, patriotism, and the religion of solidarity with one's fellow men are also heavily counted on in the new order. Every effort is made by the administration managing the economy to develop each individual's natural aptitudes and to permit him to choose the occupation in the army for which he is best fitted and which he will most enjoy. Under a program of national planning, made possible by total mobilization of the country's economic resources, the uncertainties, wastes, and periodic crises, as well as the inequities, of nineteenth-century capitalism are eliminated and an economy of scarcity gives way to an economy of abundance in which all citizens share equally. The United States, under nationalism, becomes an astonishingly affluent society, and health, harmony, and happiness prevail. In a sermon that Julian, for a small credit-card fee, hears over an ingenious telephonic device, the Reverend Mr. Barton declares proudly: "Humanity's ancient dream of liberty, equality, fraternity, mocked by so many ages, at last was realized."

Julian is bothered by the regimentation of the new system; but Dr. Leete assures him that personal freedom is zealously safeguarded in the co-operative commonwealth. The citizen may utilize his credit tickets in any way he pleases, and upon retiring from the industrial army at forty-five he may spend his time freely in leisure pursuits of his own choosing. He may, in fact, if he wishes, retire from the army at reduced pay at the age of thirty-three. Most important of all: citizens are free, after a three-year period of basic training, to select the trade, occupation, or profession for which they wish to prepare themselves. In the industrial army, in short, the system of nationalism is "elastic enough to give free play to every instinct of human nature which does not aim at dominating others or living on the fruit of others' labor." But Dr. Leete admits that universal civil (but not military: war is abolished) service is inescapable for every citizen.

> . . . to speak of service being compulsory would be a weak way to state its absolute inevitableness. Our entire social order is so wholly based upon and deduced from it that if it were conceivable that a man could escape it, he would be left with no possible way to provide for his existence. He would have excluded himself from the world, cut himself off from his kind, in a word, committed suicide.

Nevertheless, he explains, service in the army "is regarded as so absolutely natural and reasonable that the idea of its being compulsory has ceased to be thought of." Amid conditions of equality, security, and abundance, the natural nobility of human nature—which is essentially "good, not bad . . . generous, not selfish, pitiful, not cruel, sympathetic, not arrogant"—has been enabled to flower; as a consequence the nationalist order "depends in no particular upon legislation but is entirely voluntary, the logical outcome of the operation of human nature under rational considerations." (There are, apparently, no credit-card burners in Bellamy's utopia.)

Julian West was readily persuaded by the good doctor's case for nationalism. Critics of *Looking Backward* were more skeptical. They pointed out that service in an army (military or industrial), with its hierarchical ethos, scarcely encourages the kind of original thinking and independence of mind among citizens that makes for a dynamic social order. They also charged that eliminating the profit motive would retard production and that conditions of enforced equality would kill off "emulation, skill, personal enterprise" and produce "*a vast system of slavery*" in which there was neither freedom nor abundance. In responding to these criticisms, Bellamy retorted that those most concerned about freedom in the collectivist economy he advocated were entirely silent about the "sordid bondage" that the majority of people experienced under the prevailing system of monopolistic capitalism. But he also made a more positive defense of his position. "Always except this precious liberty of loafing," he wrote,

> I am quite unable to understand what liberties the nationalist plan of industrial organization curtails. Assuming that it is right to re-

quire a man to work, is it a loss of liberty to guarantee him the opportunity to work at what he likes best and can do best? Is it tyranny to insure him promotion, leadership and honor in precise proportion to his achievement? Is it a curtailment of his liberty to make him absolutely free of dependence upon the favor of any individual or community for his livelihood by giving him the constitutional pledge of the nation for it? Is it oppressive to guarantee him against loss of income in old age, and absolute security as to the welfare of his wife and children after he is gone? If to do all these things for a man means to take away his liberties and tyrannize over him, we had better get a new dictionary, for the definitions in the old ones are evidently all wrong.

Bellamy was no Marxist; his socialism was strictly homegrown. Like George and Lloyd, Bellamy was repelled by Marx's materialistic philosophy and he disliked the idea of class struggle, violent revolution, and dictatorship of the proletariat. His plan, he insisted, would involve none of these things; it would represent, in essence, the extension of the principles of the Declaration of Independence from the political to the economic realm. For a brief period, Bellamy's prescription for America's social ills seemed compelling to many Americans. More than 150 Nationalist Clubs, with several thousand members, sprang up in various parts of the country, and there were lectures, speeches, newspapers, and magazines devoted to the gradual achievement of Bellamy's program. But the movement was short-lived; by the mid-1890's it had disappeared. *Looking Backward,* however, continued to be popular into the twentieth century.

American Marxism: Daniel De Leon

The Marxian socialists saw much to criticize in Bellamy: his sympathy for religion, his rejection of economic determinism and class conflict, and the general utopian nature of his thought. Like Marxists everywhere, the American Marxists regarded their socialism as scientific, not utopian or sentimental; it was based squarely upon the scientific analysis of the laws of social development made by Karl Marx. According to Marx, the capitalist system of private ownership of the means of production and distribution was ill adapted to modern industrial life and was bound to become increasingly clumsy in its operations; it would also become steadily more oppressive as more and more people were pushed down into the ranks of the exploited proletariat. A social explosion was inevitable: the proletariat would eventually rise, take over the property of the capitalists, and establish a socialist order in which the major economic resources of society were publicly owned and managed. When, under the dictatorship of the proletariat, the last vestiges of capitalism were eliminated, the state itself (which Marx regarded as an instrument of the capitalists for exploiting the workers) would wither away, and society would move into the final stage of history, communism, a classless society in which people would live and work together in peace, harmony, and freedom.

Marxism arrived in the United States before the Civil War, but it was largely confined to immigrants from Germany and made little or no impact on American thought. The *Communist Manifesto,* written in German by Karl Marx and Friedrich Engels in 1848, was not published in an English version in the United States until 1870, and the first volume of Marx's *Capital* (1867) was not translated into English until 1887. After the Civil War, branches of Marxist groups in Europe were established in the United States, mainly in industrial centers in the East among immigrant workers, and by 1875 there were three tiny socialist organizations struggling for recognition. But the first group to win much attention outside of sectarian circles was the Socialist Labor Party, founded at a convention in Newark, New Jersey, in 1877; strictly Marxist in outlook and tightly organized and disciplined, the SLP has managed to survive to the present day.

Daniel De Leon, a West Indian–born scholar who taught international law for several years at Columbia University, gave the SLP whatever importance it acquired. De Leon started out as a supporter of Henry George and he campaigned for George when the latter ran as mayor of New York City in 1886. He also joined the Knights of Labor and, after reading Bellamy, participated briefly in the Nationalist movement. He began reading Marx in 1889, was completely won over, joined the SLP in 1890, and soon came to dominate the party. De Leon was brilliant, eloquent, and energetic; he was also dictatorial, dogmatic, and vituperative. The single-tax theory of George he came to regard as "half-antiquated, half-idiotic reasoning"; a rival in the SLP who knew a lot about the early American socialist movement was a "250 pound perambulating scrap book and historic junk shop"; and American labor leaders who did not joint the socialist movement were crooks, traitors, "labor fakirs," ignoramuses, and enemies of the people. De Leon probably came to know more about theoretical Marxism than anyone else in the United States; but he also struck out on paths of his own, and Lenin once said that he was the only thinker who added anything of importance to socialist thought after Marx. De Leon wanted capitalist society to be replaced by a system in which industrial, not geographical, constituencies formed the basis of government representation. In De Leon's commonwealth, the working people would be organized into industrial (as opposed to craft) unions and each union would elect delegates to the governing body of the country. "The parliament of civilization in America," he wrote,

> will consist, not of Congressmen from geographic districts, but of representatives of trades throughout the land, and their legislative work will not be the complicated one which a society of conflicting interests, such as capitalism, requires but the easy one which can be summed up in the statistics of the wealth needed, the wealth producible, and the work required—and that any average set of workingmen's representatives are fully able to ascertain, infinitely better than our modern rhetoricians in Congress.

De Leon advocated both economic and political action. In the economic realm, industrial unions must be organized, not to get better wages and working hours, which was a waste of time for socialists, but to prepare for the day when they became the ruling power; in the political realm, the SLP should participate in elections with the aim of capturing the presidency and Congress and then abolishing them. Though De Leon's objective was the overthrow of capitalism, he did not favor force and violence to achieve this objective.

De Leon could hardly be considered a success. The SLP won only 21,000 votes in the 1892 election (compared to the Populists' more than a million) and De Leon's efforts to gain influence in the Knights of Labor and in the AFL ended in total failure. Because of his authoritarian behavior (he was called the "New York Pope"), moreover, a group known as the Kangaroos seceded from the SLP, and they were followed within a few years by another group known as Kanglets. Most of the Kangaroos and Kanglets eventually joined Eugene Debs (who in his warmth and undoctrinaire nature was the reverse of De Leon) in the Socialist Party of America, organized in 1901. De Leon's failure to win America to socialism cannot of course be attributed to personal shortcomings. The fact that Marxism came from abroad and had a dogmatic and anti-religious temper that was distasteful to American reformers probably doomed De Leon's efforts from the outset. The fluidity of American society, the possession by American workers of the right to vote and hold office, and the fact that the American people had their own democratic ideals—the liberty, equality, and government by consent enshrined in the Declaration of Independence—also militated against the success of Marxism in America even during the darkest days of industrial depression in the nineties.

Communist Anarchism: John Most

If De Leon's socialism had little appeal for most Americans, John Most's communist anarchism seemed even less attractive. Communist anarchists like Most agreed with the Marxists on the necessity for overthrowing capitalism and replacing it with socialism and then communism, but since they regarded the state as the primary upholder of capitalism, they viewed its overthrow as their major task. The anarchists utilized two techniques for advancing their aims: (1) propaganda of the word, that is, spreading the anarchist gospel by means of speeches, lectures, pamphlets, newspapers, and books; and (2) propaganda of the deed, that is, violent resistance to established authority in the form of strikes, riots, bomb-throwing, and assassination of prominent public officials.

John Most, who made something of a stir in the United States in the Gilded Age, was a German anarchist who espoused propaganda of the deed. After suffering imprisonment on numerous occasions for anarchist agitation in Germany, Austria, and England, he came to the United States in 1882 to spread the anarchist gospel. To help the cause, he turned out a pamphlet entitled *Science of Revolutionary Warfare: A Manual of Instructions in the Use and Preparation of Nitroglycerine, Dynamite, Gun-Cotton, Fulminating Mercury, Bombs, Fuses, Poisons, Etc., Etc.*, containing chapters on how to poison bullets and daggers, where to put bombs, and how to make self-inflammable liquids for starting fires. At a congress of social revolutionaries (mostly German) in Pittsburgh in 1883, Most helped draft a manifesto (containing passages from both the Declaration of Independence and Marx) which called for the destruction of the state and of the capitalist class by all means, including force. Most wrote many pamphlets setting forth his creed; and his ideology, which wavered between socialism and anarchism for a time, finally became definitely anarchist-communist in its emphasis on opposition to the state. "Our principle," he wrote, "is: to prevent all command over man by his fellow-men, to make state, government, laws, or whatsoever form of compulsion existing, a thing of the past, to establish full freedom for all. Anarchism means first and foremost freedom from all government."

Most believed that coercive institutions corrupt the heart, and that with their elimination and the establishment of a society based on voluntary co-operation, man's basic goodness and rationality would flower. "Morally," he said, "the state, the government, and the laws are the principal causes of vice and crime. But with the cause the effect will disappear." Most abandoned propaganda of the deed after the Haymarket Square explosion in 1886, which was blamed on anarchists. But the attempt of an anarchist to kill Carnegie Steel official Henry Clay Frick in 1892 and the assassination of President McKinley by a demented anarchist in 1901 led to a crackdown by the authorities, and the anarchist movement, mainly confined to immigrants and always tiny, did not last long into the twentieth century.

Conservatism in the Churches

In varying degrees of acerbity, the reformers of the Gilded Age attacked the churches for their massive indifference to the social injustices that seemed so obvious to those who cared to look. Except for the Marxian socialists and the anarchists, most reformers (George, Lloyd, and Bellamy, for example) were generally sympathetic to religion in its broadest sense; in its institutional form, however, they regarded it as a stark betrayal of the ethical principles contained in Judeo-Christian tradition. The social conservatism of the churches was, in fact, pronounced; while not condoning the more outrageous misdeeds of businessmen like Jay Gould, clerical leaders looked with favor, even enthusiasm, on the American system of acquisition and enjoyment and pronounced it socially and morally above reproach. It seemed clear enough to those reared in the Protestant ethic:

wealth is God's reward for diligent endeavor and poverty His punish-
ment for idleness and neglect. In the long run, said Episcopal Bishop
William Lawrence, "it is only to the man of morality that wealth
comes." "Put ten thousand immoral men to live and work in one
fertile valley," he suggested, "and ten thousand moral men to live
and work in the next valley, and the question is soon answered as to
who wins the material wealth. Godliness is in league with riches."
Private property, in the view of clergymen like Lawrence, has a
divine sanction; man holds his property as a steward of the Lord and
he should accumulate it and manage it with care, wisdom, and foresight. "God has need of rich Christians," said the *Congregationalist*
in 1869, "and He makes them, and He assigns particular duties to
them." In a famous speech, "Acres of Diamonds," which he delivered
six thousand times, Baptist minister Russell Conwell exclaimed: "To
secure wealth is an honorable ambition, and is one great test of a
person's usefulness to others. Money is power. Every good man and
woman ought to strive for power, to do good with it when obtained.
. . . I say, get rich, get rich!"

On the major social issues agitating the Gilded Age, most American clergymen took the business point of view. They had tremendous
admiration for captains of industry, especially pious ones like Rockefeller, looked with acute disfavor on labor unions, regarded poverty
as little short of criminal depravity, and heartily objected to all efforts to alleviate the plight of the underprivileged except by acts of
private charity. The fact that the workingman was alienated from the
Protestant church because of its identification with business did not
disturb men like Henry Ward Beecher and De Witt Talmage. Expressing disdain for the working class, Beecher declared that "God
has intended the great to be great and the little to be little." And
Talmage announced that he wanted no working people in his congregation. "I have a good friend," he explained,

who, if he sat in the front pew in church, and a working man
should enter the door at the other end, would smell him instantly.
My friend is not to blame for the sensitiveness of his nose, any
more than you would flog a pointer for being keener on the scent
than a stupid watchdog. The fact is, if you had all the churches
free, by reason of the mixing up of the common people with the
uncommon, you would keep one-half of Christendom sick at their

stomach. If you are going to kill the church thus with bad smells, I will have nothing to do with this work of evangelization.

The Rise of the Social Gospel

Despite Talmage, there was a minority of Protestant clergymen in the Gilded Age who began to take an interest in the workingman (smells and all) and who came to believe that the church erred grievously in siding always with capital and in refusing to see labor's point of view. They observed with misgiving the growing isolation of the Protestant church from the mass of working people and they wondered whether organized religion could continue long to hold its position of moral leadership in American society if a large portion of the population stayed away from the churches. In the big cities and industrial centers, moreover, it was difficult for conscientious ministers to remain completely indifferent to the squalor, misery, disease, and crime in the burgeoning slums and working-class districts; to some of them, continued emphasis on individual salvation, in the manner of Dwight L. Moody, began to seem increasingly irrelevant to life in the big city. The violent upheavals of the period—the railroad strike of 1877, the Haymarket Square affair of 1886, the Homestead strike of 1892, and the Pullman strike of 1894—also shocked many clergymen into a realization that the problems of the age were far more complicated than they seemed to complacent Spencerians like Henry Ward Beecher, and they began taking a second look at the "labor question." There had always been social idealism as well as social conservatism in the Protestant tradition; and it is not surprising that, in an age that experienced several violent capital-labor clashes and two major industrial depressions, voices of protest about the nature of things began to be raised in the church as well as in other sectors of society.

Possibly the declining prestige of Protestant clergymen had something to do with the development of a social conscience in the American Protestant church. Once looked up to with respect and listened to with attention as the moral and intellectual leaders of their communities, Protestant clergymen found themselves being overshadowed by rich men in their congregations (the real objects of admiration for many in the Gilded Age), ignored by large numbers of American wage earners, and displaced in fields like science, philosophy, and economics, as well as in college and university life in general (in which they had once been prominent), by professionals with a secular outlook. Discussing "Our Unchurched Millions" for the *Arena* in October, 1890, Thaddeus B. Wakeman pointed out that

> If we ask, What is the creed which alone satisfies the modern American? the answer is, That which he knows to be true,—and that, in one word, is *Science*. The majority of the American people are already *practically secularists*—people of this world. . . . Our people are unconsciously welcoming the incoming sway of Science and Man; and this is proved by their absence from the churches.

If American society was becoming secularized, it was necessary, perhaps, if the church was to be heard at all, for clergymen to participate in secular as well as in religious activities. Whatever the reasons— the desire to put Protestantism again in contact with the masses and their problems, Christian idealism, the shock of social upheaval, or the wish to compensate for the clergy's loss of prestige in a secular age by asserting leadership in the social field—the fact is that a few Protestant clergymen began concerning themselves with social reform in the Gilded Age and began preaching a "Social Gospel" from their pulpits. The majority of churchmen, to be sure, continued in the old ways; but the new minority was articulate and energetic and it laid the groundwork for the transformation of the major Protestant denominations into socially conscious bodies in the twentieth century.

Like all movements, the Social Gospel movement, which began developing in the 1870's, had its conservative, liberal, and radical wings. The conservatives did not go much beyond encouraging employers to pay higher wages to quiet unrest, though there was some support for factory legislation for women and children. The liberals were thoroughgoing reformers. They read George, Lloyd, and Bellamy, sympathized with the Populists, the Knights of Labor, and the AFL, studied the new political economy diligently, and even joined the American Economic Association, where Richard T. Ely was their firm friend. Their interests were more ethical than theological and their outlook was called variously "new theology," "social theology," and "ethical theology." Most of them believed in an immanent God, working through society as well as man, emphasized Christian love, and looked forward with confidence to the steady improvement of both human nature and social relations. Washington Gladden, pastor of the First Congregational Church of Columbus, Ohio, and the most influential of all the middle-of-the-road Social Gospelers, taught that friendship, service, and good will were the essence of Christ's teachings. Among other things, Gladden, who stressed Christ's admonition to love one's neighbor as oneself, defended labor's right to organize, favored maximum-hours laws and factory inspection, and supported government regulation of natural monopolies. To the left of Gladden stood the Christian socialists. Social salvation, they insisted, lay not in superficial reforms of capitalist society, but in replacing it with a co-operative order based upon Christian principles. Social Gospel radicals like Episcopalian William Dwight Porter Bliss, Congregationalist George D. Herron, and Baptist Walter Rauschenbusch were not Marxists, for Marxist materialism and the doctrine of class war ran counter to their Christian idealism; but their condemnation of capitalism was vigorous and forthright all the same and they did not shrink from supporting candidates of the Socialist Labor Party and, later, the Socialist Party. "I was made a Christian by Karl Marx," Bliss once said, "and a Socialist by Jesus Christ." *"The worst charge that can be made against a Christian,"* said Herron, *"is that he attempts to justify the existing order."*

Most Social Gospelers rejected the old political economy. They thought that the philosophy of laissez-faire substituted Adam Smith for Jesus and minimized spiritual values. For them, the Sermon on the Mount, not *Wealth of Nations*, was to be the guide for social action. They were equally emphatic in their rejection of Social Darwinism. The "law of greed and strife . . ." said Gladden, "is not a natural law; it is unnatural; it is a crime against nature; the law of brotherhood is the only natural law. The law of nature is the law of sympathy, of fellowship, of mutual help and service." Liberals like Gladden were repelled by the idea that labor was a commodity, governed by the law of supply and demand. The workingman, they insisted, should be treated as a friend and brother, and capital-labor relations themselves should be governed by Christian love, not by profits. "The Christian moralist," said Gladden,

> is bound to admonish the Christian employer that the wage-system, when it rests on competition as its sole basis, is anti-social and anti-Christian. "Thou shalt love thy neighbor as thyself" is the Christian law, and he must find some way of incorporating that law into the organization of labor. . . . It must be possible to shape

the organization of our industries in such a way that it shall be the daily habit of the workman to think of the interest of the employer, and of the employer to think of the interest of the workman.

Gladden defended the right of workers to strike, even against businessmen in his own congregation, though he preferred, like most Social Gospelers, having labor disputes settled by arbitration; he also favored profit-sharing plans as a means of reconciling capital and labor. Gladden and his liberal associates in the Protestant church were critical of the business community for its exploitation of labor; they also condemned business for its tendency to cut corners in its efforts to make profits. They denounced the audacious derring-do of the robber barons, condemned dishonest advertising, crooked railroad practices, tricky ways of manipulating the stock market, and the bribery of politicians, and they demanded that businessmen practice "social honesty." When it came to social action the Social Gospelers took a special interest in the urban poor; they founded churches in working-class districts of the big industrial cities, established social settlements in the slums, and developed "institutional churches" with a wide range of educational, welfare, and recreational facilities available for the poor.

Through sermons, lectures, articles, books (like Charles M. Sheldon's *In His Steps,* a best-selling novel about what Jesus would do in the modern age, published in 1897), and through various reform organizations, Protestant clerical reformers, though a distinct minority in the Gilded Age, were in time to have considerable influence on middle-class America. Under their tutelage the Protestant church began moving from the Social Darwinism of Henry Ward Beecher toward the Social Gospel of Washington Gladden, and it was to become strongly oriented toward progressive reform in the twentieth century. The Social Gospel movement was primarily a Protestant phenomenon; but there were also the beginnings in the Gilded Age of a similar emphasis on social consciousness in American Catholicism and American Judaism. By the end of the century, secular leaders like Samuel Gompers, formerly critical of organized religion, were expressing gratification at the new outlook of America's religious leaders.

Chapter 6

William James
and the Open Universe

In 1908, almost two years before he died, William James observed that "the competitive regime, so idolized 75 years ago, seems to be getting wounded to death." But he added calmly: "What will follow will be something better. . . ." It was a remarkable statement coming from a man who was known for his individualism, hated "bigness and greatness in all their forms," and who once confessed that he had received his political education from E. L. Godkin and the laissez-faire-oriented *Nation*. Political and social issues were not James's primary concern, but, full of curiosity to the end, he read H. G. Wells and G. Lowes Dickinson and other critics of the competitive regime in his last years and lamented "the exclusive worship of the bitch-goddess SUCCESS," with its "squalid cash interpretation," which he regarded as America's national disease.

James had always been more open-minded about social matters than his admiration of Godkin might indicate; and, despite the aristocratic conservatism of the milieu in which he lived and worked all his life, he had never been blind to the realities existing outside of his own circle. In 1886, for example, he cautioned his brother, Henry, the novelist, against alarm over the labor upheavals of that year; he was quite sure they were "a most healthy phase of evolution . . . and

123

sure to do lots of good to all hands in the end." Though deploring anarchism, he expressed sympathy for the Knights of Labor and chided Godkin for looking on "the doings of Terence Powderly & Co. too much from without and too little from within." It was James's great gift that he could view people and things from within, that is, from their, not his, point of view. Aristocratic, dignified, urbane, cultured, and puritanic, James was at the same time warm-blooded, earthy, affectionate, exuberant, and democratic. Though the most cosmopolitan of men, he was as American as Mark Twain; he simply did not believe that America's pecuniary corruption could compare with the "corruptive geniuses of monarchy, nobility, church, army" in Europe. James believed that every thinker, even the most abstract, put the stamp of his own personality upon his philosophy; and this was surely true where he was concerned.

The Formative Years

William James was a good deal like his father, Henry James, Sr.: restless, impatient, tender, spontaneous, vivacious. He "is just like a blob of mercury," his sister Alice once said; he "would lend life and charm to a treadmill." His democratic sympathies were probably learned, at least in part, from his father, who as a Fourierist stressed brotherhood, and who believed that, for a right-minded man, a crowded Cambridge horsecar was the nearest approach to heaven on earth. James's lifelong interest in religion was also undoubtedly learned from his father, who was a disciple of the great Swedish mystic, Emanuel Swedenborg, and who wrote extensively on religious matters.

As a boy James showed artistic promise and as a young man he studied painting for a time with a professional. But he was also powerfully drawn to science and in the end decided on science as his life's work. In the fall of 1861 he enrolled in the Lawrence Scientific School at Harvard to study chemistry under Charles W. Eliot (soon to become president of Harvard); he also attended lectures by Louis Agassiz and Jeffries Wyman, and his interests gradually shifted from chemistry to anatomy and physiology and he decided to study medicine with the ultimate aim of teaching. In 1864 he entered Harvard Medical School, and after several interruptions, including a trip to Brazil with Agassiz' expedition in 1865–66 to collect zoological specimens, he took his M.D. in 1869, and then spent two years studying physiology in Germany. In 1873 he became instructor in anatomy and physiology at Harvard, and he spent the rest of his life in the academic world, moving first into the rapidly developing field of psychology and then, finally, into the field of philosophy.

James's search for a vocation had been long, tortuous, and personally agonizing, and it was accompanied by frequent bouts with ill health—eye trouble, backaches, general nervousness—which had undoubted neurotic origins. For several years James suffered from acute spells of anxiety and depression and at times he almost lost the will to live. In 1870, when he was twenty-eight, just after the death of Mary Temple, a beloved young cousin, James experienced a severe attack of panic fear which he later described anonymously in *The Varieties of Religious Experience* (1902) as an illustration of the "sick soul." The image of a young patient he had seen in an asylum (who sat all day "like a sort of sculptured Egyptian cat or Peruvian mummy, moving nothing but his black eyes and looking absolutely non-human") suddenly popped into his mind, and in his morbid identification with the patient he was reduced to "a mass of quivering fear"; after that, he said, he "awoke morning after morning with a horrible dread at the pit of my stomach, and with a sense of the insecurity of life that I never knew before...." For days afterward, James lived on the razor's edge, dreaded being alone, and marveled that other people could go around cheerfully without being aware of "that pit of insecurity beneath the surface of life." In the depths of his depression, James felt as if he were caught in a kind of deterministic straitjacket that constricted both thought and action, and it seemed to him that life without freedom was unbearable. But James had been reading the French philosopher Charles Renouvier, who made out a forceful case for freedom of the will, and he finally resolved to pull himself out of his misery by a sheer act of will. "I think yesterday was a crisis in my life," he wrote in his diary on April 30, 1870.

> I finished the first part of Renouvier's second "Essais" and see no reason why his definition of free will—"the sustaining of a thought *because I choose to* when I might have other thoughts"— need be the definition of an illusion. At any rate, I will assume . . . that it is no illusion. My first act of free will shall be to believe in free will . . . ; believe in my individual reality and creative power. My belief, to be sure, *can't* be optimistic—but I will posit life (the

real, the good) in the self-determining *resistance* of the ego to the world. Life shall [be built in] doing and suffering and creating.

James's father, who had undergone a similar experience of panic fear as a young man, was delighted by the eventual reappearance of his son's energetic and buoyant spirit. "I was afraid of interfering with it," he wrote Henry, Jr., after an animated visit from William,

> or possibly checking, but I ventured to ask what specially in his opinion had promoted the change. He said several things: the reading of Renouvier (specially his vindication of the freedom of the will) and Wordsworth, whom he has been feeding upon now for a good while; but especially his having given up the notion that all mental disorder required to have a physical basis. This had become perfectly untrue to him. He saw that the mind did act irrespectively of material coercion, and could be dealt with therefore at firsthand, and this was health to his bones. . . .

James's emotional difficulties as a young man drew him into the field of psychology, and he was eager to learn all he could about the relation between mind and body. From his own unhappy experience he developed a deep sympathy for people in trouble, and he was anxious, in his psychology and later his philosophy, to help make life (which he regarded as essentially tragic) happier and more livable for people. Freedom became the keystone of his outlook; though, as a scientist, he accepted determinism as a necessary presupposition for any generalizing about human behavior, he also insisted on preserving some measure of freedom for the individual in his system of thought. A totally determined human existence, in his opinion, would be morally meaningless.

James as a Harvard Professor

James's own life after he solved his personal problems and found his vocation was of course creative and fruitful, both personally and professionally. He married in 1878 and became a devoted husband and loving father, and he also developed into a stimulating teacher at Harvard. To his students he seemed dynamic and vibrant. "To see him," said one student, "was never to forget what it means to be alive." James let students ask questions in class, unusual in those days, walked and talked with them outside of the classroom, and entertained them at his home. He was the reverse of the pedant; in fact, he felt like a humbug as a professor, he once confessed, because so much of the paraphernalia of academic life (including what he called the "Ph.D. octopus") seemed ridiculous to him. When Gertrude Stein, a special student at Radcliffe, came to take her final examination with him, she read the questions and then wrote on her blue book, "Dear Professor James, I am so sorry but really I do not feel like an examination paper in philosophy today," and left the room. The following day she received this note from James: "Dear Miss Stein, I understand perfectly how you feel. I often feel like that myself." He then gave her the highest grade in the class. As a psychologist, James was interested both in psychical research (he attended séances and was president for a while of the American Society for Psychical Research) and in the effect of drugs on the mind. He experimented with drugs himself and on one occasion jotted down some ideas that came to him while under the influence of mescaline. When he later appended these jottings to an essay on Hegel as examples of "Hegelisms," there was considerable indignation among philosophers over his irreverence toward the great German philosopher.

James's Psychology

In 1878 James signed a contract with Henry Holt and Company to write a book on psychology for Holt's American Science Series. Twelve years later he delivered over a thousand pages of manuscript to Holt with the comment that it was "a loathsome, distended, tumefied, bloated, dropsical mass, testifying to nothing but two facts: *1st*, that there is no such thing as a *science* of psychology, and *2nd*, that W. J. is an incapable." But he also told friends that his book, which was published as *The Principles of Psychology* in 1890, might be "rather a vigorous and richly colored chunk," and in this he was quite correct. His book was acclaimed as a masterpiece both here and abroad, translated into several other languages, and soon became the leading textbook in psychology classes in American colleges and universities. James's *Principles* is a landmark in the development of modern psychology. It contains, for one thing, a summing up of all the achievements of French, German, British, Swiss, and American psychologists by the late nineteenth century and an indication of what the major problems facing James's contemporaries in psychology were. It was, in the second place, the first fully developed evolutionary psychology in which the implications of Darwinism for man's mental life were fully explored. It is, thirdly, as George Santayana (a former student of James's) observed, a work of the imagination, written with freshness, vitality, and, at times, poetic beauty. The book contains, finally, many fresh ideas and thoughtful observations about man; James's psychological insights, it has been said, "have the steadiness of a polar star."

Before presenting his own views on human consciousness in *Principles of Psychology*, James felt it necessary to say something about the automaton theory of the mind, then popular with materialists, which held that man was a "conscious automaton," that is, a mere bundle of nervous reflexes acting mechanically. According to this theory, sense organs, moved by external stimuli, awaken brain cells, brain cells awaken each other in a rational and orderly sequence, and finally the last brain vibration discharges downward into the motor tract and produces a motion or action of some kind. The movement from stimulus to response is completely automatic; thinking is not required for behavior. Consciousness, to be sure, accompanies these physiological movements, but it is a mere spectator; it is generally aware of what is going on in the body, but powerless to do anything about it. Thomas Huxley, whom James quoted on the point, thought that all states of consciousness were "immediately caused by molecular changes of the brain-substance," denied that any state of consciousness is "the cause of change in the motion of the matter in the organism," and insisted that our mental conditions are simply "the symbols in consciousness" of the changes which take place automatically in the organism. To James, the idea that consciousness possessed no causal efficacy seemed preposterous. "It is to my mind," he declared, "quite inconceivable that consciousness should have *nothing to do* with a business which it so faithfully attends." James used a Darwinian argument against the automatists. Consciousness, he pointed out, was a product of evolution just as much as the nervous system was; it must therefore have adaptive and survival value. Unless it had proved its utility and efficaciousness in the struggle for existence, it would have been eliminated by natural selection. Yet the higher the animal kingdom, the more complex and intense the consciousness. "From this point of view," wrote James, it seems an organ, superadded to the other organs which maintain the animal in the struggle for existence; and the presumption of course is that it helps him in some way in the struggle, just as they do. But it cannot help him without being in some way efficacious and influencing the course of his bodily history.

James himself took a functional view of the mind. Thinking for him was a process, not a thing; it was a function of the brain. "The bald fact," he said, "is that *when the brain acts, a thought occurs.*" Thinking, he insisted, is the biological functioning of the brain in the same way that breathing is the function of the lungs, digesting the function of the stomach, and seeing the function of the eyes. Like breathing, digesting, and seeing, thinking enables man to adapt to his environment and it is therefore essential to his survival. But James's view of human consciousness as an instrument for human adaptation was not purely utilitarian. He regarded the brain tissue as highly unstable and productive of many spontaneous variations, but he did not think that all of the variations that survived the struggle for existence and shaped human consciousness did so because of their contribution to adaptation on the part of the living organism; some variations, he was convinced, persisted as accidental by-products or "side effects" of the evolutionary process, neither furthering nor hindering the organism's ability to survive. James thought there were important elements in human consciousness—logical, mathematical, aesthetic, and moral—which were quite non-utilitarian in nature but which make certain modes of thinking about the world "natural" to human beings. But that human consciousness, with all of its characteristics, non-utilitarian as well as utilitarian, was the product of evolution James had no doubt. He was a thorough Darwinist and he regarded it as a grievous shortcoming in Louis Agassiz, whom he otherwise admired, that he closed his mind to the doctrine of evolution.

When it came to analyzing the content of human consciousness, James utilized introspection; he began with what everyone "directly knows, namely his total concrete states of mind." The total and concrete way of regarding the mind's changes was for James the only valid one: "Now we are seeing, now hearing; now reasoning, now willing; now recollecting, now expecting; now loving, now hating, and in a hundred other ways we know our minds to be alternately engaged." James's view represented a sharp break with the atomistic view of ideas held by John Locke and the traditional British empiricists. Locke looked upon the mind as a *tabula rasa* (blank tablet), passively receiving simple and discrete sense impressions from the external environment and then combining these simple ideas into complex ideas by certain mechanical laws of association. But James denied that simple and isolated ideas actually ever occur naturally in consciousness; simple ideas are, in fact, abstractions made from the welter of thoughts, feelings, and impressions contained in consciousness. "Consciousness, then," said James,

> does not appear to itself chopped up in bits. Such words as "chain" or "train" do not describe it fitly as it presents itself in the first instance. It is nothing jointed; it flows. A "river" or a "stream" are the metaphors by which it is most naturally described. *In talking of it hereafter, let us call it the stream of thought, or consciousness, or of subjective life.*

The mind, in James's psychology, consists of a continuous and ever changing flow of thoughts in which no segment of the flow is completely identical with what went before. We may think about the same object more than once; but each time our thinking about it (because of our physical condition, recollections, environmental situation, etc.) will be somewhat different from what it was previously. Novelty, in the form of ever fresh states of mind, is perpetually seeping into our consciousness.

According to James, the wonderful "stream of consciousness" is made up of flights and resting places. The resting places, which he called the "substantive parts" of consciousness, are occupied by thoughts of definite things, abstract and concrete, which "can be held before the mind for an indefinite time, and contemplated without changing." The places of flight, which he called the "transitive parts" of consciousness, "are filled with thoughts of relations, static or dynamic, that for the most part obtain between the matters contemplated in the periods of comparative rest." Thinking, James said, tends at all times toward some other substantive part than the one from which it has just been dislodged; and the main use of the transitive parts of consciousness is to lead us from one substantive conclusion to another. That consciousness contains substantive parts— thoughts of people, things, events—was easy enough to grasp; but that it also possessed transitive states—feelings of the relations between objects in the external environment—was more difficult to accept. But James was insistent on the point. "If there be such things as feelings at all," he said,

> *then so surely as relations between objects exist* in rerum natura, *so surely, and more surely, do feelings exist to which these relations are known.* There is not a conjunction or a preposition, and hardly an adverbial phrase, syntactic form, or inflection of voice, in human speech, that does not express some shading or other of relation which we at some moment actually feel to exist between the larger objects of our thought. . . . We ought to say a feeling of *and,* a feeling of *if,* a feeling of *but,* and a feeling of *by,* quite as readily as we say a feeling of *blue* or a feeling of *cold.*

Relations of every sort—of time, space, cause, difference, likeness, change, rate—between objects are directly experienced in consciousness. We have, that is to say, an immediate experience of spatial relations and directions, of temporal relations of past and present, and of all other relations between things. James was the most radical of empiricists.

In addition to transitive flights and substantive perchings, James called attention to several other modifications of consciousness, for which there was no precise name, but which he regarded as just as important as the transitive states. There is the attitude of expectancy which we have when we hear such exclamations as "Wait!," "Hark!," or "Look!" There is the feeling, intensely active, which we have when we are trying to recall a forgotten name or word. There is also the feeling of tendency, that is, the feeling we have when we are about to say something, but have not yet formed the words. James thought that a goodly portion of our psychic life was made up of these "rapid premonitory perspective views of schemes of thought not yet articulate" and that psychology must recognize their importance for thinking. Traditional psychology confined itself to discussing separate images of things, said James, and hence

> talks like one who should say a river consists of nothing but pailsful, spoonsful, quartpotsful, barrelsful, and other moulded forms of water. Even were the pails and pots all actually standing in the stream, still between them the free water would continue to flow. It is just this free water of consciousness that psychologists reso-

lutely overlook. Every definite image in the mind is steeped and
dyed in the free water that flows around it.

James called the halo of relations around an image in the stream of
consciousness a "psychic overtone" or "fringe," and he thought that
psychologists who overlooked these overtones were doomed to super-
ficiality.

James not only criticized Lockian psychology for its simplistic
view of consciousness; he also criticized it for depicting the mind as
a passive *tabula rasa*. For James the mind was active, not passive; as
we have seen, he insisted that it had causal efficacy, that is, had the
power to produce changes in bodily conditions. The efficacy of consciousness, according to James, comes from the fact that the mind is
a *selecting* agency. "Whether we take it in the lowest sphere of sense,
or in the highest of intellection . . ." said James, "the item emphasized
is always in close connection with some interest felt by consciousness
to be paramount at the time." James's belief that consciousness selects
for special attention, in accordance with its varied interests, certain
items from its experience and ignores or suppresses all the rest is basic
to his psychology, and later to his philosophy. Whether he is discussing sensation, perception, conception and memory, or, indeed, ethics,
aesthetics, science, and philosophy, James never fails to note the selective industry of the human mind. From the lowest to the highest
levels of intellection, the mind is always interested more in some
features of its experience than in others, and all the time it is thinking,
it is welcoming and rejecting, that is, it is making choices. Our senses
respond to certain movements in the outside world and ignore the
rest as if they did not exist; then, out of the sensations transmitted to
our consciousness by the sense organs, our attention selects certain
ones (which happen to interest us practically) as worthy of notice,
individualizes them, and gives them names; in reasoning about these
individualized sensations, the mind again picks and chooses; and
picking and choosing are also involved in aesthetics and ethics as in
rational thought. The mind thus

is at every stage a theatre of simultaneous possibilities. Consciousness consists in the comparison of these with each other, the selection of some, and the suppression of the rest by the reinforcing
and inhibiting agency of attention. The highest and most elaborated mental products are filtered from the data chosen by the

faculty next beneath, out of the mass offered by the faculty below that, which mass in turn was sifted from a still larger amount of yet simpler material, and so on. The mind, in short, works on the data it receives very much as a sculptor works on his block of stone. . . . We may, if we like, by our reasonings unwind things back to that black and white jointless continuity of space and moving clouds of swarming atoms which science calls the only real world. But all the while the world *we* feel and live in will be that which our ancestors and we, by slowly cumulative strokes of choice, have extricated out of this, like sculptors, by simply rejecting certain portions of the given stuff. . . .

The mind, in short, is an active, interested, and selective instrument of human adaptation and survival. It is teleological in character; it pursues ends—practical, moral, aesthetic, and theoretical—and chooses means for the achievement of these ends. The enhanced dignity given to man by James's activist view of consciousness is clear enough. Not so clear, perhaps, is the severe blow that James's view gave to the Platonic notion that abstract ideas are fixed, unchanging, and eternal; but it was as heavy a blow as that given by Darwin to the belief in the fixity of species. This was to become more apparent when James turned his attention to specific philosophical problems.

Motives for Philosophizing

The *Principles of Psychology* contains the germs of all the ideas—pragmatism, pluralism, radical empiricism, pure experience—which James was to develop at length later in life when he moved from psychology into philosophy. In a real sense James never abandoned psychology; psychology and philosophy were always closely linked in his mind. James thought there were motives for thinking in philosophy, as in everything else; on the highest as well as the lowest levels of intellection we think in order to satisfy deep-seated needs. On a practical level, James's point is obvious: we become hungry or thirsty and seek some way of satisfying our desire for something to eat or drink. When it came to philosophy and science, however, James's point seemed outrageous to many people. But James insisted that all thinking, even the most theoretical, is in some sense wishful. No system of thought, however abstract or recondite, is the result of pure reason untouched by human desires and preferences. When two or more theories are proposed, each accounting equally well for the facts, the philosopher or scientist will select the one that pleases him the most, or, as James put it, satisfies his "sentiment of rationality" the most fully. Philosophers and scientists, said James,

> desire to attain a conception of the frame of things which shall on the whole be more rational than that somewhat chaotic view which every one by nature carries about with him under his hat. But suppose this rational conception attained, how is the philosopher to recognize it for what it is, and not let it slip through ignorance? The only answer can be that he will recognize its rationality as he recognizes everything else, by certain subjective marks with which it affects him. When he gets the marks, he may know that he has got the rationality.
>
> What, then, are the marks? A strong feeling of ease, peace, rest, is one of them. The transition from a state of puzzle and perplexity to rational comprehension is full of lively relief and pleasure. . . . This feeling of the sufficiency of the present moment, of its absoluteness,—this absence of all need to explain it, account for it, or justify it,—is what I call the Sentiment of Rationality. As soon, in short, as we are enabled from any cause whatever to think with perfect fluency, the thing we think of seems to us *pro tanto* rational.

An Open Universe

When it comes to metaphysics, some thinkers, according to James, get satisfaction out of conceiving of the universe we live in as bound together into a majestic unity of some kind, and they view the world as one, not many; others prefer novelty and diversity to unity, and they refuse to conceive of the plurality of things as being totally swallowed up in some kind of monolithic system. James thought the pluralistic view of the universe was just as rational and empirically valid as the monistic view.

James's own preference was for an "open universe." He had a temperamental dislike for closed systems of thought which claimed to explain everything in the universe, once for all, according to a few basic principles or according to one big principle. "The reader," he warned in the preface to *Principles of Psychology*, "will in vain seek for any closed system in the book." Once, when he bought a farm in

Chocorua, New Hampshire, as a summer home for his family, he told his sister Alice: "Oh, it's the most delightful house you ever saw; has fourteen doors all opening outside." His sister reflected: "His brain isn't limited to fourteen, perhaps unfortunately." The door of James's mind always opened outward. He took a delight in new facts, experiences, and ideas, and he had a deep aversion to imprisoning the rich details of human life in a totally unified system with all the doors locked and the keys thrown away. ("Isn't it abominable," he said to a friend facetiously, "that everybody is expected to spell the same way?") James's universe was an evolutionary one; it was continually changing, growing, and developing, and nothing in it was absolutely fixed and certain. In James's universe there was a place for novelty, chance, and freedom; the future was to a large extent unpredictable.

James vigorously discarded what he called "block universes," that is, systems of thought based on universal determinism. According to block-universe theories (whether in religion, philosophy, or science), the world is a tightly knit system in which everything is related to everything else and in which all that takes place does so because of immutable laws fixed for all eternity. The will of God, implacable fate, Absolute Mind, or the inexorable laws of matter in motion, according to these theories, determine what happens at every stage of development in the world. The Calvinist belief that all happenings have been predestined by an omnipotent God for His own mysterious purposes was of course distasteful to James; but so was the far less harsh concept of God as an Eternal Knower who apprehends all reality (which must therefore be all of a piece) in a flash. The concept of the Absolute, which philosophers substituted for the anthropomorphic God, was equally unpalatable to James. Josiah Royce, James's friend and colleague at Harvard, insisted that an Absolute Idea (or Absolute Mind, Being, or Person) underlies the constitution of nature and of human society and unites them into an all-inclusive order; but James could not accept this view of things. He argued genially but firmly with Royce over the Absolute for years. "The Absolute must get fun out of being you," he once teased Royce. "Damn the absolute!" he exclaimed on another occasion. "The 'through-and-through' universe," said James in 1884 of monistic theories depicting the complete interconnectedness of everything,

seems to suffocate me with its infallible impeccable all-pervasiveness. Its necessity, with no possibilities; its relations, with no subjects, make me feel as if I had entered into a contract with no

reserved rights, or rather as if I had to live in a large seaside board-
ing-house with no private bed-room in which I might take refuge
from the society of the place. . . . The "through-and-through" philosophy . . . seems too buttoned-up and white-chokered and clean-
shaven a thing to speak for the vast slow-breathing unconscious
Kosmos with its dread abysses and its unknown tides.

In James's opinion, monistic and absolutistic philosophies not only
gave too neat, tidy, and elegant a picture of the vast, sprawling, and
rowdy universe that we experience in our everyday lives; they also
destroyed man's freedom by their insistence on all-relatedness and
all-pervasive interdependence. What place for freedom was there in
a universe whose course was inexorably determined by God's will,
Absolute Being, or fixed laws governing the movements of matter?

James did not reject all determinism, for he realized that uniform-
ities and necessities of some kind are essential to any kind of orderly
(and especially scientific) thinking; but he did reject *universal* determinism—the linking of everything into a block universe—in all its
forms. By depriving man of freedom, according to James, universal
determinism made illusions out of both moral responsibility and
human creativity, and it took the heart out of man's struggle against
evil and his search for the good, the true, and the beautiful. James
himself, having experienced almost total paralysis of will during his
emotional crisis of 1870, could live only in a universe in which freedom was a reality and the creative energies of the individual counted
for something. For this reason he was exasperated by Herbert Spencer's monistic evolutionary philosophy, which was such a rage among
Americans in the Gilded Age. Spencer's efforts, in *First Principles*, to
account for everything in the universe by a vague, all-inclusive evolutionary law (whose parody by Thomas Kirkman James liked to quote)
was even more irritating to him than Royce's Absolute. The margins
of James's copy of Spencer's book are filled with expletives: "absurd";
"trebly asinine"; "damned scholastic quibble"; "the ass"; "curse his
metaphysics"; "good God!"

In an essay on "Great Men and Their Environment" (1880), James
vigorously assailed Spencer's theory that historical change is due,
not to the actions of great men, but to the impersonal movement of
social evolution. The great man, said Spencer, is a product of society,
and before he can affect society, society must produce him. "All those
changes of which he is the proximate initiator," according to Spencer,

"have their chief causes in the generations he descended from. If there is to be anything like a real explanation of those changes, it must be sought in the aggregate of conditions out of which both he and they have arisen." But James thought that to explain great men and their influence in terms of "aggregate conditions" was like explaining them in terms of God's will, fate, or Absolute Mind. It contained the "enormous emptiness" of abstract propositions that explain everything in general and nothing in particular. Though James did not deny the importance of environmental factors in shaping people, he was anxious to see that the individual was not swallowed up in the sweeping and impersonal generalizations of Spencerian philosophy. James was impressed by spontaneous variations in human thinking. New ideas, he thought, spring up as "accidental outbirths of spontaneous variation in the functional activity of the excessively instable human brain," and they make a difference in social development. Society may accept or reject the new ideas put forward by outstanding individuals; but if it accepts them, they will have a fermentative effect and society will be modified in "entirely original and peculiar ways." James did not confine his theory of creative individuality entirely to superior minds; he took account of the contributions of all individuals to social change. "There is little difference between one man and another," he declared; "but what little there is, *is very important.*" Each individual is in some respects unique and he may add his bit, however small, to social change. And by recognizing the significance of unusually gifted individuals in history, "each one of us," he said, "may best fortify and inspire what creative energy may lie in his own soul."

The individual, then, is central to James's philosophy. He lives in an open, plastic, unfinished universe in which his ideas, choices, and actions are meaningful. What he thinks and what he does have some effect on the movement of things in the universe. Thinking and acting were closely linked in James's philosophy. "The knower," he once said, "is the doer." Ideas for James were guides for action; they were instruments enabling man to deal fruitfully with his experience. Abstract, as well as simple, ideas are instruments of adaptation and plans of action. Abstract ideas (like the law of gravitation) are generalizations made by the mind to introduce some kind of order into the endless sequence of sense impressions which man perceives and they help man to come to grips with the perpetual flux of sense experience. General ideas are never absolutely and entirely true, for the human mind can never grasp the totality of reality; they are only tentatively true, and they may have to be modified (as Newton's law of gravitation was modified by Einstein's relativity theory) in the light of new information. But whatever unity there is in the universe, James said, has been introduced by man himself. When creative thinkers like Newton and Darwin select certain portions of reality and unify them into the law of gravitation and the law of natural selection, they are introducing something new into the universe with important consequences for the future. Even such common-sense categories as "things," "mind," "body," and "matter," James suggested, were creations of "prehistoric geniuses whose names the night of antiquity has covered up; they may have been verified by the immediate facts of experience which they first fitted; and then from fact to fact and from man to man they may have *spread*, until all language rested upon them and we are now incapable of thinking naturally in any other terms." It is by creative thinking and acting that man participates in the growth and development of the universe, for man's ideas do make a difference in what happens in the world. But man's ideas must be verified by experience; they must put him into fruitful relation with reality and satisfy some human need, physical or intellectual.

Pragmatism

How do we judge the validity of an idea? How do we know whether an idea is true or false? "The truth of a thing or idea," wrote James around 1875, "is its meaning, or its destiny, that which grows out of it." Truth, in other words, is prospective; it has to do with what happens to an idea when it is put to use. James called his view of truth "pragmatic" (practical), and he freely admitted that he had borrowed the term from Charles S. Peirce. Peirce, a brilliant though somewhat eccentric philosopher and mathematician whose unusual gifts James fully appreciated, had been talking about "pragmatism" in the early seventies; in 1878 he published an essay on "How to Make Our Ideas Clear" in the *Popular Science Monthly,* in which he stated that our beliefs are really rules for action and that to develop a thought's meaning we need to determine what conduct it is fitted to produce. James used Peirce's suggestions as a point of departure for his own philosophizing, but he made entirely original contributions of his own to an understanding of the meaning of truth; and the pragmatism that he developed later in life was quite different from what Peirce had had in mind in 1878.

The truth of an idea, James declared, depends on its concrete results when it is put into practice; if the idea puts one into a satisfactory relation with reality, then that idea may be judged true, and if it doesn't, the idea is false. (If an idea has no practical consequences at all when put to work, it is meaningless.) Truth and falsity are thus properties of ideas and can be determined only by getting down to concrete cases. In ascertaining the validity of an idea, therefore, one must ask himself what practical difference the idea will make in experience. The pragmatic method, James emphasized, was an attitude of orientation: "*The attitude of looking away from first things, principles, 'categories,' supposed necessities; and of looking towards last things, fruits, consequences, facts.*" The origin of an idea, its basic premises, its internal consistency or coherence, its logicality or reasonableness, and its elegance are all of secondary importance; the main thing about an idea is its practical consequences (in terms of the sensations it will produce and the behavior it will evoke) when put to work in the stream of experience. "Grant an idea or belief to be true," James's pragmatist says, "what concrete difference will its being true make in any one's actual life; how will the truth be realized? What experiences will be different from those which should obtain if the belief were false? What, in short, is the truth's cash-value in experiential terms?" And his answer is: "*True ideas are those that we can assimilate, validate, corroborate, and verify. False ideas are those that we can not.*" If I see a small, round, thin white object and decide that it is a cigarette, there is only one way, ultimately, in which I can find out whether my idea is valid: pick it up and try to smoke it. If it is truly a cigarette, what I experience when I try to light and smoke it will be quite different from what happens if it is chalk, candy, glass, or grass. We don't, to be sure, have to follow out all of our ideas to their termination in sense experience every hour of the day and every day of the week; we take it for granted that the concepts we use are perceptually based and act accordingly. "Truth," James explained,

> lives, in fact, for the most part on a credit system. Our thoughts and beliefs "pass," so long as nothing challenges them, just as banknotes pass so long as nobody refuses them. But this all points to direct fact-to-face verifications somewhere, without which the

fabric of truth collapses like a financial system with no cash-basis whatever. You accept my verification of one thing, I yours of another. We trade on each other's truth. But beliefs verified concretely by *somebody* are the posts of the whole superstructure.

Somewhere, somehow, and sometime, that is to say, an idea must terminate in a particular fact if it is to be meaningful. James's view has been called "radical empiricism" because of its emphasis on sense experience, but the term "pragmatism" became more popular.

An idea for James was really a kind of hypothesis which was to be tested in much the same way as a scientific hypothesis is tested in the laboratory. James's pragmatic method was in many respects an extension of the scientific method to all ideas. But James thought that the truth of an idea consisted of much more than some sensory experience that we can predict in our minds or actually undergo if we trace an idea's effects in the workaday world. The truth of an idea, he concluded, is identical with the verification process itself. Truth is dynamic, not static; it's a process, not an entity. It involves the very process of verification by which we move successfully from abstract concept to concrete fact. "The truth of an idea," said James,

> is not a stagnant property inherent in it. Truth *happens* to an idea. It *becomes* true, is *made* true by events. Its verity *is* in fact an event, a process: the process namely of its verifying itself, its veri-*fication*. Its validity is the process of its valid-*ation*.

An idea's truth consists of all the concrete experiences that we have while we are verifying it: in the case of the cigarette idea, how the little white thing feels, smells, and tastes when we pick it up and put it into our mouth, what happens when we apply a lighted match to its tip, what sensations we have when we inhale it, and any other experiences we have, in both the long and the short run, in connection with it. The truth of an idea, from this point of view, is always tentative and provisional, not absolute and final, for it is forever open to modification by new experiences and verifying processes. The very process of testing out an idea, moreover, may lead us to new truth and end by changing reality. (Medical research on the effect of smoking on health may drastically alter our idea of what a cigarette is and produce changes in our smoking habits.) "Why may not thought's mission be to increase and elevate," asked James, "rather than simply

to imitate and reduplicate, existence?" James was certain that thinking and knowing did have such an "elevating" function. "In our
cognitive as well as in our active life we are creative," he said. "We
add, both to the subject and to the predicate part of reality. The
world stands really malleable, waiting to receive its final touches at
our hands. Like the kingdom of heaven, it suffers human violence
willingly. Man *engenders* truth upon it."

The view that man "engenders truth" upon reality by generating
ideas—scientific, moral, aesthetic, as well as practical—and trying
them out in the world would, James thought, "add both to our dignity
and to our responsibility as thinkers." To call James's pragmatism,
as some critics have, a justification for an ethic of sheer expediency
and self-aggrandizement is to misunderstand and distort his meaning.
James had the highest moral and intellectual standards, labored tire-
lessly to illuminate our understanding of man and the universe, and
hoped that with knowledge and insight man could create a better
world. Put to the pragmatic test, an ethic of sheer expediency may be
shown to destroy the mutual trust on which to some degree all society rests; the highest ideals, conversely, may be shown, by their
effect on human behavior, to have the greatest value for humanity.

The Right to Believe

James was interested in religion as well as in psychology, philosophy,
and science. "Religion," he once said, "is the great interest of my
life"; "the life of it as a whole," he also said, "is mankind's most important function." James was not concerned with organized religion;
his interest was in personal religious experiences and in individual
beliefs about the nature of things which transcend sense experience.
Like Asa Gray, Joseph Le Conte, and other religiously minded scientists, James wanted to bring about a reconciliation between science
and religion, but he wanted to do it in a way that would not do violence to empirically validated scientific ideas. He sought, in short, a
pragmatic justification for religious faith. Faith, for James, was a
"working hypothesis," and he believed man had just as much right to
adopt working hypotheses, subject to the test of experience, in religion as he did in science. *"If theological ideas prove to have a value
for concrete life,"* he wrote, *"they will be true, for pragmatism, in the
sense of being good for so much. For how much more they are true,
will depend entirely on their relations to the other truths that also*

have to be acknowledged." The Fiske–Le Conte notion of a God immanent in the universe did not appeal to James; like all monistic outlooks, it seemed to imprison man in a closed system and deprive him of his freedom and responsibility. It also raised the problem of evil (if a benevolent spirit is inherent in the universe, why is it that there is so much evil—physical pain, death, natural calamities overwhelming the just and the unjust alike—in the world?) in an acute form. Asa Gray's argument from design was also quite unsatisfactory to James, for Darwin's emphasis on the role of chance variations in the evolutionary process was a fundamental part of James's own philosophy. "From the order of the world," said James of the design argument, "there is no path to God by coercive reasoning, or even by strong analogy or induction." But religion, like science, James was convinced, satisfied certain human needs and it must be taken seriously by the pragmatist. Where science satisfies the intellectual and aesthetic passion for order and unity and economy of thought, religion fulfills the emotional need for some kind of moral meaning in the universe at large. In times of trouble, religion provides comfort and consolation; in times of heroic endeavor (James's own favorite mood), religion gives assurance that the struggle for high moral ideals, against overwhelming odds, is not absurd. "That we believe in God . . ." said James,

> is not due to our logic, but to our emotional wants. . . . The world is a datum, a gift to man. Man stands and asks himself, "What is it?" Science says molecules. Religion says God. Both are hypotheses. Science says, "You can't deduce or explain anything by yours." Religion says, "You can't inspire or console by yours." What is *worth* most, is, after all, the question. Molecules can do certain things for us. God can do other things. *Which things* are worth the most?

Both were eminently worthwhile hypotheses for James.

James himself was convinced of the reality of another world beyond the natural world with which the scientist deals. "I firmly disbelieve myself," he wrote,

> that our human experience is the highest form of experience extant in the universe. I believe rather that we stand in much the same relation to the whole of our universe as our canine and feline

do to the whole of human life. They inhabit our drawing rooms and libraries. They take part in scenes of whose significance they have no inkling. They are merely tangents to curves of history, the beginnings and ends and forms of which pass wholly beyond their ken. So we are tangent to the wider life of things.

But James was never precise about the "wider life of things" which he thought transcended the natural world. Sometimes he simply referred to it as a "*more.*" But it was, he suggested, a spiritual order in which the riddles of the natural order were explained; and it was also an order that was friendly to man's moral ideals and perhaps actively assisted him (possibly by inspiring him with courage, energy, and endurance) in the struggle against evil. If belief in such an order gave meaning to life and made life better worth living, then, James insisted, such a belief had pragmatic value. "Probably to almost every one of us here," he told a Harvard student group, "the most adverse life would seem well worth living, if we only could be *certain* that our bravery and patience with it were terminating and eventuating and bearing fruit somewhere in an unseen spiritual world." There might be one God; or there might be a plurality of higher powers in the unseen spiritual world co-operating with human beings and helping them in the fight against the forces of darkness. And if God helps man, perhaps man helps God in the endless struggle for something better in the world. "I confess," wrote James,

> that I do not see why the very existence of an invisible world may not in part depend on the personal response which any one of us may make to the religious appeal. God himself, in short, may draw vital strength and increase of very being from our fidelity. For my own part, I do not know what the sweat and blood and tragedy of this life mean, if they mean anything short of this. If this life be not a real fight, in which something is eternally gained for the universe by success, it is no better than a game of private theatricals from which one may withdraw at will. But it *feels* like a real fight,—as if there were something really wild in the universe which we, with all our idealities and faithfulnesses, are needed to redeem. . . .

There are undoubted ironies in James's treatment of religion. Though James thought that our passional natures are decisive when it comes to religion, his own concept of God was mainly dictated by the intellectual requirements of his system of thought, not by any profound religious experience that convinced him of the reality of such a God. James's God was finite, temporal, and limited; He was not, that is to say, responsible for evil, nor did He stand in the way of chance, novelty, freedom, and the possibility of creative activity by man. James's religion, furthermore, had to be compatible with empirically validated scientific generalizations about the universe; and it had also to fit comfortably into his open universe. These are the specifications of a philosopher, not a devout believer. James made little use of what he once called the "will to believe," though he vigorously defended the right of others to exercise it freely. Perhaps he best summed up his own personal outlook when he responded to a query about his religious faith toward the end of his life. ". . . My personal position is simple," he wrote,

> I have no living sense of commerce with God. I envy those who have, for I know the addition of such a sense would help me immensely. The Divine, for my *active* life, is limited to abstract concepts which, as ideals, interest and determine me, but do so faintly, in comparison with what a feeling of God might effect, if I had one. It is largely a question of intensity, but differences of intensity may make one's whole centre of energy shift. Now, although I am so devoid of *Gottes-bewusztsein* [consciousness of God] in the directer and stronger sense, yet there is *something in me* which *makes response* when I hear utterances made from that lead by others. I recognize the deeper voice. Something tells me, *"thither lies truth"* . . . Call this, if you like, my mystical *germ*.

Radical Empiricism and Pluralism

James's "mystical germ" made him extremely sensitive to the inner life of the individual of which religion takes account but which philosophy ordinarily overlooks. The real world, as the individual directly experiences it, is "various, tangled, painful," and it cannot be captured by science; yet in its warmth, intimacy, and immediacy, it has a ring of authenticity about it which our impersonal scientific generalizations (colossally important for human life though these are) do not possess. In the deep privacy of every person's heart, James thought, there are unsharable experiences and voiceless intuitions that our abstract ideas can never quite get hold of. James thought that the "thin and noble abstractions" of philosophy were remote from the "big blooming buzzing confusion" of our immediate sensory life, and that if philosophers were to achieve "more solid and real constructions," they must "get into as close contact as realistic novelists with the facts of life." To *be*, he once said, is more important than to *define being*. "It would be an awful universe," he groaned, "if *everything* could be converted into words, words, words." (Unlike many twentieth-century existentialists, James avoided cluttering up reality with technical and frequently incomprehensible verbiage.) Knowledge about a thing (reading a bill of fare) is no substitute for direct acquaintance with a thing (eating an egg), and philosophers err seriously, James said, when they emphasize concepts (ideas and thoughts) at the expense of percepts (sensations and feelings).

What it all comes to is this: James was a radical empiricist. His philosophy began and ended in sense experience. Though he did not deny the importance of concepts in getting us around the manifold of sense experience with convenience and dispatch and in revealing profound aspects of reality to us, he also insisted that living perceptions are equally important for understanding reality and that, in some crucial respects, the deeper features of reality are found only in perceptual experience. "Conceptual knowledge," he said,

> is forever inadequate to the fulness of the reality to be known. Reality consists of existential particulars as well as of essences and universals and class-names, and of existential particulars we become aware only in the perceptual flux. The flux can never be superseded. We must carry it with us to the bitter end of our cognitive business, keeping it in the midst of the translation even when the latter proves illuminating, and falling back on it alone when the translation gives out.

Toward the end of his life, James even suggested that "pure experience," a kind of basic neutral stuff, may be the ultimate datum in the universe, and that it may be taken as mind in one context and as matter in another.

James was a pluralist as well as a radical empiricist to the end. Reality for him could never be a single, all-inclusive systematic whole; it was a strung-along, incompletely integrated, and loosely connected stream of experience full of change and striving. James admitted that pluralistic empiricism "offers but a sorry appearance. It is a turbid, muddled, gothic sort of affair, without a sweeping outline and with little pictorial nobility"; but he thought it vastly preferable to the monistic block. In James's "pluriverse," each part of the world was connected in some ways with other parts, but there was not complete interconnectedness. James did believe, to be sure, that a process of unification, largely through man's efforts, was continually taking place in the world; but he thought that total unity would forever elude mankind. "Ever not quite!" he quoted Benjamin Paul Blood, a pluralistic mystic whom he befriended, as having said, and he commented:

> This seems to wring the very last panting word out of rationalistic philosophy's mouth. It is fit to be pluralism's heraldic device. There is no complete generalization, no total point of view, no all-pervasive unity, but everywhere some residual resistance to verbalization, formulation, and discursification, some genius of reality that escapes from the pressure of the logical finger, that says "hands off," and claims its privacy, and means to be left to its own life. In every moment of immediate experience is [something] absolutely original and novel. "We are the first that ever burst into this silent sea." Philosophy must pass from words, that reproduce but ancient elements, to life itself, that gives the integrally new.

James also liked another statement of Blood's: "There is no conclusion. What has concluded, that we might conclude in regard to it?" The universe was open for James to the day he died.

James did not pretend to have said the last word about any of the matters that engaged his lifelong attention; psychology and philosophy remained open for him to the end. In 1909, a year before his death, he attended an international conference of psychologists meeting at Clark University in Worcester, Massachusetts, and there he met Sigmund Freud, as well as Carl Jung, Ernest Jones, and other psychoanalytic disciples of Freud. Though he was disturbed by Freud's dogmatism and had reservations about "symbolism" as a method of psychology, James expressed hope afterward that "Freud and his pupils will push their ideas to their utmost limits. . . . They can't fail to throw light on human nature. . . ." "The future of psychology," he told Ernest Jones, "belongs to your work." Freud, who didn't much like Americans, returned to Europe with high respect for James.

He never forgot a scene that occurred one day when he and James were on a walk together. James stopped suddenly, Freud recalled, handed him a bag he was carrying, and asked him to walk on, saying that he would catch up with Freud as soon as he had gotten over an attack of angina pectoris which was just coming on. "He died of that disease a year later," wrote Freud; "and I have always wished that I might be as fearless as he was in the face of approaching death."

Chapter 7

Oliver Wendell Holmes, Jr., and the Path of the Law

On March 7, 1900, the Bar Association of Boston gave a dinner in honor of Oliver Wendell Holmes, Jr., who had been appointed Chief Justice of the Supreme Judicial Court of Massachusetts seven months earlier. In his address that evening, Holmes reminisced briefly about his sixteen years as associate justice on the court and then said something about life in general. "Life is action," he told the lawyers,

> the use of one's powers. As to use them to their height is our joy and duty, so it is the one end that justifies itself. . . . Life is an end in itself, and the only question as to whether it is worth living is whether you have enough of it.

Reading Holmes's speech afterward, William James expressed disappointment that the new Chief Justice had taken the occasion to "celebrate mere vital excitement, *la joie de vivre,* as a protest against humdrum solemnity." To James, the moralist, Holmes's views seemed "curiously childish"; mere excitement, he exclaimed, was "an immature ideal, unworthy of the Supreme Court's official endorsement."

James and Holmes

James had forgotten his own protest against the humdrum solemnity that he encountered at Chautauqua, New York, when he went there to lecture in July, 1896. The sheer blamelessness of the place left James panting for excitement. "The flash of a pistol," he wrote his wife, "a dagger, or a devilish eye, anything to break the unlovely level of 10,000 good people—a crime, murder, rape, elopement, anything would do." But James was a meliorist, for all his bluster, and it was inevitable that he should find the views of Holmes, a Darwinian skeptic who was wary of moral idealism and humanitarian aspirations, somewhat jarring. Holmes and James had much in common, but they had never been able to see entirely eye to eye with one another about things even when they were close student friends. In an argument they had as young men, James once insisted that "feeling counts," and Holmes retorted: "To know is not less than to feel." Still, when Holmes was studying law at Harvard after the Civil War and James was in medical school, the two had become friends and developed real affection and esteem for each other. James thought Holmes a "first-rate article" (though "perhaps too exclusively intellectual") and he loved to "jaw" with him about their "dilapidated old friend the Cosmos." There were frequent bull sessions lasting far into the night in which Holmes and James tried to "evolve cosmos out of Chaos"; and when James went abroad for study there were long letters in which the two men continued their philosophical discussions. The time came, however, when "law—law—law," as Holmes put it, replaced metaphysics as Holmes's major preoccupation. ". . . I now go on," he wrote James in 1868,

> with an ever increasing conviction that law as well as any other series of facts in this world may be approached in the interests of science and may be studied, yes and practised, with the preservation of one's ideals. I should even say that they grew robust under the regimen,—more than that I do not ask.

James thought Holmes was too ambitious for personal glory; "He is a powerful battery," he remarked, "formed like a planing machine to gouge a deep self-beneficial groove through life." He also thought Holmes was overworking; but he was impressed by Holmes's diligence nonetheless. "This must lead," he predicted, "to Chief Justice, U.S. Supreme Court."

Though Holmes and James drifted apart after they left school, they never entirely lost touch with each other. In some respects, too, they shared a common outlook, and Holmes himself is sometimes described as a legal pragmatist. Like James, Holmes rejected absolutes. "The truth to me," he said, "is what I can't help believe; but I do not suppose that my can't helps are compulsory for the universe." Holmes once said that he could write all he knew on half a sheet of paper, but that he would need the other half on which to write, "I'm not sure!" He was willing, he said, to "leave absolute truth for those who are better equipped." Holmes also shared James's distrust of excessive formalism in thinking. "To rest upon a formula," he said, "is a slumber that, prolonged, means death." His belief that to act "is to affirm the worth of an end, and to persist in affirming the worth of an end is to make an ideal" comes pretty close to what James said in his famous essay on the "Will to Believe"; to some extent, moreover, Holmes shared James's individualism. ("Deep-seated preferences," he said, "can not be argued about—you can not argue a man into liking a glass of beer.") Nevertheless, Holmes and James were quite at variance in their outlooks. Holmes read James's essays and books and expressed some sympathy for pragmatism, but he found James's defense of the right to believe in religion soft and sentimental. He was always more of a skeptic than James about everything (except science), including freedom; at the same time he had a way of celebrating sheer physical exuberance that was appalling to James.

Holmes's War Experience

Holme's tributes to the life of joyous action, which James thought overdone, were undoubtedly based on his experience as a soldier during the Civil War. Holmes always looked back to the Civil War with nostalgia. In a Memorial Day address in 1884, he declared: "I think that, as life is action and passion, it is required of a man that he should share the passion and action of his time at the peril of being judged not to have lived." Then he went on to say that "the generation that carried on the war has been set apart by its experience. Through our great good fortune, in our youth our hearts were touched with fire. It was given to us to learn at the outset that life is a profound and passionate thing." Holmes had an aristocratic view of war: war, he thought, by giving people a feeling of being part of "an unimaginable whole," lifted them out of the morass of selfish materialism and pleasure seeking into a world in which honor, courage, self-sacrifice, and manly heroism counted for something. (James acknowledged that this could be so, but he sought a "moral equivalent for war.") Holmes had enlisted in the army toward the end of his senior year at Harvard, served three years with the 20th Massachusetts Volunteers, and was wounded three times. Back in Boston, after leaving the service in July, 1864, the handsome young ex-soldier liked to shock young ladies by calling war an "organized bore," but he did not really think this was so. In the army he had faced pain and death with honor and fortitude and he was proud of his war record.

The Civil War was in some respects the greatest influence on Holmes's outlook. For all of his hard-boiled realism and his skepticism about universal moral ideals, Holmes had a tendency in later years to romanticize, even sentimentalize, about war; and he always took special pleasure in reminding humanitarian reformers that life was hard and tough and full of suffering and that struggle was inherent in human existence. In a famous Memorial Day address on "The Soldier's Faith" in May, 1895, Holmes deplored the growing belief that war was wicked and foolish and bound to disappear. The struggle for life, he insisted, is "the order of the world, at which it is vain to repine"; man's destiny is battle and his highest ideals are drawn from war. A world of universal peace, plenty, and comfort, at which reformers appeared to be aiming, seemed dull, flat, and unprofitable to Holmes. Life without "the divine folly of honor" would be unendurable. "I do not know what is true," Holmes told his audience,

> I do not know the meaning of the universe. But in the midst of doubt, in the collapse of creeds, there is one thing I do not doubt . . . and that is that the faith is true and adorable which leads a soldier to throw away his life in obedience to a blindly accepted duty, in a case which he little understands, in a plan of campaign of which he has no notion, under tactics of which he does not see the use.

To James such notions seemed like the rankest kind of irrationalism, and the "will to believe" which he defended was cautious and tentative indeed compared to the blind fighting faith that Holmes found so inspiring. Holmes acknowledged that war, "when you are at it, is horrible and dull." But when it is over, he said, "you see that its message was divine." That war was elevating and ennobling Holmes never had any doubt. "In this snug, oversafe corner of the world we need it," he said,

> that we may realize that our comfortable routine is no eternal necessity of things, but merely a little space of calm in the midst of the tempestuous untamed streamings of the world, and in order that we may be ready for danger. . . . For high and dangerous action teaches us to believe as right beyond dispute things for which our doubting minds are slow to find words of proof. Out of heroism grows faith in the worth of heroism. The proof comes later and even may never come. Therefore I rejoice at every dangerous sport which I see pursued. The students at Heidelberg, with their sword-slashed faces, inspire me with sincere respect. I gaze with delight upon our polo-players. If once in a while in our rough riding a neck is broken, I regard it, not as a waste, but as a price well paid for the breeding of a race fit for headship and command.

Such sentiments were outrageous to James; and they represent, of course, only one aspect of Holmes's philosophy of life.

Legal Scholarship

After getting out of the service, Holmes entered Harvard Law School, took his law degree in 1866, was admitted to the bar the following year, and began practicing in Boston. He also became heavily involved in legal scholarship. In 1869 he undertook the preparation of a new edition of Chancellor Kent's famous *Commentaries on American Law* (which was published in 1873) and in 1870 he began a three-year stint as editor of the *American Law Review*, for which he also wrote distinguished essays and comments in the 1870's. "His whole life, soul and body," William James's mother noted, "is utterly absorbed in his *last* work upon his Kent." When Holmes had dinner with the Jameses, they were amused to see him carry his Kent manuscript around in a green bag wherever he went. "He started to go to Will's room to wash his hands," Mrs. James reported, "but came back for his bag, and when we went to dinner, Will said, 'Don't you want to take your bag with you?' He said, 'Yes, I always do so at home.' His pallid face, and this fearful grip upon his work, makes him a melancholy sight." Holmes's ambitions as a young man were colossal; he had concluded that "a man may live greatly in the law," and he was determined to live greatly. Living greatly for Holmes meant achieving distinction in the world of thought as well as the world of action; many years later he spoke of "the secret isolated joy of the thinker who knows that, a hundred years after he is dead and forgotten, men who never heard of him will be moving to the measure of his thought . . ." Holmes was to know something of this joy. His lectures for the Lowell Institute in Boston in the winter of 1880–81 were well received, and his influential book *The Common Law* (1881), based on the Lowell lectures, was regarded as the foremost contribution to legal thought and scholarship appearing in the English-speaking world in the late nineteenth century.

Legal Realism and Social Darwinism

Holmes was a "legal realist," that is, he took a practical, scientific, and empirical rather than an abstract, metaphysical, and formal approach to the law, and he kept his eyes on the clash of social interests underlying legal and constitutional issues. Early in his career, it is true, he concerned himself with the problem of classification, and in 1870 he published an essay on "Codes, and the Arrangement of the Law," in which he proposed a classification of the law based on duties rather than rights. But he soon abandoned this rather taxonomic effort for more empirical concerns, and in some lectures on jurisprudence which he gave at Harvard in the spring of 1872 (summarized in the *American Law Review* for October, 1872) he showed his real talent: the ability to cut through to the heart of things in finding out what the law is actually all about.

Holmes's point of departure was the Austinian conception of law. John Austin, influential British writer on jurisprudence, had defined law as the command of the sovereign (supreme political power) in society. The courts, according to Austin, represent the sovereign; hence their decisions are commands of the sovereign and constitute law. The decisions of the courts may be influenced by the mores of society, but these mores are only motives for decisions, not laws in themselves. Not until mores are incorporated into rules laid down by the courts and officially proclaimed can they be regarded as laws, that is, as commands of the sovereign speaking through the courts. Holmes regarded the Austinian definition of law as too narrow and oversimplified. Customs and traditions, he pointed out, frequently have as much compulsory power over people's behavior as court rulings and statutes do. Moreover, previous court decisions (precedents) and statutes enacted by legislatures can be just as much motives for the decisions made by judges as the customs and usages of society are. "What more indeed is a statute," Holmes asked,

> and in what other sense law, than that we believe that the motive which we think that it offers to the judges will prevail, and will induce them to decide a certain case in a certain way, and so shape our conduct on that anticipation. A precedent may not be followed; a statute may be emptied of its contents by construction; or may be repealed . . . after we have acted on it; but we expect the reverse, and if our expectations come true, we say that we have been subject to law in the matter in hand. It must be remembered . . . that in a civilized state it is not the will of the sovereign that makes lawyers' law, even when that is its source, but what a body of subjects, namely, the judges, by whom it is enforced, *say* is his will. The judges have other motives for decisions, outside their own arbitrary will, beside the commands of their sovereign. . . . The only question for the lawyer is, how will the judges act? Any motive for their action, be it constitutional statute, custom, or precedent, which can be relied upon as likely in the generality of cases to prevail, is worthy of consideration as one of the sources of law, in a treatise of jurisprudence.

The suggestion that, practically speaking, what the law is depends on our prediction of how the courts will rule in given instances was to be explored at greater length by Holmes later on.

Holmes's legal realism was based squarely on a Darwinian view of things. Holmes read Spencer's *First Principles* like so many other Americans during the Gilded Age and he took for granted thereafter the application of evolution to law, as well as to other social institutions. The concept of the struggle for existence, moreover, confirmed what he had learned during the Civil War about the primacy of force in human affairs. Since he was also a devout Malthusian, impressed by nature's cruelty and convinced that social reformers (most of whom he regarded as humbugs) could do little to soften the harshness of life, he came close at times to articulating Social Darwinism in its most brutal form. Holmes was unusual in taking an evolutionary view of the law at a time when most Americans looked upon the law (and especially the U.S. Constitution) as a body of fixed principles almost sacred in nature. He was also unusual, even among Social Darwinists, in his habit of stripping away the rhetoric by which social questions are described and trying to get at the realistic forces at work beneath.

Holmes's legal philosophy is seen clearly in his comments on the Gas-Stokers case, which agitated Great Britain for some time, in the *American Law Review* for July, 1873. In the fall of 1872, leaders of the Gas-Stokers Union, which had gone on strike in London, were convicted of conspiracy for violating their contracts of employment and sent to jail for a year. A storm of protest followed; the judge was castigated for imposing the sentence and the law by which the strikers were convicted was called "class legislation." In his unsigned comments on the case, Holmes admitted freely that class legislation was involved. "But it is no sufficient condemnation of legislation," he said, "that it favors one class at the expense of another; for much or all legislation does that. . . ." In every society, according to Holmes, there is a struggle for power taking place, and the more powerful interests at any given time "must be more or less reflected in legislation; which, like every other device of man or beast, must tend in the long run to aid the survival of the fittest." The objection to class legislation, he added, "is not that it favors a class, but either that it fails to benefit the legislators, or that it is dangerous to them because a competing class has gained in power, or that it transcends the limits of self-preference which are imposed by sympathy." Holmes saw nothing reprehensible about self-preference—"In the last resort a man rightly prefers his own interest to that of his neighbor"—though he acknowledged that it must be tempered by sympathy. As for the utilitarian view that laws are to be judged by their contribution to the greatest good of the greatest number, Holmes subjected this to Darwinian questioning also. "Why should the greatest number be preferred?" he asked.

> Why not the greatest good of the most intelligent and most highly developed? The greatest good of a minority of our generation may be the greatest good of the greatest number in the long run. But if the welfare of all future ages is to be considered, legislation may as well be abandoned for the present. If the welfare of the living majority is paramount, it can only be on the ground that the majority have the power in their hands. The fact is that legislation in this country, as well as elsewhere, is empirical. It is necessarily

made a means by which a body having the power, puts burdens which are disagreeable to them on the shoulders of somebody else. Communism would no more get rid of the difficulty than any other system unless it is limited or put a stop to the propagation of the species. And it may be doubted whether that solution would not be as disagreeable as any other.

Holmes never lost sight of the power relations at the heart of society and he was impatient all his life with efforts of sentimentalists to minimize them or to conceal them under a moralistic covering. Unlike most Social Darwinists, however, Holmes accepted the quest for power by labor as well as by capital (though his sympathies were generally with the latter) as normal, natural, and entirely in accord with Darwinian principles. There was no Social Darwinist quite like Holmes.

Holmes's Darwinism pervades his classic, *The Common Law*. Self-interest, on the part of both the individual and the state, he thought, is the major factor in the struggle for survival. Early in the book he announced frankly his opinion that "the *ultima ratio*, not only *regum*, but of private persons, is force, and that at the bottom of all private relations, however tempered by sympathy and all the social feelings, is a justifiable self-preference." When a man is in the middle of the ocean on a plank, said Holmes, and a stranger tries to get hold of it, the man will push him off to save his own skin. "When the state finds itself in a similar position," he added, "it does the same thing." Holmes thought it possible (though not probable) that the time might come when man's social instincts would control his actions absolutely. "But they have not yet done so," he said, "and as the rules of law are or should be based upon a morality which is generally accepted, no rule founded on a theory of absolute unselfishness can be laid down without a breach between law and working beliefs."

In his analysis of the common law, Holmes never deviated from his basic assumption that a "justifiable self-preference," moderated by social sympathies, motivates men's behavior and that it is quite in accord with Darwinian principles for men to struggle for their own interests in society. He specifically rejected the Kantian imperative—the idea that man, being a person, should always be treated as an end in himself, and never as a means to some other end—and, by implication, the entire Christian ethic of self-sacrifice. He also called in question the belief that in all free communities, citizens have equal rights to life, liberty, and personal security; society cheerfully overrides all of these rights, he declared, whenever it thinks its survival is at stake. "No society has ever admitted that it could not sacrifice individual welfare to its own existence," he declared firmly.

If conscripts are necessary for its army, it seizes them, and marches them, with bayonets in their rear, to death. It runs highways and railroads through old family places in spite of the owner's protest, paying in this instance the market value, to be sure, because no civilized government sacrifices the citizen more than it can help, but still sacrificing his will and his welfare to that of the rest.

Holmes of course placed a high value on civility, tolerance, and mutual respect in social relations; but he never lost sight of the configurations of power which underlie and shape the cultural order. Where most American Social Darwinists paid at least lip service to Christian ideals, Holmes never pretended that the Darwinian view and Christian ethics could be reconciled in any serious sense.

The Common Law

The common law, when Holmes began studying it in the early 1870's, was in considerable disarray—"chaos without an index," as someone put it. Holmes hoped, by a painstaking analysis of the history and structure of the common law, to discover its basic concepts and, by making these explicit, introduce some kind of order into the law which would be both intellectually satisfying and practically useful. Holmes was familiar with the efforts of Jeremy Bentham and the utilitarians to reform the law in the interest of better procedures and more rational objectives (though he regarded their work as essentially pre-Darwinian). He also knew the work of John Austin, and though, as we have seen, he took exception to much of what Austin said, he admired his accomplishments in the field of analytic jurisprudence. He had also studied Sir Henry Maine's *Ancient Law*, that epoch-making study of the ancient laws of Rome; and in some respects he was motivated by a desire to do for the common law of England what Maine had done for Roman law.

Holmes was interested in both history and analysis; history was indispensable for understanding why the common law was what it was. But history was to be a tool for analysis, not an end in itself, for

Holmes's interest was primarily that of a jurist, not a legal historian. Holmes brought to his task an amazing fund of information. He had mastered the details of the English common law while working on his annotation of Kent's *Commentaries* and he also knew Roman law thoroughly and was well acquainted with the work of German scholars in this field. When Holmes launched his study of the common law, he knew that some English jurists wanted to use Roman law to bring order into the common law of England, but he was strongly opposed to this approach. Roman law had gotten heavily involved in Kantian and Hegelian metaphysics at the hands of German scholars, and Holmes, an empiricist with strong anti-metaphysical feelings, was anxious to keep the common law completely free of Kantian imperatives and Hegelian absolutes. For this reason, his tendency was to minimize Roman influences on English law and to emphasize its Teutonic origins.

Holmes's *Common Law* was a milestone in American legal development and many of its ideas have become an essential part of American thinking about the law. Holmes began the book by explaining that his object was to present a general view of the common law, and that to accomplish his task he needed other tools beside logic. "It is something to show that the consistency of a system requires a particular result," he said, "but it is not all." Then came the most famous passage in the book:

> The life of the law has not been logic: it has been experience. The felt necessities of the time, the prevalent moral and political theories, intuitions of public policy, avowed or unconscious, even the prejudices which judges share with their fellow-men, have had a good deal more to do than the syllogism in determining the rules by which men should be governed. The law embodies the story of a nation's development through many centuries, and it cannot be dealt with as if it contained only the axioms and corollaries of a book of mathematics. In order to know what it is, we must know what it has been, and what it tends to become.

In the examination of early forms of liability, criminal law, torts, and contracts which follows, Holmes saw the common law as tending to become increasingly objective in its standards. He used both logic and historical experience in presenting his thesis.

In the first chapter, "Early Forms of Liability," Holmes established the point that in the development of the law, new wine is continually being poured into old bottles. Just as the clavicle in the cat survives from some earlier creature to which a collarbone was serviceable, so precedents survive in the law long after they have outlived their usefulness and the reason for their original existence has been forgotten. "The customs, beliefs, or needs of a primitive time," said Holmes,

> establish a rule or formula. In the course of centuries the custom, belief or necessity disappears, but the rule remains. The reason which gave rise to the rule has been forgotten, and ingenious minds set themselves to inquire how it is to be accounted for. Some ground of policy is thought of, which seems to explain it and to reconcile it with the present state of things; and then the rule adapts itself to the new reasons which have been found for it, and enters on a new career. The old form receives a new content, and in time even the form modifies itself to fit the meaning which it has received.

Holmes thought the moral language appearing in many of our rules of law was a survival from ancient times and that it no longer possessed much meaningfulness. Our modern system of private liability for the consequences of a man's acts, he said, did have its origin in the notion of actual intent and actual personal culpability, but this was because the early forms of legal procedure were based on primitive animism and on the passion for revenge. Primitive peoples, according to Holmes, ascribed deliberate and malevolent intent to moving things (animate and inanimate)—animals, falling trees, ships—which harmed people, held them morally responsible, and insisted on wreaking vengeance on them. The animal that killed a man was slain and cast beyond the borders; the tree that fell on a man was cut to pieces and its chips scattered to the winds. The owner of the offending thing was expected to surrender it to the injured party or to pay some kind of compensation in order to buy off the vengeance. Today, said Holmes, a man is quite properly bound at his peril to keep his cattle from trespassing; he is also liable for damage done by his dog or by any fierce animal, "if he has notice of a tendency in the brute to do the harm complained of." Why is he liable? Because he is personally guilty of carelessness or neglect in handling his animals? Not according to Holmes. Considerations of public policy, not personal blameworthiness, have come to dictate that the law hold him liable for harm inflicted by his animals on innocent people. The standard is objective and social, not subjective and individual. Nevertheless, the moral terminology—which had its origins in the desire for revenge on offending things in olden times—persists and objective rules are explained (inaccurately, in Holmes's opinion) by moral considerations. Holmes wanted to divest the law of its moral coloring, as much as possible, so that more purely external legal standards could be established. The separation of law and morals, he thought, would make possible a more scientific legal system and one that would serve human needs in modern times more adequately.

Having established the proposition that the law has been progressively moving away from the belief that an offender is guilty of moral turpitude and evolving toward more objective standards of fault, Holmes proceeded to apply his thesis to the criminal law, to torts (civil wrongs), and to contracts. In criminal law, he accepted prevention of crime, not reform of the criminal or retribution for the wrong he has done, as the chief justification for society's insistence on punishing the criminal. "For the most part," he said, "the purpose of the criminal law is only to induce external conformity to rule." This is a social objective; the public safety, not individual regeneration, is its highest consideration. The law is concerned with the consequences of actions which are harmful to society, not with personal morality. "In directing itself against robbery or murder . . ." explained Holmes, the purpose of criminal law "is to put a stop to the actual physical taking and keeping of other men's goods, or the actual poisoning, shooting, stabbing, and otherwise putting to death of other men. If those things are not done, the law forbidding them is equally satisfied, whatever the motive."

How does the law attempt to prevent actions deemed injurious to society? By rendering certain acts criminal because they are done under circumstances in which they are likely to cause some harm that the law seeks to prevent. The law deals with conduct, not conscience; it proscribes deviations from certain standards of behavior. These standards depend ultimately upon the moral sense of the community; as Holmes put it, the "first requirement of a sound body of law is, that it should correspond with the actual feelings and demands of the community, whether right or wrong." The average person with ordinary intelligence and understanding is expected to observe his society's rules of conduct. If he acts imprudently and causes injury, he may be punished, no matter how innocent his intentions. At his peril a citizen must behave in the way a reasonable and prudent member of his society would behave: he must know the law of his community, and be able to calculate the consequences flowing from courses of action which he chooses to initiate. If a workman on a housetop at midday knows that the space below is a street in a large city, he knows facts from which a man of average understanding would infer that there are people below. He should make that inference; in fact, he is chargeable with knowledge of that fact whether he makes the inference or not. If, then, he throws a heavy beam down into the street, he performs an act that a person with ordinary intelligence would foresee is likely to cause serious injury or death. And if death is caused by his act, he is guilty of murder even if he did not foresee the event and his intentions were not homicidal. On the other hand, if the workman has reasonable cause to believe that the space below is a private junkyard from which all people are excluded, then, if he throws the beam down and it happens to hit someone, his action is a mere misadventure, not murder.

Holmes applied the same external test to torts and to contracts that he did to criminal law. The law, he insisted, "only works within the sphere of the senses. If the external phenomena, the manifest acts and omissions, are such as it requires, it is wholly indifferent to the internal phenomena of conscience." Despite the moral phraseology—negligence, fraud, malice, intent—used in the law of torts, an objective standard of blame can be found in this department of law as in the criminal law. Generally speaking, in the law of torts, as in criminal law, a man is liable if he injures another party in circumstances in which the average citizen, the ordinary man of intelligence and prudence, would be regarded as answerable. Ordinary liabilities in tort, in other words, arise from failure to comply with fixed and uniform standards of conduct prescribed by the community which a prudent man is presumed and required to know. "If the act was voluntary," said Holmes, "it is totally immaterial that the detriment which followed from it was neither intended nor due to the negligence of the actor." This means that a defendant in tort who is morally above reproach may be required by the law to make good another man's loss simply because he is the person responsible for the injury. A man who is accident-prone is continually hurting himself and others without meaning to; but his "slips are no less troublesome to his neighbors than if they sprang from guilty neglect." His neighbors, accordingly, "require him, at his proper peril, to come up to their standard, and the courts which they establish decline to take his personal equation into account." In Holmes, the social always takes precedence over the individual. "The standards of the law are standards of general application," he declared. "The law takes no account of the infinite varieties of temperament, intellect, and education which make the internal character of a given act so different in different men. It does not attempt to see men as God sees them. . . ." In civil, as in criminal law, then, Holmes's objective theory discarded the concept of *mens rea* (evil intent), made so much of by Austin, as a relevant factor.

When it came to contracts, Holmes sought to achieve objectivity by means of his famous "risk" theory. The essence of a contract, he said, is the assumption of a risk by a promisor that a certain event will take place involving a promisee; if the event does not come about, the promisee has a right to sue the promisor. Contracts, in short, consist of making arrangements for the future. In making a contract, the promisor assures the promisee that a future event or state of things will come to pass; if the promised event fails to take place, the law makes the promisor pay damages for the injury or detriment the promisee has suffered by the failure. The law "does not inquire, as a general thing," said Holmes,

> how far the accomplishment of an assurance touching the future is within the power of the promisor. In the moral world it may be that the obligation of a promise is confined to what lies in the reach of the will of the promisor. . . . But unless some consideration of public policy intervenes, I take it that a man may bind himself at law that any future event shall happen. He can therefore promise it in a legal sense.

Holmes's denial that there was any legal duty to perform a contract elicited considerable criticism; but it was entirely consistent with his theory that objectivity in standards of contract liability made risk, rather than performance, the heart of contractual undertakings.

Prediction Theory of the Law

In a lecture on "The Path of the Law" (perhaps the most famous one he ever gave) at the Boston University School of Law in January,

1897, Holmes transformed his "risk" theory of contracts into a "prediction" theory and then made it applicable to the law as a whole. "The duty to keep a contract at common law," he said, "means a prediction that you must pay damages if you do not keep it—and nothing else." Elaborating:

> If you commit a tort, you are liable to pay a compensatory sum. If you commit a contract, you are liable to pay a compensatory sum unless the promised event comes to pass, and that is all the difference. But such a mode of looking at the matter stinks in the nostrils of those who think it advantageous to get as much ethics into the law as they can.

Holmes, for his part, was determined to remove ethics from the law as much as he could. The object of the study of law, he announced, is prediction: "the prediction of the incidence of the public force through the instrumentality of the courts." The means of the study, he said,

> are a body of reports, of treatises, and of statutes, in this country and in England, extending back for six hundred years, and now increasing annually by hundreds. In these sibylline leaves are gathered the scattered prophecies of the past upon the cases in which the axe will fall. These are what properly have been called the oracles of the law. For the most important and pretty nearly the whole meaning of every new effort of legal thought is to make these prophecies more precise, and to generalize them into a thoroughly connected system. . . . It is to make the prophecies easier to be remembered and to be understood that the teachings of the decisions of the past are put into general propositions and gathered into textbooks, or that statutes are passed in a general form.

Holmes did not hesitate to apply his prediction theory to legal duties and rights, which in his day were heavily entangled in metaphysical and absolutistic systems of thought. The primary rights and duties with which jurisprudence is concerned, he said, are nothing but prophecies. A legal duty for Holmes was "nothing but a prediction that if a man does or omits certain things he will be made to suffer in this or that way by judgement of the court; and so of a legal right." (In an essay on "Natural Law" appearing in 1918, he put it more starkly: ".... for legal purposes a legal right is only the hypostasis of a prophecy—the imagination of a substance supporting the fact that the public force will be brought to bear upon those who do things said to contravene it. . . .") Summarizing his prediction theory, Holmes had this to say: "Take the fundamental question, What constitutes the law? . . . The prophecies of what the courts will do in fact, and nothing more pretentious, are what I mean by the law." This was Holmes's legal realism—and his legal pragmatism—at its farthest reach.

In "The Path of the Law," Holmes restated several of the themes that he had explored in some detail in *The Common Law*. Regarding the separation of law and morals, he confessed frankly that he thought the law would probably benefit "if every word of moral significance could be banished . . . and other words adopted which should convey legal ideas uncolored by anything outside the law." He also emphasized the evolutionary nature of the law, denied that systems of law could be "worked out like mathematics from some general axioms of conduct," and added a skeptic's warning: ". . . certainty generally is an illusion, and repose is not the destiny of man." He also placed great emphasis on the necessity of delving into history in order to discover why a rule of law has taken its particular shape and to decide whether it is still relevant to current needs:

> When you get the dragon out of his cave on to the plain and in the daylight, you can count his teeth and claws, and see just what is his strength. But to get him out is only the first step. The next is either to kill him, or to tame him and make him a useful animal. . . . It is revolting to have no better reason for a rule of law than that so it was laid down in the time of Henry IV. It is still more revolting if the grounds upon which it was laid down have vanished long since, and the rule simply persists from blind imitation of the past.

In his 1897 lecture, as in *The Common Law*, Holmes regarded the social advantage, not private interest, as the primary concern of the law, and insofar as he encouraged a rational study of the law in order to bring it in accord with modern public needs, he may be regarded as a reformer. But in his apparent willingness to accept community standards as they prevail at any given time as the norm for the external authority of the law, and in his indifference to social reform, Holmes was unmistakably a conservative. His prediction theory may have accurately described the law, at least from the lawyer's point of view; but it prescribed nothing as far as the future was concerned. On the other hand, a man with Holmes's views of the law was not likely to stand in the way of social reform either as a lawyer or as a judge. He took a laissez-faire attitude toward social change.

Massachusetts Judge

Holmes became a judge shortly after publication of *The Common Law*. His book was hailed by scholars in the United States and abroad as a major piece of legal scholarship, quickly translated into several foreign languages, and it was followed by an appointment to the faculty of Harvard Law School. But Holmes served only a few months as a law professor. In December, 1882, "by a stroke of lightning which changed all the course of my life," he was appointed associate justice of the Supreme Judicial Court of Massachusetts by Governor Long. Holmes could have had a distinguished career as a scholar at Harvard, but he left the academy for the bench, partly, as he told James Bryce, because he "did not think one could without moral loss decline any share in the practical struggle of life which naturally offered itself and for which he believed himself fitted." The opportunity "to think under fire" had a tremendous appeal for Holmes. He spent twenty years on the Massachusetts bench (the last three as chief justice) and during that period wrote more than 1,300 decisions. Most of his opinions dealt with cases involving private law; but some of the most important had to do with matters of public law. As a Massachusetts judge he was able to weave some of the basic ideas contained in *The Common Law* into the practical workings of the law of his state. Holmes was one of the most distinguished state judges in American history; even if he had not joined the U.S. Supreme Court in 1902, his reputation would have been assured.

The views that Holmes displayed on the Massachusetts Supreme Court foreshadowed those that he was to express as a member of the U. S. Supreme Court after 1902: a realistic view of individual rights, friendliness to labor, willingness to allow experiments in social-welfare legislation whether he approved them personally or not, and, in general, insistence that judges should refrain from interfering with the actions of legislatures where no constitutional provision was violated. As to the matter of personal rights, Holmes believed that the rights enjoyed by citizens were social, not "natural," and that they depended for their existence on the willingness of the community to enforce them. "It is only tautologous to say," he declared in 1888, "that the law knows nothing of moral rights unless they are also legal rights . . ." Individual rights, in his opinion, must give way to the social good when "the general benefit and improvement" of the community is involved. In one case with which he dealt, the owner of a lot in a cemetery owned by the town of Lawrence complained that the town had built a wall in front of his lot and closed the avenue; but Holmes upheld the town and refused to order the place restored to its original condition. In another case, when a man in Newton owning pigs that were polluting the water supply was asked to remove them and refused to do so, Holmes held that the city had the right to take the land in order to get rid of this nuisance.

In his labor decisions, Holmes won a reputation as a radical (despite his conservative economic views) among ultra-conservatives because he thought organizations of laboring men were just as legitimate as organizations of employers and because he defended the right to peaceful picketing, boycotts, and the closed shop. His dissent in *Vegelahn v. Guntner* (1896) became something of a classic. The majority of the court held that picketing by strikers, though done peacefully, intimidated the employer and was therefore illegal; but Holmes declared that peaceful picketing was an entirely lawful method for labor to use in its confrontation with capital. If picketing hurt business, said Holmes, this was simply part of the price society must pay for the benefits of free competition. Holmes held that free competition—he called it "the battle of trade"—included the struggle between employers and employees as well as the struggle between rival employers; he even suggested that the expression "free competition" be replaced by the Darwinian term "free struggle for life" in order to clarify this point. Holmes went on to say that combination in labor, as in capital, was inevitable in modern industrial society and that it was futile to resist it. "One of the eternal conflicts out of which life is made up," he said,

is that between the effort of every man to get the most he can for his services, and that of society, disguised under the name of capital, to get his services for the least possible return. Combination on the one side is patent and powerful. Combination on the other is the necessary and desirable counterpart, if the battle is to be carried on in a fair and equal way.

Holmes was of course no radical. In *Plant v. Woods* (1900) he upheld strikes and boycotts as means of achieving the closed shop, but he also, in an aside, revealed his basic economic conservatism. Though reiterating his belief that the strike is "a lawful instrument in the universal struggle of life," he also called it pure fantasy to suppose that

> there is a body of capital of which labor as a whole secures a larger share by that means. . . . Organization and strikes may get a larger share for the members of an organization, but, if they do, they get it at the expense of the less organized and less powerful portion of the laboring mass.

Holmes, in short, subscribed to the wages-fund theory of orthodox economists; still, this did not prevent him from siding with labor in this and other cases.

In his dissent in *Commonwealth v. Perry* (1891), Holmes not only sided with trade unions; he also showed his openness to the idea of state regulatory legislation. The case involved a state law, designed to protect weavers, prohibiting employers from withholding any part of a worker's wages because of imperfection in his work. The majority of the court voted to nullify the law on the ground that it interfered with "liberty of contract" and thus violated the Declaration of Rights of the Massachusetts Constitution. Holmes cut through the language of natural rights to the heart of the issue. "I suppose," he said, "that this act was passed because the operatives, or some of them, thought that they often were cheated out of a part of their wages under a false pretense that the work done by them was imperfect, and persuaded the Legislature that their view was true." Then he added: "If their view was true, I cannot doubt that the Legislature could deprive employers of an honest tool, which they were using for a dishonest purpose, and I cannot pronounce the legislation void, as based on a false assumption, since I know nothing about the matter one way or the other."

Holmes's judicial toleration of legislative action came out again when the Massachusetts House of Representatives asked the advice of the court in 1892 as to the constitutionality of a statute empowering cities and towns to buy and sell fuel or to establish and maintain municipal fuel yards. Where the majority of Holmes's colleagues reported unfavorably, Holmes could see no reason for opposing such legislation. "I am of the opinion," he said,

> that when money is taken to enable a public body to offer to the public without discrimination an article of general necessity, the purpose is no less public when that article is wood or coal than when it is water, or gas, or electricity, or education, to say nothing of cases like the support of paupers or the taking of land for railroads or public markets.

The legislature, Holmes thought, had the power to enact the statute; as for its necessity or expediency, that was not the business of the court to decide. Holmes had no sympathy for what was called "populistic" legislation; but he had a large tolerance for social experiments that popularly elected legislatures might choose to make and a firm belief that judges should not permit their personal economic prejudices to intrude themselves into their judgments on constitutional questions. "In my opinion," he said in 1894, in approving a statewide referendum on woman suffrage,

> the Legislature has the whole law-making power except so far as the words of the Constitution expressly or impliedly withhold it, and I think that in construing the Constitution we should remember that it is a frame of government for men of opposite opinions and for the future, and therefore not hastily import into it our own views, or unexpressed limitations derived merely from the practice of the past.

Holmes was to carry his insistence on judicial self-restraint to the highest court in the land.

Laissez-Faire and Constitutional Law

In his lecture on "The Path of the Law" in 1897, Holmes noted the increasing tendency of people "who no longer hope to control the legislatures to look to the courts as expounders of the Constitutions. . . ." And he found it cause for criticism that "in some courts new principles have been discovered outside the bodies of those instruments, which may be generalized into acceptance of the economic doctrines which prevailed about fifty years ago, and a wholesale prohibition of what a tribunal of lawyers do not think about right." Holmes had in mind the growing practice in American courts (both state and federal) during the Gilded Age of reading the laissez-faire doctrines of Herbert Spencer into state constitutions and into the federal Constitution itself in order to override laws regulating business enacted by state legislatures. The U. S. Supreme Court took the lead in Spencerizing American constitutional law in the late nineteenth century. In carrying out this objective, justices like Stephen J. Field, David J. Brewer, and Rufus W. Peckham displayed habits of mind which were the reverse of those that Holmes regarded as essential for realistic and impartial judgments on the part of members of the bench. Where Holmes was a legal realist, Field and his colleagues talked about natural law and natural rights and avoided meeting the social realities of industrial America head on and discussing considerations of social advantage frankly and fairly. Where Holmes urged judicial restraint and tolerance of legislative action, Field and his associates engaged in judicial activism and made the courts, instead of the legislatures, the final arbiters when it came to crucial social issues.

The instrument of the laissez-faire activists on the U. S. Supreme Court was the Fourteenth Amendment, a Reconstruction amendment added to the U.S. Constitution in 1868 with the primary purpose of protecting Negro civil rights against violations by the states. Their interpretation of this amendment was inspired, ingenious, and breathtaking. In 1873, Justice Field announced that the inalienable rights mentioned in the Declaration of Independence (life, liberty, and the pursuit of happiness) had been incorporated into the U. S. Constitution by means of the Fourteenth Amendment. "That amendment," he declared, "was intended to give practical effect to the declaration of 1776 of inalienable rights which are the gifts of the Creator, which the law does not confer, but only recognizes." The inalienable rights of the Declaration of Independence were given an economic twist by Field; their major purpose, he said in 1884, was to safeguard the right to engage in the "common business and callings of life, the ordinary trades and pursuits," without government interference.

In construing the Fourteenth Amendment as a guarantee for laissez-faire liberty, Field and his associates found the following sentence in the amendment of crucial importance:

No state shall make or enforce any law which shall abridge the privileges or immunities of citizens of the United States; nor shall any state deprive any person of life, liberty, or property without due process of law, nor deny to any person within its jurisdiction the equal protection of the laws.

After some efforts at pouring inalienable-rights–laissez-faire content into the phrase "privileges and immunities of citizens of the United States," Field and the other justices began concentrating on what is called the due-process clause of the amendment: "nor shall any state deprive any person of life, liberty, or property without due process of law." In an extremely important opinion rendered in the Slaughterhouse cases in 1884, Justice Field moved with ease and confidence from the inalienable rights of the Declaration of Independence to the "just liberty" of Adam Smith's *Wealth of Nations,* and from there to the liberty mentioned in the due-process clause. His conclusion was that the due-process clause was intended to protect "the right of men to pursue their happiness, by which is meant the right to pursue any lawful business or vocation, in any manner not inconsistent with the equal rights of others," against "any arbitrary invasion by State authority."

After 1873, when he first began construing the Fourteenth Amendment as a charter for laissez-faire liberty, Justice Field elaborated on his interpretation of the due-process clause in a series of influential opinions that gradually won the majority of the court over to his point of view. The liberty of the due-process clause, he said, involves more than freedom from physical restraint; it includes the liberty of the individual "to pursue such callings and avocations as may be most suitable to develop his capacities, and to give to them their highest enjoyment." (Eventually it came to include liberty of contract, the right of workers and employers to agree on terms of employment without interference by labor unions or government officials.) The due-process clause, moreover, protects property against more than arbitrary seizure by governmental authorities; it safeguards it against government regulation. In Field's opinion, "all that is beneficial in property arises from its use, and the fruits of that use; and whatever deprives a person of them deprives him of all that is valuable in the title and possession." For legislation to prescribe rules and regulations for the management of business was for Field as much a violation of property rights as actual confiscation; property was secure only if government, state and federal, followed a hands-off policy.

Field thought that the due-process clause gave the same protection for liberty and property to persons organized into corporations as it did to those doing business as individuals. In 1882 he declared that "it would be a most singular result if a constitutional provision intended for the protection of every person against partial and discriminating legislation by the states, should cease to exert such protection the moment the person becomes a member of a corporation." The "person" mentioned in the due-process clause, in short, was intended to apply to corporations as well as to individuals. "Whatever acts may be imputed justly or unjustly to corporations," said Field, "they are entitled when they enter the tribunals of the nation to have the same justice meted out to them which is meted out to the humblest citizen. There cannot be one law for them and another law for others." Field was determined to see that corporate enterprise enjoyed the same protection of the due-process clause as the humblest citizen in the land, *e.g.*, the Negro, for whom the clause was originally written.

One other phrase in the due-process clause of the Fourteenth Amendment needed interpreting: the very meaning of "due process" itself. The court's understanding of "due process" had to be updated if the economic interpretation of such words as "liberty," "property," and "person" was to subserve laissez-faire purposes. Due process of law traditionally had referred to procedural safeguards for citizens against arbitrary arrest and imprisonment. In his *Commentaries on the Constitution* (1833), for example, Justice Joseph Story had declared that due process of law "affirms the right of trial according to the process and proceedings of the common law." But a procedural use of due process was scarcely adequate for Field's purposes; if it was to be utilized as a general limitation on legislative power over American business enterprise, it must be given a *substantive* interpretation, that is, it must permit the justices to examine the actual *substance* of legislative enactments to see whether they squared with laissez-faire liberty. Chief Justice Morrison R. Waite had resisted this interpretation at first. In *Munn v. Illinois* (1877), Waite upheld the right of state legislatures to enact "Granger laws," that is, laws regulating rates charged by railroads and grain elevators, because these enterprises were "clothed with a public interest." The whole matter of "Granger laws" he regarded as a political, not a legal, question. He acknowledged that regulatory power on the part of state legislatures might be abused; but that, he said, "is not argument against its existence. For protection against abuses by legislatures the people must resort to the polls, not to the courts." Field vigorously dissented from Waite's view. "If this be sound law," he said, "if there be no protection, either in the principles upon which our republican government is founded or in the prohibitions of the Constitution against such invasion of private rights, all property and all business in the State are held at the mercy of a majority of its legislators. . . ." Field did not trust the majority and he wanted the Supreme Court to protect the property interests of the minority against regulatory action by the majority acting through state legislatures. He did not deny that the states, under what was called their "police power," could take action to protect the health, morals, safety, and welfare of their citizens; but he interpreted this police power very narrowly. When it came to business enterprise, he wanted the due-process clause of the Fourteenth Amendment to afford the completest protection possible against social-welfare laws and regulatory legislation that state legislatures might take it into their heads to enact.

By the end of the century, Field's views had come to dominate the thinking of the U.S. Supreme Court. In his *Lectures on the Fourteenth Article of Amendment to the Constitution of the United States* (1898), William Guthrie noted that American constitutional history during the previous thirty years had been "little more than a commentary on the Fourteenth Amendment." Out of a total of more than six hundred Fourteenth Amendment cases handled by the Supreme Court from 1868 to 1910, only twenty-eight involved the rights of Negroes. (Field was popular in the South for defending the rights of former rebels just after the Civil War and he increased his popularity when, in a dissenting opinion in 1880, he declared that the state of Virginia was not compelled to accept Negroes as jurors.) The Fourteenth Amendment thus became a Magna Carta for American business; under it, corporations could challenge laws that they disapproved with a strong likelihood that the federal courts would find them unconstitutional under the Fourteenth Amendment. Not only did the Supreme Court become a bulwark for big business and a foe of the general-welfare state in this fashion; state courts, following the lead of the Supreme Court, also came to place limits on the scope of social and economic measures enacted by state legislatures. Under the inalienable-rights–laissez-faire interpretation of the Fourteenth Amendment, state and federal courts nullified laws designed to protect the worker and put him in a little better bargaining position *vis-à-vis* his employer.

Holmes's Judicial Restraint

Holmes heartily disapproved of the increasing tendency of judges during the Gilded Age to let their own personal economic predilections affect their decisions on questions of law. Commenting on Field's dissent in *Munn v. Illinois,* he noted that legislation regarding prices had been "common to all periods of the English law" and that even if rate regulation was something new, the circumstances giving rise to it were equally novel. "If the railroads and elevators have a constitutional right to charge what they please," he said,

> it is just as truly a right to destroy the property of others as a right to make noxious vapors would be. In such cases, it is immaterial that there is no statutory monopoly, so long as there is actual power on one side and actual dependence on the other. It was objected that the question what was a reasonable charge, was a judicial question. But the legislature did not attempt to say what should be charged: it only fixed a limit and there was nothing to show that this was not considerably higher than the reasonable charge. . . . Of course, the question may be raised where to draw the line; but no experienced lawyer is disturbed by that, for he is aware that the best-settled legal distinctions illustrate the Darwinian hypothesis no less than the diversities of species.

But Field simply would not have grasped Holmes's point; he was thoroughly pre-Darwinian in his thinking.

When Holmes joined the Supreme Court in 1902, by appointment of Theodore Roosevelt, he took with him the Darwinian awareness of struggle and change, the social realism, and the judicial humility regarding legislative matters which he had shown on the Supreme Judicial Court of Massachusetts. (He also took along his graceful literary style and his gift for what he called "aperçus," which make his Supreme Court opinions a delight to read.) Because the court was dominated by the Field view of the Fourteenth Amendment when he became an associate justice, Holmes inevitably became "the Great Dissenter."

Holmes's most famous dissent—one of the most famous in the history of the court—came in the Lochner case in 1905, when a majority of the court voted to overrule a New York law, providing for a ten-hour day and a sixty-hour week in the baking industry, on the ground that it violated liberty of contract. "This case," announced Holmes at the outset, "is decided upon an economic theory which a large part of the country does not entertain." Going on to point out that his own personal opinion of New York law had "nothing to do with the right of the majority to embody their opinions in law," Holmes reminded his colleagues that there was nothing novel about legislative interference with liberty of contract:

> The liberty of the citizen to do as he likes so long as he does not interfere with the liberty of others to do the same, which has been a shibboleth for some well-known writers, is interfered with by school laws, by the Post-Office, by every State or municipal institution which takes his money for purposes thought desirable, whether he likes it or not.

Some regulatory laws, said Holmes,

> embody convictions or prejudices which judges are likely to share. Some may not. But a constitution is not intended to embody a particular economic theory, whether of paternalism and the organic relation of the citizen to the State or of laissez faire. It is made for people of fundamentally differing views. . . .

As to the constitutional issue on which the Lochner case was decided, "The Fourteenth Amendment," said Holmes flatly, "does not enact Mr. Herbert Spencer's *Social Statics*." But Spencer was to outlast Holmes on the court; Holmes retired in 1932, but it was not until the late 1930's that the Supreme Court began coming around to his view of the Fourteenth Amendment.

Chapter 8

Thorstein Veblen
and the Leisure Class

On February 10, 1897, Bradley Martin, wealthy businessman from Albany, New York, and his wife threw a lavish costume ball in Manhattan at which they attempted to reproduce the splendor of Versailles. "... I doubt if even the Roi Soleil himself ever witnessed a more dazzling sight," wrote Bradley's brother Frederick afterward.

The interior of the Waldorf-Astoria Hotel was transformed into a replica of Versailles, and rare tapestries, beautiful flowers and countless lights made an effective background for the wonderful gowns and their wearers. I do not think there has ever been a greater display of jewels before or since; in many cases the diamond buttons worn by the men represented thousands of dollars, and the value of the historic gems worn by the ladies baffles description. My sister-in-law personated Mary Stuart, and her gold embroidered gown was trimmed with pearls and precious stones. Bradley, as Louis XV, wore a Court suit of brocade, and represented a gentleman of the period.... The power of wealth with its refinement and vulgarity was everywhere. It gleamed from countless jewels, and it was proclaimed by the thousands of orchids and roses, whose fragrance that night was like incense burnt on the altar of the Golden Calf. . . . Everyone said it was the most brilliant function of the kind ever seen in America, and it certainly was the most talked about.

Two years later, Macmillan published a puzzling book, *The Theory of the Leisure Class,* written by an equally puzzling writer, Thorstein Veblen, filled with passages that, though phrased in dispassionate and matter-of-fact language, seemed to be commenting satirically on the doings of people like the Bradley Martins. "Conspicuous consumption of valuable goods is a means of reputability to the gentleman of leisure," wrote Veblen, who taught economics at the University of Chicago.

As wealth accumulates in his hands, his own unaided effort will not avail to sufficiently put his opulence in evidence by this method. The aid of friends and competitors is therefore brought in by resorting to the giving of valuable presents and expensive feasts and entertainments. Presents and feasts had probably another origin than that of naive ostentation, but they acquired their utility for this purpose very early, and they have retained that character to the present; so that their utility in this respect has now long been the substantial ground on which these usages rest. Costly entertainments, such as the potlatch or the ball, are peculiarly adapted to serve this end. The competitor with whom the entertainer wishes to institute a comparison is, by this method, made to serve as a means to the end. He consumes vicariously for his host at the same time that he is a witness to the consumption of that excess of good things which his host is unable to dispose of single-handed, and he is also made to witness his host's facility in etiquette.

Conspicuous consumption as a means of reputability? Putting opulence in evidence? Consuming vicariously? Witnessing a host's facility in etiquette? What kind of language was this for a professional economist? And what about the other strange phrases in the book: pecuniary emulation, instinct of workmanship, invidious distinction, archaic traits, non-invidious interest? And the continual references to predatory barbarism in discussions of modern pecuniary culture? Above all, what was one to make of passages on the relation between parks and cow pastures, the relative reputability of cats and dogs, the contribution of corsets and walking sticks to status, the role of college football in inculcating predatory habits, and the way in which English orthography obeyed the law of conspicuous waste?

Veblen and the Reviewers

It was difficult for some reviewers of *Theory of the Leisure Class* to gauge Veblen's intentions accurately. Was he writing as a satirist? As a social critic? As a humanitarian reformer? Or—given the obscurity of some portions of the book—was he simply a clumsy stylist who had failed to express himself clearly? Veblen himself repeatedly disclaimed all value judgments; his purposes, he said, were purely scholarly, analytical, and scientific. In a chapter on conspicuous consumption, he admitted that his use of the term "waste" carried an undertone of disapproval, but he insisted that he didn't mean it that way. "The exigencies of language," he explained, "make it impossible to avoid an apparent implication of disapproval of the aptitudes, propensities, and expressions of life here under discussion." But, he hastened to add, he was interested in neither eulogy nor deprecation; the purpose of his book was to examine leisure-class habits solely from the point of view of economic theory. Still, for all of his protestations of objectivity, Veblen scarcely sounded like the scientific analyst he claimed to be when he lumped the "ideal pecuniary man" with the "ideal delinquent," declared that lawyers are "exclusively occupied with the details of predatory fraud, either in achieving or in checkmating chicane," remarked (in a discussion of "devout observances") that "the consumption of goods and efforts in the service of an anthropomorphic divinity means a lowering of the vitality of the community," and (in a chapter on the "higher learning") said that "the cap and gown, and the more strenuous observance of scholastic proprieties which came with them," were floated into our colleges on a "tidal wave of reversion to barbarism" after the Civil War.

The reviewer of Veblen's book for the *Yale Review* wasn't fooled a bit; he got enough of Veblen's point to be thoroughly hostile. He called Veblen a dilettante, said his references to economics were "ill-considered and vicious," characterized his language as "futile, archaic, and cumbrous," said the book contained "ex-cathedra propositions, often of a revolutionary and startling nature," and blasted

Veblen for bringing sociology into disrepute "among careful and scientific thinkers." Other reviewers were equally shocked and angry. But Lester Ward liked the book and did a favorable review for the *American Journal of Sociology;* and William Dean Howells, in two essays for *Literature,* was glowing in his praise. Howells liked Veblen's "clear method," "graphic and easy style," and "delightful accuracy of characterization." "In the passionless calm with which the author pursues his investigation," he said, "there is apparently no animus for or against a leisure class. It is his affair simply to find out how and why and what it is. If the result is to leave the reader with a feeling which the author never shows, that seems to be solely the effect of the facts." Howells, like Ward, interpreted the book mainly as a discussion of the life of luxury lived by the upper classes, and many readers followed him in this interpretation. The *Yale Review* writer was unquestionably closer to the mark in detecting propositions of a "revolutionary and startling nature" in the book. Nevertheless, Howells' review helped make the book something of a sensation. But Howells—and others—were curious about the author. Veblen's name, Howells declared, "is newer to me than it should be, or than it will hereafter be to any student of our status." But despite the success of his first book, Veblen was not to become very well known to many people. None of his subsequent books was to become anywhere near as popular as *Theory of the Leisure Class.* The radical nature of what he was saying and the complicated, involuted, and frequently obscure way in which he expressed his ideas prevented a wide following.

People who encountered Veblen at every stage of his life found him as baffling as some of the passages in his books. As a boy he was regarded as the "oddest" of the Veblens; and while teaching at the University of Chicago he seemed remote, aloof, and withdrawn to his colleagues. Students found him "an exceedingly queer fish." He never gave an examination, and at the end of the semester, reported one of his students,

> he would say that with our permission he would register "C" grade for each of us to conform to the necessary ritual of university life . . . Very commonly with his cheek in his hand, or in some such position, he talked in a low, placid monotone, in itself a most uninteresting delivery. . . . We never did really know him or much about him personally.

But Veblen had a whimsical side to him for all his seeming solemnity, and at times it found an outlet in practical jokes. Once when he was out walking he came across a hornets' nest and a little later he met a farmer carrying an empty sack. Veblen asked the farmer if he could borrow the sack for a while, and when the farmer consented he took the sack, returned to the nest, and put the hornets into the sack. He then walked back to the farmer, handed him the sack, and said "thank you." The farmer, it is said, spent years looking for Veblen. In a way, this episode symbolizes Veblen's entire career: he was always slipping hornets' nests into sacks and handing them to people. His comments on modern business civilization were hornets' nests tossed among the purveyors of conventional use and wont in this country. Veblen was, as Wesley Mitchell (an economist who studied under him) said, a "disturbing genius"; and what he had to say continues to be disturbing to those who are struck by the irrationality of much of what passes for common sense in contemporary American culture.

The Education of Thorstein Veblen

Veblen was a "Norskie." The fourth son of Norwegian immigrants, he was born on an eighty-acre farm in Wisconsin in 1857 and his boyhood was spent on farms in Wisconsin and, later, Minnesota, to which the family moved in 1865. He did not like the farmwork and he spent much of his time reading in the hayloft; but he did have a mechanical bent and he enjoyed tinkering with his father's farm machinery. Veblen's parents had emigrated to the United States from Norway ten years before his birth and they brought with them the ideals and traditions of the *bonde*, the independent Norwegian farmer, who stressed economy and self-sufficiency and regarded the business classes of the towns as exploitive and parasitic. The *bonde-kultur* to which his parents clung in America was of crucial import- ance in Veblen's life. Though he freed himself from the superstitious aspects of the *bonde's* outlook (as his father had before him), he thoroughly absorbed the *bonde's* hatred of waste, his hostility to absentee ownership, his disdain for town merchants, and his distrust of the market economy of the city with its treacherous credit system. Until he was seventeen and went away to school, Veblen never really left Norway. His father had no contacts outside of the Norwegian community (and few inside of it), never learned English, and hired a tutor to teach the children Norwegian grammar and literature.

Reared in complete isolation from native Americans, Veblen as a young man did not feel completely at home outside of his Norwegian community, and even after he left home he always remained something of an outsider. He never lost touch with Norwegian culture; as an adult he continued to read Norwegian newspapers, translated Icelandic sagas as a hobby, and sometimes put on a heavy Norwegian accent to impress people. His lifelong sense of alienation was probably psychological as well as cultural; but the cultural isolation he experienced as a boy surely exacerbated his personal aloofness and helps explain why he was able to detect aspects of American life which eluded most Americans. His feeling of being an outsider also probably heightened the skeptical, iconoclastic turn of mind which he shared with his father. He once said that he got all of his basic ideas from his father.

When Veblen entered Carleton College Academy, a small Congregational school, in 1874, he spoke very little English. But he learned rapidly. His intellectual precocity had long been apparent. John Bates Clark, who was professor of political economy and history at Carleton, regarded Veblen as his brightest student, though he also thought him quite out of place in a school that boasted it was "thoroughly *Christian,* and distinctly and earnestly evangelical." Veblen was not only out of sympathy with the religious orientation of Carleton; he also took exception to the conservative economic views of the faculty and made no secret of his liking for Henry George's *Progress and Poverty.* He had little regard for the faculty (except for Clark), mainly devout Congregational ministers; for the curriculum, which stressed the classics, religion, and moral philosophy; or for his fellow students, to whom he seemed a strange mixture of conceit, good-natured indolence, and cynicism. On his own he read Spencer, Mill, Hume, Rousseau, Huxley, and others who were omitted from the courses taught at Carleton. At the weekly public declamation exercises, he solemnly delivered papers on "A Plea for Cannibalism," "An Apology for a Toper," and "The Face of a Worn-Out Politician," and, when queried about his intentions, claimed he was simply engaged in scientific observation. He made only one friend at Carleton: Ellen Rolfe, niece of the president, brilliant, witty, and equally a misfit. At student gatherings the two spent all of their time together apart from the others and gave the impression that they disdained the other students. Veblen graduated from Carleton in 1880, taught school for a year, and then entered Johns Hopkins University to study philosophy. His stay at Johns Hopkins was brief, but while he was there he took a course in political economy under Richard T. Ely and attended lectures on logic by Charles Peirce. From Hopkins Veblen went to Yale to study philosophy under Noah Porter and he wrote a doctoral dissertation on Kant and Spencer. Porter looked on Veblen as by far his most brilliant student and Veblen regarded Porter as an able thinker, though he thought his views were out of date. Veblen also admired William Graham Sumner and Sumner was tremendously impressed by one of Veblen's papers. A doctoral degree in 1884 and excellent letters of recommendation failed to get Veblen a teaching position in philosophy after leaving Yale. College teachers, especially in philosophy, were still largely drawn from the ranks of theology students; and the prospect of having a "Norskie," especially one with agnostic views, did not seem enticing to American colleges at this time. Veblen returned to his home in Minnesota in frustration and bitterness.

Veblen was almost as much a misfit within his Norwegian community in Minnesota as he was outside of it. He was regarded as conceited and lazy by the neighbors and even by some of the members of his family. "He read and loafed," said one brother, "and the next day, he loafed and read." Though he did hack writing for a time and invented agricultural implements (but was too late in patenting them), he spent most of his time with books. He read everything he could lay his hands on: novels, poetry, and Lutheran hymnbooks as well as treatises on economics, sociology, and anthropology. In 1888 he and Ellen Rolfe were married and arrangements were made to get him a position as economist with the Atchison, Topeka, and Santa Fe Railway, of which Ellen's uncle was president. But the railway got into financial difficulties and the job fell through. Veblen then settled down with his wife on her father's farm in Stacyville, Iowa, and continued his reading and loafing. With his wife he studied Greek and Latin and botany. The two also read Bellamy's *Looking Backward* together and Ellen regarded it as "the turning-point of our lives." At this time Veblen also began reading widely in the field of economics and he conceived the idea of making a critical study of modern business enterprise. Further efforts to get college teaching positions came to naught, and at length, after seven years of enforced idleness, Veblen decided to return to the academic world as a graduate student with the hope of eventually obtaining a teaching position.

In 1891, Veblen appeared in the office of J. Laurence Laughlin (old-school economist who refused to join the American Economic Association) at Cornell University wearing a coonskin cap and corduroy trousers and announced mildly: "I am Thorstein Veblen." Laughlin was startled, but, after some conversation, impressed, and he obtained a special grant for Veblen to study economics at Cornell. An article by Veblen on socialism plus some notes on technical economic subjects for professional journals convinced Laughlin that Veblen showed great promise, and when he went to the newly founded University of Chicago in 1892 to head the economics department, he took Veblen with him. At the University of Chicago, Veblen, who was now thirty-five, was at first only a fellow (with a salary of $520 a year), not a member of the faculty. Nevertheless, he did most of the editorial work for the *Journal of Political Economy* and taught a course in socialism; but no one could decide whether Veblen was a socialist or not (he was). He also continued to publish essays and reviews of a high intellectual order in economic journals, began to be noticed by the faculty, and in 1895 was promoted to instructor and assigned the courses in economic theory required for advanced degrees.

Professor Veblen

Veblen did not attract many students at Chicago or at any of the other schools where he subsequently taught. A few of the abler students were impressed by his vast erudition, his free-ranging spirit, his originality, and his sly humor, but most students found him languid, dull, almost inarticulate, and impossible to take notes from. He spoke in a low monotone, paid little attention to the students, and sometimes gave the impression he had fallen asleep. Veblen kept his classes small by asking prospective students if they could read French and German and whether they were well versed in psychology and philosophy. On one occasion he told a sorority girl who wanted to take a course of his: "I don't say that I will fail any member of a sorority or fraternity, but no member of such an organization has ever yet passed one of my courses." On another occasion he asked an extremely devout student to calculate for the class the value of her church in terms of kegs of beer. When one diligent student asked him to repeat something he had said in class, Veblen said, "I don't think it is worth repeating."

Veblen seemed to regard the paraphernalia of academic life—class rolls, examinations, and grades—as optional eccentricities and he thought faculty committees were committees for "sifting sawdust." He almost never took class attendance and students doubted whether he ever read their examination papers; they all got C, whatever they did. To a student who complained that Veblen's was the only low grade he received at Chicago, Veblen explained: "My grades are like lightning. They are liable to strike anywhere." But when another student told Veblen he needed a high grade in order to graduate, Veblen cheerfully raised it from "medium" to "superior," and when this did not suffice, to "excellent," leaving the dean's office quite mystified. Once Veblen encountered a Phi Beta Kappa student who could not harness a horse; vastly amused, he told one of his classes about it. When one student contended that "maybe that wasn't his line," Veblen insisted, "He was just a fine Phi Beta Kappa." "Professor Veblen," asked a student who encountered him on campus, "do you ever take anything seriously?" "Yes," responded Veblen, "but don't tell anybody." Veblen was more interested in the welfare of his students than they realized; frequently, without their knowing it, he attempted to help them professionally. With the passage of time, moreover, he gradually developed a loyal following among younger economists who had studied with him. But he remained a remote figure even to those who knew him best.

Economics as an Evolutionary Science

There are passages in *The Theory of the Leisure Class*, which he began writing late in 1895, and in his later books, which give the impression that Veblen regarded the United States as a kind of vast theater of the absurd. His subject was modern capitalism but he had the pecuniary culture of the United States chiefly in mind. He wrote with wit, satire, irony, and at times with acerbity, despite his disclaimers of moral engagement. At the same time he wrote with utter seriousness. He was a professional scholar, thoroughly at home with the technical data of psychology, sociology, anthropology, and philosophy, as well as of economics, and his book displays a tremendous amount of learning.

Veblen's aim was to illuminate our understanding of modern civilization by examing its basic springs of action and propounding a theory of how and why it got to be what it was. A series of articles appearing in professional journals prior to the appearance of *The Theory of the Leisure Class* foreshadowed both the method and some of the substance of the book. In the most important of these, "Why Is Economics Not an Evolutionary Science?" (1898), Veblen was above all insistent that economics must profit from Darwin's method. To be truly evolutionary, he said, economics must avoid such abstractions as economic man and conditions of perfect competition and concentrate on what actually goes on in the economic world. It must also rid itself of all natural-rights and natural-law concepts, for these, in Veblen's opinion, were obsolete hangovers from eighteenth-century thought and utterly unscientific. The economist's primary concern was with process and development; but he should avoid teleology like the plague. Insofar as the economist views social development from the point of view of over-all purpose, direction, or goal (as natural-law thinkers do), he is preventing economics from being a truly evolutionary science. To be a thoroughgoing evolutionist, according to Veblen, the economist must follow closely in the footsteps of Darwin: he must eliminate the idea of antecedent design or inherent progress from his thinking about economic development, just as Darwin eliminated design from his thinking about organic development.

Veblen thought that both the classical economists and the historical economists fell grievously short of Darwinian standards. Neither concerned themselves with a scientific study of economic sequences: changes in society's methods of turning material things to account and alterations in habits of thought on which economic changes (including changes in the mechanical process of industry) depend. The evolutionary economist, in Veblen's opinion, has the task of describing the changing character of economic relations, but he must do more than that: he must also formulate a theory to explain the economic process, just as Darwin formulated a theory to account for organic change. Evolutionary economics, said Veblen, must achieve a theory about the "process of cultural growth as determined by the economic interest" which will explain the connection between modern economic conditions and earlier ones. "It is necessarily the aim of such an economics," he said, "to trace the cumulative working-out of the economic interest in the cultural sequence. It must be a theory of the economic life process of the race or the community."

Veblen was an "institutionalist" as well as an evolutionist; indeed, he is sometimes regarded as the father of institutional economics in the United States. Economic institutions (organized ways of doing things), not economic men, were the center of his interest. Veblen was also a "cultural organicist"; he did not think that economic behavior could be understood in isolation from other forms of behavior. The economist, he believed, must examine economic institutions within their cultural context; he should seek to discover the interrelation between economic and non-economic aspects of society and trace the ramifications of economic behavior throughout culture as a whole. Because of his method of viewing economic institutions in their cultural setting, Veblen is sometimes regarded as a sociologist rather than an economist. The subtitle of *The Theory of the Leisure Class*, however, is "An Economic Study of Institutions."

Did Veblen actually have a scientific theory to explain the sequence of economic events the way Darwin had a scientific theory to explain the sequence of organic events? He certainly thought he did, just as Karl Marx thought he did. Like Marx, Veblen regarded technological innovation as a basic factor in initiating social change; but where Marx saw the struggle between economic classes as the key to social evolution, Veblen emphasized the distinction between productive and non-productive groups (in somewhat the fashion of the Populists) and the way in which the non-producers dominated and shaped society in all of its aspects and prevented it from adjusting to technological change. Veblen's theory was that the "leisure class"—the class that abstained from all productive work—had had a decisive effect on historical development. In *The Theory of the Leisure Class*, Veblen attempted to explain the origin and nature of this class, describe the changing forms it took at different stages of social development, and show the extent to which it continued to shape culture in the modern world.

Veblen's continual protestations of objectivity and neutrality in his analysis of the leisure class must be understood in the light of his desire to present a scientific theory about the social world as convincing as Darwin's was about the natural world. But one would have to be the most devout and uncritical of Veblenians to believe that he actually succeeded in his purpose. His analysis is shot through with likes and dislikes. He made no secret, for example, of his belief that most leisure-class activities were horrendously wasteful; and though he insisted that he was using the word "waste" in a technical, not pejorative, sense, we are not convinced, especially when we find him saying frankly that leisure-class expenditure "does not serve human life or human well-being on the whole." But if Veblen was less scientific than he thought he was, he was surely, in his own fashion, more objective than most other American social analysts thought they were. He saw many significant things on the American scene which escaped other observers; and the pertinence of much of what he said about Gilded Age America—as well as about America in the twentieth century—is undeniable.

Origin of the Leisure Class

Veblen thought that the leisure class appeared at a relatively late date in history. Like Lewis Henry Morgan, he distinguished three major stages in social evolution, each containing two substages: savagery (earlier and later), barbarism (predatory and quasi-peaceable), and modern pecuniary culture (subdivided into an earlier handicraft era and the present business era). The leisure class, according to Veblen, did not appear as a distinct institution until the period of predatory barbarism; it was during this period, moreover, that the chief habits of mind of the modern businessman and his characteristic ways of behaving were developed.

The initial stage of social development—peaceful savagery—was a kind of golden age for Veblen. During this stage, men lived together in peace and harmony. Primitive men were poor, to be sure, and their lives were lived simply and inelegantly; but they were pacific, co-operative, and hard-working. During the stage of peaceful savagery, there was very little ownership, class distinctions were non-existent, women were socially equal with men, and everyone worked for the benefit of the group. Man's "instinct of workmanship"—his inborn taste for effective work and his distaste for waste, inefficiency, and futile effort—found its outlet in employments that went to further the life of the community. "What emulation of an economic kind there is between the members of such a group," said Veblen, "will be chiefly emulation in industrial serviceability. At the same time the incentive to emulation is not strong, nor is the scope for emulation large." Confronted by force or fraud, the peaceful savage could only respond with "a certain amiable inefficiency."

There was no amiable inefficiency about the predatory barbarians who came to the fore during the second stage of social evolution. Force and fraud as well as unrelenting emulation became the main features of human life with the passing of peaceful savagery and the rise of predatory barbarism. The movement of culture from a peaceful to a predatory phase, according to Veblen, rested on a change in spiritual outlook, and this in turn was an outgrowth of changes in the material circumstances of the group. "Predation," said Veblen,

> can not become the habitual, conventional resource of any group or class until industrial methods have been developed to such a degree of efficiency as to leave a margin worth fighting for, above the subsistence of those engaged in getting a living. The transition from peace to predation therefore depends on the growth of technical knowledge and the use of tools. A predatory culture is similarly impracticable in early times, until weapons have been developed to such a point as to make man a formidable animal. The early development of tools and of weapons is of course the same fact seen from two different points of view.

It was during the transition of society from a peaceable to a consistently warlike habit of mind that the leisure class gradually took shape. Two conditions were necessary for its emergence: (1) the community had to be of a predatory habit of life (engaged in war or in the hunting of large game or both), with men in it accustomed to inflicting injury by force and strategem; and (2) subsistence had to be obtainable easily enough to permit the exemption of some members of the community from productive work. The leisure class— which Veblen defined as any class not engaged in productive labor— was originally made up of barbarian warriors; they were released from productive work in order to engage in warfare. The drudgery of preparing food and clothing fell to the lot of women, the weaker sex, and it became something no self-respecting warrior would have anything to do with. In war, the barbarian fighter captured all kinds of useful goods from the enemy and he also seized and brought home enemy women (and later enemy men) who could be held as slaves and put to work performing menial tasks.

Veblen linked the institution of private property (and also the institution of marriage) with war and predation. Individual ownership began, he said, with the practice of seizing women from the enemy as trophies and holding them as captives; and the possession of female captives

> gave rise to a form of ownership-marriage, resulting in a household with a male head. This was followed by an extension of slavery to other captives and inferiors, besides women, and by an

extension of ownership-marriage to other women than those seized from the enemy. . . . From the ownership of women the concept of ownership extends itself to include the products of their industry, and so there arises the ownership of things as well as of persons.

The ownership of persons and things became important less as a means of satisfying the barbarian warrior's personal needs than as tangible evidence of his skill in battle. The barbarian warrior accumulated property, not through productive efforts of his own, but through theft, exploit, and plunder, and the possession of captive women and booty seized from the enemy showed his strength and prowess and brought him glory and prestige. The predatory traits displayed by the warrior came to be greatly admired and productive traits, identified with women and slaves, greatly deprecated. The distinction between employments involving exploit (worthy) and those involving drudgery (unworthy) continued into the handicraft era and beyond. Productive labor came to be regarded as shameful and degrading because of its identification with women and slaves, and conspicuous abstention from it came to be absolutely essential for a superior man.

Veblen thought that the distinction between exploit and drudgery had persisted into modern times in the distinction between business (which is predatory in nature and is interested in getting something for nothing) and industry (which displays productive traits and is concerned with the making of tangible goods). The business-industry dichotomy was fundamental to Veblen's thought. He believed that the crucial problems arising in the capitalistic system—poverty, unemployment, periodic depressions—grew out of the way business, in its desire for inordinate profits, restricted production and prevented industry from developing an economy of abundance. His identification of the modern businessman with the predatory warrior of barbarian times and his insistence that modern business possessed predatory traits—ferocity, cunning, trickiness, and ruthlessness—naturally infuriated many of his readers.

Pecuniary Emulation and Conspicuous Leisure

The main motive for ownership, according to Veblen, was emulation. With the development of the institution of private property, "pecuniary emulation" became a major feature of man's social life. The possession of wealth conferred honor and an "invidious distinction" began to be made between people on the basis of their possessions. Under the regime of individual ownership, the struggle for pecuniary reputability became unremitting. People sought to accumulate property in order

> to rank high in comparison with the rest of the community in point of pecuniary strength. So long as the comparison is distinctly unfavourable to himself, the normal, average individual will live in chronic dissatisfaction with his present lot; and when he has reached what may be called the normal pecuniary standard of the community, or of his class in the community, this chronic dissatisfaction will give place to a restless straining to place a wider and ever-widening pecuniary interval between himself and this average standard.

The instinct of workmanship (that propensity for purposeful activity and repugnance for all futility of effort), which in peaceful savage times led people to engage in co-operative productive enterprise, now tended to shape itself into a straining to excel others in pecuniary achievement by acquiring and accumulating goods. Abstention from productive work, however, was *de rigueur* for members of the leisure class, for labor was associated with weakness and subjection to a master and thus a mark of inferiority. Members of the leisure class must therefore not only display their wealth for all to see; they must also put their leisure on display. What Veblen called "conspicuous leisure," that is, ostentatious abstention from labor, became the "conventional mark of superior pecuniary achievement and the conventional index of reputability."

Conspicuous leisure is not leisure enjoyed for its own sake; it is non-productive consumption of time which is intended to advertise a man's superior status. Beginning in the period of quasi-peaceable barbarism, conspicuous exemption from all useful employment became a characteristic feature of leisure-class life. Abstention from labor was not only meritorious and honorific; it was, in fact, a requisite for decency. Sometimes, Veblen said, the feeling that manual labor is shameful becomes so strong that it may even overwhelm the instinct of self-preservation. Certain Polynesian chiefs, for example, "under the stress of good form, preferred to starve rather than carry their food to their mouths with their own hands." There was also a French king, according to Veblen, who lost his life through an excess of moral stamina in the observance of good form. In the absence of the functionary whose office it was to shift his master's seat, the king sat uncomplaining before the fire and suffered his royal person to be toasted beyond recovery. But in so doing he saved his Most Christian Majesty from menial contamination.

But the leisure-class gentleman does not sit around doing nothing; his workmanship instinct bars him from mere idleness. He must find something to do, and it is perfectly proper for him to busy himself with occupations that are not tainted with productive labor. Warfare, for one thing, is perfectly suited to him, for war is obviously futile, predatory, and non-productive, and hence highly esteemed. He may also engage in such occupations as government, sports (especially the chase), and devout observances, none of which bear the stigma of being connected with the production of serviceable goods. Because of their obvious non-productiveness, such occupations as war, government, sports, and priestly service become monopolies of the leisure class and are regarded as the most honorable of all occupations. But what is the leisure-class gentleman to do in the privacy of his home? How is he to make it clear in public that he does not spend any of his time in private in productive employments? To get this point across, the leisure-class gentleman must master a great deal of useless information when he is at home which he may parade in public as "serviceable evidence of unproductive expenditure of time." Among other things, he acquires a mastery of "what is known as manners and breeding, polite usage, decorum, and formal ceremonial observances generally," as well as knowledge of "the dead languages and the occult sciences; of correct spelling of syntax and prosody; of the various forms of domestic music and other household art; of the latest proprieties of dress, furniture, and equipage; of games, sports, and fancy-bred animals, such as dogs and race-horses."

The pecuniary respectability of the leisure-class gentleman is also enhanced by the activities of other members of his household. With the passage of time, the wives and daughters of leisure-class gentlemen come to be exempt from industrial employment. It becomes apparent to the head of the house that it lowers his own prestige to have his wife engage in useful labor; it also occurs to him that when he is too busy (in non-productive pursuits) to indulge in much conspicuous leisure himself, he may do so, indirectly, through his wife and children. The wife is thus assigned the task of engaging in "vicarious leisure" as a means of enhancing the standing of her husband. The leisure-class gentleman also acquires a host of servants—valets, footmen, butlers—whose conspicuous abstention from productive labor give further evidence of his wealth and power. Veblen decided that the vicarious leisure performed by housewives and servants was so important that it entitled them to be classified as "a subsidiary or derivative leisure class" whose job was to contribute to the reputability of the "primary or legitimate leisure class."

Conspicuous Consumption and Conspicuous Waste

During the higher stage of barbarian culture (the quasi-peaceable feudal period), new practices were developed by members of the leisure class to advertise their status. One of them Veblen called "conspicuous consumption." Conspicuous consumption—the consumption of goods beyond those needed for subsistence in order to impress people—was added to conspicuous leisure (and, in fact, gradually superseded it) as a major feature of leisure-class life. The consumption of expensive goods was an evidence of wealth and it became honorific; conversely, the failure to consume in due quantity and quality became a mark of inferiority and a demerit. The quasi-peaceable gentleman of leisure, said Veblen, "consumes freely and of the best, in food, drink, narcotics, shelter, services, ornaments, apparel, weapons and accoutrements, amusements, amulets, and idols or divinities." He also "becomes a connoisseur in creditable viands of various degrees of merit, in manly beverages and trinkets, in seemly apparel and architecture, in weapons, games, dances, and the narcotics." Not only did chiefs, kings, and nobles compete with one another in showing off their many servants, elegant castles, magnificent furnishings, costly clothes and jewels, and rare foods; they also gave away expensive presents and threw lavish parties in order to enlist the aid of friends and neighbors in the work of consuming extravagantly. They depended, too, on their wives and children, as well as on their servants and retainers, to help publicize their wealth and status by engaging in vicarious consumption.

Conspicuous leisure, which involved a waste of time and effort, and conspicuous consumption, which involved a waste of goods, inevitably produced another leisure-class practice: "conspicuous waste." Conspicuous waste, with its subsidiary, vicarious waste, became a primary means of making an "invidious pecuniary comparison" with others. What Veblen termed the "law of conspicuously wasteful expenditure of time and substance" came to govern the leisure-class household. The more wasteful anything was, the more prestige it brought. Conspicuous waste not only displayed the owner's wealth; it also showed his contempt for mere productive effort. Fox hunting was more prestigious than deer hunting because it was so obviously non-productive and wasteful of time and effort; butlers and footmen gave the owner more honor than a cook because they accorded so perfectly with the "law of wasted effort." Still, the instinct of workmanship (with its aversion to waste of effort and substance) could not be denied, even under these adverse circumstances. It worked itself out in make-believe: "in 'social duties,' and in quasi-artistic or quasi-scholarly accomplishments, in the care and decoration of the house, in sewing-circle activity or dress reform, in proficiency at dress, cards, yachting, golf, and various sports" and in other "inanities."

Pecuniary Canons of Taste

Veblen did not believe that habits of conspicuous leisure, consumption, and waste were confined to the upper classes. The pecuniary standard of living established by the wealthy leisure class, he pointed out, gradually came to affect all classes of society. The members of each stratum of society, he said, "accept as their ideal of decency the scheme of life in vogue in the next higher stratum, and bend their energies to live up to that ideal." No class of society, not even the poorest, will deny itself all conspicuous consumption, even though indulging in it may mean stinting on basic necessities. Among laborers and handicraftsmen of the towns, for example, and among the lower middle classes of the cities, the practice of "dram-drinking, 'treating,' and smoking in public places" was the customary way of displaying pecuniary decency. In all classes, moreover, pecuniary canons of taste have become predominant in modern times; costliness, waste, and ineptness have become the major elements in the aesthetic standards of most people.

For Veblen pecuniary criteria determined the views of most people as to what is beautiful in furniture, houses, parks, gardens, and domestic animals. Pecuniary standards of taste also explained, he thought, the following curiosities: elaborate church buildings ("constructed and decorated with some view to a reputable degree of wasteful expenditure"); elegant priestly vestments ("notoriously expensive, ornate, and inconvenient"); notions of divinity (God on a throne "with a profusion of the insignia of opulence and power, and surrounded by a great number of servitors," with the shimmer of precious metals in the background); preference for costly hand-wrought silver spoons over machine-made spoons of similar appearance and utility; the belief that the high gloss of a gentleman's hat or of a patent-leather shoe is beautiful while a similarly high gloss on a threadbare sleeve is not; and the feeling that feminine beauty involves delicate hands and feet, a slender figure, and a constricted waist, because these things obviously place a woman above all suggestion of vulgarly productive labor.

Veblen regarded woman's dress as of special interest to the economist. In November, 1894, he published an essay on "The Economic Theory of Woman's Dress" in the *Popular Science Monthly* and he used it as the basis for a long analysis of "Dress as an Expression of the Pecuniary Culture" in *Theory of the Leisure Class*. Veblen thought that clothing and dress were two different things; while clothing is useful and serviceable, dress has as its primary purpose the revelation of the wealth and status of the wearer. In the case of the leisure-class woman who is trying to advertise vicariously the pecuniary decency of the head of the house, three basic principles govern the selection of her costume: obvious expensiveness, novelty (which insures that it will quickly go out of style), and sheer ineptitude (proving that the wearer can't possibly do any useful work when so dressed). Veblen believed that gentlemen's dress—the patent-leather shoe, the stainless linen, the lustrous cylindrical hat, and the walking stick—was similarly designed to show that the leisure-class man consumes without producing; but he thought that woman's dress went even further than man's did in demonstrating the wearer's abstinence from productive employment, and he cited elaborate head-dresses, long hair, high heels, long skirts, and corsets in making his point.

In addition to studying dress from the point of view of economic theory, Veblen also spent considerable time examining the pecuniary and predatory habits of mind involved in devout observances and in the higher learning. He thought that anthropomorphic religion was replete with barbarian notions of status and emulation and that it was entirely unsuited to the exigencies of modern industrial life

(which, in fact, Veblen believed worked steadily toward secularization of thought). Education, too, in his opinion, was vitiated by leisure-class ideals, occupying itself with classical lore, dead languages,
academic ritual, fraternities, and athletics, and inculcating predatory
traits, rather than spreading the kind of scientific and technical
knowledge that would further adaptation to modern industrial circumstances and enhance the industrial efficiency of the community.

Veblen, in short, thought that pecuniary habits of thought, born in
the age of predatory barbarism and persisting in modern business
civilization, were unfitted to modern industrial conditions, and that
by their pervasive influence on the culture of a community like the
United States they prevented the effective response of people to the
requirements of the present. The pecuniary ideals and predatory traits
of the leisure class were responsible, he thought, for economic mal-
adjustment in modern society. Sheltered from economic realities by
its exemption from industrial work, the leisure class took a conservative view of change, strove to perpetuate obsolescent principles from
the past, and worked to retard social evolution. The characteristic
attitude of the leisure class, said Veblen,

> may be summed up in the maxim: "Whatever is, is right"; whereas
> the law of natural selection, as applied to human institutions, gives
> the axiom: "Whatever is, is wrong." Not that the institutions of to-
> day are wholly wrong for the purposes of the life of to-day, but
> they are, always and in the nature of things, wrong to some ex-
> tent. They are the result of a more or less inadequate adjustment of
> the methods of living to a situation which prevailed at some point
> in the past development; and they are therefore wrong by some-
> thing more than the interval which separates the present situation
> from that of the past. . . . The institution of a leisure class, by
> force of class interest and instinct, and by precept and prescriptive
> example, makes for the perpetuation of the existing maladjustment
> of institutions, and even favours a reversion to a somewhat more
> archaic scheme of life. . . .

What Veblen said about the leisure class was meant, of course, to
apply with equal force to the modern business classes, for he regarded
the latter as spiritual descendants of the predatory barbarian. Business was predatory in Veblen's scheme of thought and industry was
productive; and by its parasitic control of industry, business pre-

vented industrial engineers from achieving full production and thus kept America (and other capitalistic societies) in a state of chronic crisis and misery.

The Values of Veblen

Veblen was convinced that the traits displayed in the peaceable-savage stage of social evolution—good will, honesty, sympathy, concern for the group—were better suited to modern collective industrial life than the predatory traits—ferocity, self-seeking, clannishness, disingenuousness—developed in barbarian times. True, such traits do not appreciably advance the life of the individual. The individual, in fact,

> fares better under the regime of competition in proportion as he has less of these gifts. Freedom from scruple, from sympathy, honesty, and regard for life, may, within fairly wide limits, be said to further the success of the individual in the pecuniary culture. . . . It is only within narrow limits, and then only in a Pickwickian sense, that honesty is the best policy.

Nevertheless, such "archaic" traits as truthfulness, peaceableness, good will, and a non-emulative and non-invidious interest in people and things do facilitate life in the community and they therefore possess value for the collective life process. The collective interests of modern communities, moreover, center in industrial efficiency and these interests are best served by honesty, diligence, peacefulness, and an absence of self-seeking. Veblen insisted that the economic man, "whose only interest is the self-regarding one and whose only human trait is prudence," was absolutely useless for the purpose of modern industry. "It may even be said," he added, "that in the modern industrial communities the average, dispassionate sense of men says that the ideal human character is a character which makes for peace, good-will, and economic efficiency, rather than for a life of self-seeking, force, fraud, and mastery."

It was Veblen's firm belief—and he stated it repeatedly—that modern industry requires "an impersonal, non-invidious interest in the work in hand." He acknowledged that there were some survivals of this non-invidious interest even in his own day, but he did not regard them as sufficient for the purposes of social efficiency. In some of the churches, he conceded, charity, social good-fellowship, and human solidarity were emphasized; in leisure-class circles, moreover, there were individuals here and there, especially women, whose temperaments were "reminiscent of the ante-predatory culture," and they could be found involved in charity work and sometimes even in various schemes for social betterment. But the pecuniary canons of conduct prevailing in capitalistic culture, he insisted, prevented non-invidious traits from having free play. The result was that charitable and philanthropic enterprises were contaminated by motives of an emulative or invidious origin and they failed to be of any real service to the community.

The only hope, so far as Veblen could see, was the replacement of the captains of industry and finance by technicians and engineers as the dominant force in modern society and the release of industry from the control of business enterprise. But this could occur only when scientific and matter-of-fact habits of thought, growing out of close association with the impersonal, mechanical processes of modern industry, had come to replace the animistic and predatory thinking surviving from the barbarian stage of culture. Veblen did not give the impression that he thought this would happen in the near future, and he also hastened to make it clear that his attitude was "morally colourless" in any case. But Veblen's values—peace, good will, mutual service, social solidarity, scientific truthfulness, and economic efficiency—emerge clearly enough in *Theory of the Leisure Class*, and it is difficult to understand how so many of his contemporary readers were misled by his pose of moral detachment.

Veblen's later books were primarily elaborations of themes he had explored in his first and most famous book. In *The Theory of Business Enterprise* (1904) he made a detailed—and devastating—study of business enterprise which stressed the incompatibility of investment for profit with the machine process and predicted the "natural decay" of business enterprise under the discipline of the machine. He was misunderstood, as usual, by some readers; socialists resented his "sarcastic, cynical style" and investors wrote asking his advice on how to make money. (A book of his on Germany appearing during World War I was praised by one government agency and pronounced subversive by another.) His favorite book was *The Instinct of Workmanship* (1914)—he called *Theory of the Leisure Class* "that chestnut"— in which he explored man's propensity for meaningful activity, which he regarded as innate, at some length and linked it with two other instincts that he regarded as fundamental to man: the parental bent (a concern for the welfare of the human race) and idle curiosity (a disinterested zeal for truth). A close student of James's *Psychology*, Veblen derived his notion of idle curiosity from the non-utilitarian aspects of mental life, which James thought originated as accidental by-products of the evolutionary process. Veblen also published a book on *The Higher Learning in America* (1918), in which he showed how business principles and pecuniary ideals prevented universities from fulfilling their proper function of advancing pure science and objective scholarship. It was his bitterest book. The original manuscript was so vitriolic—he intended to subtitle it "A Study in Total Depravity"—that a friend persuaded him to tone it down before publishing it.

Veblen's own experiences in the groves of higher learning were not happy. He remained a stranger to most students and faculty wherever he taught, and it was not until late in life that he began to receive the recognition he thought he deserved. But after World War I he did begin to achieve some fame in the world of letters. The playwright Maxwell Anderson reported that when he asked a friend if he had read *Theory of the Leisure Class*, the man replied: "Why, no. Why should I? All my friends have read it. It permeates the atmosphere in which I live." In the pages of *Smart Set*, H. L. Mencken reported in 1919 that "everyone of intellectual pretensions" was reading Veblen, and that there were "Veblenists, Veblen clubs, Veblen remedies for all the sorrows of the world," and even "Veblen Girls—Gibson Girls grown middle-aged and despairing." In the 1920's some of the younger economists wanted to propose Veblen's name for president of the American Economic Association, but Veblen flatly refused the nomination. "They didn't offer it to me when I needed it," he told a friend sourly. He died, lonely and neglected, in August, 1929, just before the Great Crash.

Graham Wallas once expressed the wish that someone would write a book called *The Secret of Veblen*, setting forth Veblen's main ideas clearly and accurately. But Veblen's ideas—despite his at times obscure way of putting things—were never a secret. In all of his writings he made it clear that he loathed business enterprise and that he reserved his affection for the values he believed had existed in man's peaceful savage state. Veblen thought that peacefulness and workmanship were more natural to man than fraud and predation, and he gave the impression, from time to time, that he thought the industrial process would bring these qualities into prominence again. Though socialists were bewildered by his circumlocutive and ironic style, Veblen was without question a socialist from the outset of his career. But though he admired Marx, he was no orthodox Marxist. He was too pessimistic to share Marx's teleological view of history and he could not accept Marx's belief that the working classes (which Veblen called "the underlying population") would eventually rise and overthrow the bourgeoisie (Veblen's "vested interests"). Veblen thought the working classes were too affected by leisure-class ideals to think of revolting.

Implicit in Veblen's analysis of modern industrial society was the idea that the production engineer might push the businessman aside, take control of production, and build a better social order. But Veblen had no great hopes in this direction: "the production engineers," he said toward the end of his life, "are a scattering lot of fairly contented subalterns, working piecemeal under orders from the deputies of the absentee owners. . . ." Moreover, though he insisted that machine industry cuts away the spiritual foundations of business enterprise by inculcating skeptical, matter-of-fact, and materialistic attitudes, he also seemed to think that business might be able to find ways of surviving the process. The "natural decay" of business enterprise following from the discipline of the machine could be checked, he suggested, by the adoption of aggressive and warlike national policies, which would revive the barbaric virtues of "allegiance, piety, servility, graded dignity, class prerogative, and prescriptive authority. . . ."

Though an outsider all of his life, Veblen was thoroughly American in at least one important respect: he cherished such traditional American ideals as liberty, equality, democracy, and economic wellbeing. But he firmly denied that these ideals could be achieved by war and predation.

Chapter 9

The Day of the Saxon

In April, 1898, Congress declared war on Spain and the United States embarked on the most popular of all her many wars. The Spanish-American War was, as John Hay put it gratefully, a "splendid little war." Even for the American people, who rather enjoy war and take a romantic view of it, there was something almost utopian about this war: it lasted only ten weeks; it was thoroughly covered, in press and periodical, by reporters like Richard Harding Davis and artists like Frederick Remington; it produced heroes like Commodore George Dewey and colorful outfits like Theodore Roosevelt's Rough Riders; it contained dramatic episodes like the so-called charge up San Juan Hill and spectacular victories like Dewey's at Manila Bay; and it ended triumphantly in the acquisition of a fine empire in the Caribbean and in the Pacific. After the Spanish War, Americans could never quite get over the feeling that war can and should be short, easy, and glamorous, and that if it is not, there are nefarious forces at work somewhere in the land.

War, Freedom, and Race

The Spanish-American War was, above all, an outlet for the vast stores of melodramatic idealism animating the American people. For most Americans, the Spanish War was fought to free Cuba from intolerable Spanish rule; and the encounter with Spain seemed to represent the classic American idealistic dichotomy: liberty vs. slavery, independence vs. tyranny, civilization vs. barbarism, humanity vs. brutality. The president of Oberlin College spoke for many Americans when he called the war "the last great struggle between the Middle Ages and the Declaration of Independence, between the Inquisition and the common school, between the rack and toleration, between the Duke of Alva and George Washington, between Philip the Second and Abraham Lincoln." It is possible, to be sure, that the long-range objectives of the governing elite in challenging Spain in the Caribbean and in the Pacific were primarily economic in nature. After the Great Depression of 1893–97, increasing numbers of businessmen and politicians had reached the conclusion that expanded foreign markets (particularly in eastern Asia) were indispensable to the health of the American economy, and many of them thought that overseas possessions advanced foreign trade. Still, the rationale for the war and the territorial expansion accompanying it was made only partly in economic terms. The ideology of freedom unquestionably played a major role in shaping American thought about the conflict and in winning popular support for the war.

Freedom, of course, meant several things to the American people. It meant, first and foremost, national independence and government by consent, which the Declaration of Independence had proclaimed as the highest political goals for all men. It also included the civil liberties and legal rights embodied in the Bill of Rights. But freedom was above all economic in nature for most Americans: it involved private property, free enterprise, and opportunities for material gain. Most Americans thought that political rights, civil liberties, and private enterprise were all of a piece and that it was not possible to have one without the other. Many Americans also gave a Social Darwinist twist to the idea of freedom: they looked upon it as an achievement of the "fittest" races and peoples (principally Anglo-Saxons) and they thought that the United States, as an Anglo-Saxon nation, was its special champion throughout the world. From this point of view, freedom (in any of its forms) was a privilege, not a universal right; it was the special prerogative of Anglo-Saxons at home and abroad. But not all Americans were Social Darwinists; nor were all of them of British descent. Some Americans spoke of freedom in universal terms; and others, especially if not Anglo-Saxons, extended the meaning of the term to include at least themselves. Thus non-Anglo-Saxons joined Anglo-Saxons in rallying around the banner of liberty, especially in wartime. Opinions as to who was fit for freedom depended on who was doing the fitting.

For the majority of Americans, then, the Spanish-American War was in some sense a fight for freedom. The Reverend John Henry Barrows announced that victory in the war against Spain would mean an expansion of "toleration, education, freedom, justice, equality, and opportunity" into "vast areas that have been desolated or undeveloped." Chauncey Depew called American soldiers "saints of liberty" and said they had the mission of transforming Cubans, Puerto Ricans, Hawaiians, and Filipinos into "free agents of right and justice." And Congressman Jonathan P. Dolliver of Iowa thought that the American republic, in taking on Spain, was simply acting as "an instrument in the divine hand for enlarging the area of civilization and for widening the outlook of human liberty." Thus bands played, flags flew, and young men throughout the country rushed to the colors. And T. R., who unlike many of his friends did not go in for mere spectator sports, ran around the Navy Department like a little boy on roller skates until he had perfected plans for exchanging his desk job for action at the front.

Amid the paeans to freedom, justice, and humanity in press and pulpit and on platform and podium, American blacks as well as whites flocked to the colors. For colored Americans responding to President McKinley's call for volunteers, the slogan *Cuba libre* took on special meaning, for they realized that nearly all the leaders of the Cuban revolt against Spain and most of the fighters in the Cuban army of liberation were Negroes and mulattoes. In Cuba, Negro American contingents participated in action at El Caney, Las Guasimas, and San Juan Hill, and Negro cavalry units were credited with saving the Rough Riders from annihilation at Las Guasimas. "One of the most gratifying incidents of the Spanish War," said the *Review of Reviews* in October, 1898,

has been the enthusiasm that the colored regiments of the regular army have aroused throughout the whole country. Their fighting at Santiago was magnificent. The Negro soldiers showed excellent discipline, the highest qualities of personal bravery, very superior physical endurance, unfailing good temper, and the most generous disposition toward all comrades in arms, whether white or black.

Roosevelt's Rough Riders have come back singing the praises of the colored troops. There is not a dissenting voice in the chorus of praise. . . . Men who can fight for their country as did these colored troops ought to have their full share of gratitude and honor.

At the end of the war, Booker T. Washington called for "the blotting out of racial prejudices" as the next logical step in America's fight for freedom.

Washington's plea was to go unheeded. Given the racial attitudes of American whites in the late nineteenth century, it would have been a miracle if the efforts of American blacks to prove their patriotism in the Spanish War had received more than passing recognition. In October, 1898, the very month in which Washington made his plea, there were two race riots in the South, and in November came the terrible outburst in Wilmington, North Carolina, in which a white mob killed and wounded scores of Negroes and chased hundreds out of town. It was one thing to fight for "an enlargement of the area of human freedom" abroad (as a Southern journalist glowingly described America's "world mission"); it was quite another to concern oneself with freedom at home. In the 1890's, freedom for the Negro was being steadily circumscribed in the South by force, fraud, intimidation, and Jim Crow laws; and in the North the Negro was scarcely treated as an equal even by the best intentioned whites. During the Spanish-American War, the Negro soldier met with repeated rebuffs and indignities as well as occasional commendations: slurs on his manhood by Southern newspapers, outright hostility when passing through Southern cities en route to ports of embarkation, ill-concealed doubts by white officers as to his intellect and capacity for leadership, and severe restrictions on his opportunities to rise in the armed forces. Hardest of all to bear, perhaps, was T. R.'s turnabout after the war in his attitude toward the blacks in his outfit. In his farewell address to the Rough Riders at the close of the war, he called the Negro soldiers "an excellent breed of Yankees"; writing in *Scribner's Magazine* the following year, however, he cast doubts on their courage and said they were "peculiarly dependent on their white officers."

"It is a sorry, though true fact," wrote Lewis H. Douglass (son of the famous ex-slave Frederick Douglass), on November 17, 1899, "that whatever this government controls, injustice to dark races prevails. The people of Cuba, Porto Rico, Hawaii and Manila know it well as do the wronged Indian and outraged black man in the United

States." When McKinley promised the Filipinos life, liberty, and the pursuit of happiness after the war, Douglass could not conceal his bitterness. American expansion into the Philippines and other parts of the world, he insisted, would not mean an expansion of freedom; it would mean an "extension of race hate and cruelty, barbarous lynchings and gross injustices to dark people."

Douglass was all too prescient. American suppression of the Filipino insurrection after the Spanish War turned out to be brutal and bloody; and the acquisition of an empire containing millions of colored people—"a varied assortment of inferior races," according to the *Nation*—gave an added boost to the doctrine of white supremacy in all parts of the country. (During the pacification of the Philippines, white soldiers commonly referred to Filipinos as "niggers.") "No Republican leader . . . will now dare to wave the bloody shirt and preach a crusade against the South's treatment of the negro," taunted Senator Benjamin Tillman of South Carolina. "The North has a bloody shirt of its own. Many thousands of them have been made into shrouds for murdered Filipinos, done to death because they were fighting for liberty." By the end of the century it was the day of the Saxon in the North as well as in the South; and the American Negro reached the low point of his existence as a freedman in the United States. There were, to be sure, friendliness and good will toward Negroes as well as scorn and contempt for them among American whites in the late nineteenth century; nevertheless, a vast indifference and astonishing insensitivity, as well as open dislike bordering on the pathological, had come to prevail throughout the land by the 1890's and Lewis Douglass did not err in stressing the latter.

Southern Views of Race

From a Southerner came what was perhaps the most vitriolic book on race to appear between the Civil War and the Spanish-American War: Hinton Rowan Helper's *Nojoque; A Question for a Continent* (1867). Helper was no fool; a North Carolinian who had blasted slavery in 1857 (*The Impending Crisis*) for its injurious effects on Southern life, he had been loyal to the Union during the Civil War and served as consul in Buenos Aires. In *Nojoque,* he did not retreat from his position of hostility to slavery; but his contempt for the Negro, scarcely concealed in *The Impending Crisis,* had come to assume monstrous proportions by the end of the Civil War. The chapter titles indicate the quality of his thinking: "The Negro, Anthropologically Considered—An Inferior Fellow Done For"; "Black; A Thing of Ugliness, Disease, and Death"; "White; A Thing of Life, Health, and Beauty"; "The Servile Baseness and Beggary of the Blacks." Helper did not advocate mere segregation and suppression; he called for outright expulsion of blacks from the United States and hoped for their eventual extermination throughout the world. His great dream was for the day when "the whole habitable globe shall be peopled exclusively by those naturally and superlatively superior races—the pure White Races—to whom we are indebted for all human achievements. . . ."

Few American whites went as far as Helper. His views were regarded as outlandish even by people in the South who were convinced that the Negro was inferior to the white. After the Civil War, some Southerners, in fact, strongly urged that the black man be given some of the freedom that American whites possessed as their birthright. In Kentucky, Protestant Episcopal Bishop Thomas U. Dudley, a native of Virginia who had served in the Confederate Army, insisted after the war that the Negro was a citizen possessing constitutional rights and that he needed all the help he could get from whites— "personal, individual, patient, loving help, that he may be fitted to exercise his covenanted rights, and to do the duties which these rights impose." Bishop Dudley was repelled by the idea of miscegenation and he had some doubts about the Negro's ability to progress morally; still, he regarded segregation as a mistaken policy, whether in church or on public transportation, and he insisted that it would prevent the Negro from bettering himself. Lewis Harvie Blair, well-to-do Virginia businessman who, like Dudley, had fought for the Confederacy, also insisted that the interest of the South lay in

> enfranchising, not coercing the Negroes, in inviting, not repelling their co-operation; in encouraging them to vote and participate in public affairs; in making them feel that they have a country and are not despised aliens in their native land, and that they have rights inalienable and not with a string to them and the string in our hands.

Blair thought that repression of the Negro and racial bigotry had a pernicious effect on the welfare of the South as a whole, and in 1889 he published a book setting forth his views entitled *The Prosperity of the South Dependent upon the Elevation of the Negro.*

Many Southern politicians also rejected Helper's philosophy in the postwar period. Conservative upper-class leaders who came into power at the end of Reconstruction had previously raised the cry of white supremacy against the carpetbaggers; once in power, however, some of them sought to enter into a limited co-operation with the Negro for political purposes. Men like Wade Hampton of South Carolina, L. Q. C. Lamar of Mississippi, and Alexander H. Stephens of Georgia supported the Negroes' right to vote and run for office and saw to it that they received minor appointments in local government. These men did not, moreover, insist on strict segregation, and they were willing to tolerate a good deal of mixing of the races in public places. The motive of such conservatives was mainly economic; they needed Negro votes in their struggle with agrarian-minded Southerners who were opposed to their pro-business orientation. In general, Southern conservatives who were willing to work with Negroes took a paternalistic view of the matter. They regarded the Negro as lower than the white, but they thought he deserved certain limited rights appropriate to his subordinate station in life. They also thought the superior race had obligations as well as privileges, and that one of its primary duties was to look out for the welfare of the underprivileged black. "The Negro race is under us," explained Governor Thomas G. Jones of Alabama. "He is in our power. We are his custodians . . . we should extend to him, as far as possible, all the civil rights that will fit him to be a decent and self respecting law-abiding and intelligent citizen. . . . If we do not lift them up, they will drag us down." But the conservative-Negro alliance was short-lived. To defeat the Populists, who made a strong bid for Negro support in the 1890's, the conservatives began warning against threats to white supremacy, and they came, in the end, to support disfranchisement and strict segregation of the Negro in the South.

American Negroes had a far firmer Southern friend in the novelist George Washington Cable, whose books about the Creoles made him one of the most popular writers of his day. Cable was a native of Louisiana, the son of slave-owning parents, and he had fought in the Confederate Army and been wounded twice. Never abandoning his deep affection for the South, Cable nevertheless came gradually after the war to the conclusion that slavery had been a monstrous evil, that any caste system involving the subordination of one race or class to another violated the "faith of our fathers," and that simple justice, as well as the welfare of the South, and of the nation as a whole, called for the extension of full civil rights to the freedman. Cable repeatedly

urged Southerners to get rid of the idea of caste, which had caused
so much misery and oppression, once for all. "Is the 'Southern' instinct
not cunning enough," he asked in 1882, "to snuff out the stupid wick-
edness of exalting and abusing our fellow humans class by class and
race by race instead of man by man?" To the question "Who—if not
the intelligent—are to rule?" Cable responded: *"All!* All are to rule.
That order of society is the best, and that order of society only is
American, where the intelligent are so hemmed in with the unintelli-
gent that they cannot afford to let them rest in their unintelligence."

In 1885 Cable published an essay on "The Freedman's Case in
Equity" in the *Century Magazine,* which roused a storm in the South.
In the essay he characterized the prevailing caste distinctions in the
South as "gross, irrational, unjust, and inefficient," said they were
contrary to "the eternal principles of justice," and declared his conviction that "whatever elevates the lower stratum of the people lifts
all the rest, and whatever holds it down holds all down." Cable
denied that his objective was social equality; social relations, he said,
were purely matters of private choice and had nothing to do with the
civil rights that should be accorded all American citizens. When it
came to civil rights—the Negro's right to free and unrestricted access
to such public facilities as schools, libraries, courthouses, railroads,
steamers, theaters, and concert halls—Cable was uncompromising;
"every interest in the land," he declared, "demands that the freedman
be free to become in all things, as far as his own personal gifts will
lift and sustain him, the same sort of American citizen he would be
if, with the same intellectual and moral caliber, he were white."
Cable was attacked as a traitor to his section by many irate Southerners, but he also received letters from Southern whites endorsing
his views; and his belief that there was a "silent South"— Southerners
who agreed with him but dared not speak up—encouraged him to
continue his efforts on behalf of the Negro to the end of the century.

Mark Twain, a Missourian, was as firm a friend of the Negro as
Cable. Like Cable, Twain had been reared in a slaveholding community, and he came only gradually as an adult to realize the injustice of slavery. After the Civil War he did what he could toward
"the reparation" that he thought was "due from every white to every
black man" for having enslaved him. He put two Negroes through college, helped raise money for Booker T. Washington's work, and
lectured to Negro churches whenever he was asked (even though too
busy to speak to white congregations); more important, in his novels,

lectures, essays, and sketches, he punctured the romantic view of the Old South, blasted slavery, satirized racial prejudice, and, in his portrayal of such characters as Jim in *Huckleberry Finn*, emphasized the innate dignity and love for freedom of the Negro American. Twain once told his daughter Jean that "white was not a favorite complexion with God," since he made so many dark-skinned people, "two-thirds, you see, of the human race"; and he toyed with the idea of doing an ironic sketch about how Negroes came to dominate the South and enforced segregation on the whites. Twain was appalled by the increase in lynchings in the later years of the nineteenth century and he made plans to write a history of lynching called "The United States of Lyncherdom." He once proposed that American missionaries in China come home to take up their work among American lynchers. "O kind missionary," he said, "O compassionate missionary, leave China! Come home and convert these Christians!"

Tom Watson of Georgia was as appalled by lynching (in which his own state stood high) as Twain was. The foremost leader of Southern Populism, Watson in 1893 urged the People's Party to "make lynch law odious to the people," and in 1896 the Georgia People's Party platform denounced lynch law and called for justice for the Negro. Watson believed in class struggle, not racial strife; the poor and oppressed of both races, he thought, could work amicably together on the basis of common interests and common grievances. In an article on "The Negro Question in the South" for the *Arena* in September, 1893, Watson said that the accident of color was irrelevant to the economic interest of farmers, sharecroppers, and laborers, and that the poor of both races were, in fact, kept apart only so that they might be "separately fleeced" of their earnings. "You are made to hate each other," he told them, "because upon that hatred is rested the keystone of the arch of financial despotism which enslaves you both. You are deceived and blinded that you may not see how this race antagonism perpetuates a monetary system which beggars you both."

Watson was confident that the Populist Party could settle the race question:

First, by enacting the Australian ballot system. Second, by offering to white and black a rallying point which is free from the odium of former discords and strifes. Third, by presenting a platform immensely beneficial to both races and injurious to neither. Fourth, by making it to the *interest* of both races to act together for the success of the platform. Fifth, by making it to the *interest* of the colored man to have the same patriotic zeal for the welfare of the South that the whites possess.

The question of social equality, according to Watson, "does not enter into the calculation. That is a thing each citizen decides for himself. . . . Each citizen regulates his own visiting list—and always will." With the failure of Populism in Georgia and elsewhere, Watson abandoned his dream of uniting poor whites and blacks in a crusade against industrial capitalism, and he came gradually to take up the hatred and prejudice that he had denounced so forthrightly in the early 1890's. The time came when he praised lynch law and said that Booker T. Washington was as "imitative as an ape" and "as bestial as a gorilla."

Race Attitudes in the North

Negrophobia was by no means confined to the South. In 1868, John Van Evrie, a New York physician who had favored slavery and championed the South during the Civil War, published a book on *White Supremacy and Negro Subordination*, which, though more moderately phrased than *Nojoque*, was as contemptuous of the Negro as Helper's book. Unlike Helper, Van Evrie did not call for expelling Negroes from the land. God and nature, he said, had intended white and black to live in juxtaposition; the black man, however, was destined for a strictly subordinate position. Van Evrie thought there were six distinct races of men and he listed them in the order of their supposed ability: Caucasian or white, Mongolian, Malay or Oceanic, the aboriginal American, the "Esquimaux," and the Negro or typical African. He did not think well of any race but the Caucasian (he thought Confucius was a Caucasian), but he regarded the Negro as "lowest and inferior to all." To prove his point he presented many "facts" about the Negro—he doesn't feel pain, he can't stand up straight, he can't speak English or sing properly because his vocal cords are inferior, etc.—illustrating the Negro's inferiority. Van Evrie's conclusion from his collection of old (Caucasian) wives' tales was that subordination was the Negro's normal condition and that slavery hadn't been so bad after all.

If Van Evrie can be considered an ignoramus, what is one to say of Frederick L. Hoffman, naturalized citizen of German origin and

statistician for the Prudential Insurance Company of America? Hoffman, who thought the Negro a poor insurance risk, utilized the
statistical method to study the *Race Traits and Tendencies of the
American Negro* and had his findings published by the American
Economic Association in 1896, but he scarcely did better by the
Negro than Van Evrie did. Hoffman, it is true, did not share Van
Evrie's superstitious dislike of the Negro, but his thesis, in the end,
was just as silly as Van Evrie's; undoubtedly more pernicious, too, in
its effects, for the absence of rancor, the air of detachment, and the
statistical tables (based mainly on the census of 1890) which he used
probably made his book persuasive to well-meaning people who
would have been repelled by the imbecilities of Helper and Van
Evrie. Ever since emancipation, according to Hoffman, the Negro
because of "inherited organic weakness" had been deteriorating, both
physically and morally, and there was every reason to suppose that he
would eventually die out. "It is not in the *conditions of life*," Hoffman
insisted,

but in *the race traits and tendencies* that we find the causes of the
[Negro's] excessive mortality. So long as these tendencies are
persisted in, so long as immorality and vice are a habit of life of
the vast majority of the colored population, the effect will be to increase the mortality by hereditary transmission of weak constitutions, and to lower still further the rate of natural increase, until
the births fall below the deaths, and gradually extinction results.

Hoffman thought that race amalgamation, as well as vice and immorality, was contributing to the Negro's decline. Intellectually, he
said, the mulatto is superior to the pure-blooded Negro, but physically and morally he is inferior; with race mixing, then, an "inferior
degree of vital power" results and Negro mortality increases rapidly.
Hoffman did not regret this tendency, for it meant the triumph of the
whites, or Aryans, as he called them. The Aryan race, he said jubilantly,

is possessed of all the essential characteristics that make for success in the struggle for the higher life, in contrast with other races
which lack in either one or the other of the determining qualities. . . . Here, in the contrast between the white and colored races,
we have the most complete historical proof of race superiority,

a superiority extending into all the intricate and complex phenomena of life. Wherever the white man has gone, he has become the master of the conditions of life. The whole history of Anglo-Saxon conquest and colonization is one of endless proof of race superiority and race supremacy. In countries where the very forces of nature were at first against him, he has, after years of struggle, gained his end and mastered the conditions of life surrounding him.

Reviewing Hoffman's book, Professor Kelly Miller of Howard University pointed out that crime grows out of social conditions, not race traits, declared that immorality is a human, not a race, trait, and said that if the low industrial efficiency of Negroes was due to race traits, it should be attributed to "the domineering and intolerant race traits" of whites who denied Negroes an equal chance. He also presented a table showing that the death rate of Germans was just as high as that of Negroes, and asked: "If race traits are playing such havoc with the Negroes in America, what direful agent of death, may we ask the author, is at work in the cities of his own fatherland?" But American whites read Hoffman—and Van Evrie—not Kelly Miller.

The kind of thinking about race found in Hoffman and Van Evrie did not, of course, completely dominate Northern attitudes in the Gilded Age, for there were Northerners, especially during the Reconstruction period, who thought far better of the Negro than this and who had greater hopes for his future. During Reconstruction, radical Republicans like Thaddeus Stevens and Charles Sumner championed the freedman's right to vote as well as a whole range of civil rights designed to make him a first-class citizen, and they also exerted their efforts to advance his health, education, and welfare. With the end of Reconstruction, however, most Northerners placed the re-establishment of sectional harmony above the welfare of the Negro and they acquiesced in the gradual consolidation of white supremacy in the South after the Compromise of 1877. Beginning with Rutherford B. Hayes, American presidents adopted a let-alone policy toward the South, and though they continued to pay lip service to the civil rights guaranteed the Negro by law, they made no serious effort to uphold these rights. At the same time the Supreme Court gradually nullified or drastically curtailed the rights of Negroes which radical Reconstructionists had written into the fourteenth and fifteenth amendments to the Constitution. A few people protested the abandonment of the freedman by the federal government, but most Northerners lost interest in the Negro. When Booker T. Washington, speaking in Atlanta, Georgia, in September, 1895, accepted a subordinate position for his people, at least for the time being, and urged the Negro to put all his efforts into improving himself economically rather than striving for political and social equality, there was general approval in the North as well as in the South.

In the North, too, most whites came to share the view of the Negro held by white supremacists in the South. Northern newspapers played up Negro crimes, used such pejorative terms as "burly negro," "negro ruffian," and "colored cannibal" in their news stories, and printed anecdotes, jokes, and cartoons containing such words as "coon," "darky," "pickaninny," and "nigger." Similar expressions—as well as the popular stereotype of the Negro as "lazy, improvident, child-like, irresponsible, chicken-stealing, crap-shooting, policy-playing, razor-toting, immoral and criminal"—appeared in articles, short stories, and poems in respectable magazines like *Harper's, Scribner's, Century,* and *Atlantic Monthly.* The derogatory stereotype of the Negro also came to prevail on the stage, in minstrel shows, and in novels. Even well-meaning American whites came to accept Negro inferiority as an indubitable fact and to favor at least some degree of segregation. Edward Bellamy, for example, thought it necessary to provide for a separate colored industrial army in his utopian commonwealth.

Belief in white (or Caucasian or Aryan or Teutonic or Anglo-Saxon) superiority shaped the attitudes of most Americans toward the Indians and Chinese in this country as well as toward the "new" immigrants who began coming to the United States in the 1880's. For most whites, the American Indian was peculiarly base, treacherous, and bloodthirsty; and the Chinese were barbaric, superstitious, and practically subhuman. As for the Italians, Poles, Russian Jews, Serbians, Hungarians, and other people from southern and eastern Europe, sociologist Edward A. Ross thought they were of "low mentality," economist Francis Walker called them "beaten men from beaten races; representing the worst failures in the struggle for existence," and Thomas Bailey Aldrich called them "human gorillas." Aldrich, editor of the *Atlantic Monthly* from 1881 to 1890, was so repelled by the new immigrants that he wrote a poem entitled "Unguarded Gates," in which he beseeched "O Liberty, white goddess," to consider whether it was wise to leave American gates open to the "wild motley throng" coming here with its "unknown gods and rites," its "tiger passions," and its "accents of menace alien to our air."

William James was appalled by the prejudices (including anti-Semitism) which he encountered in the United States in the late nineteenth century. "In God's eyes," he insisted, "the differences of social position, of intellect, of culture, of cleanliness, of dress, which different men exhibit...must be so small as practically quite to vanish." American intellectuals in particular, James thought, should be mindful of man's "ancestral blindness" toward his fellow men and strive themselves to live by "sympathies and admirations, not by dislikes and disdains." James found the cult of the Anglo-Saxon (especially popular in old-stock patrician circles in the East) thoroughly distasteful. "If the Anglo-Saxon race would drop its sniveling cant," he wrote, after reading Rudyard Kipling's poem "The White Man's Burden" (which appeared in *McClure's Magazine* in February, 1899), "it would have a good deal less of a burden to carry." Then he added indignantly: "We're the most loathsomely canting crew that God ever made."

The Cult of the Anglo-Saxon

The doctrine of Anglo-Saxon superiority was not new in the Gilded Age. Belief that Anglo-Saxons were uniquely gifted with a love of liberty and a capacity for self-government was an old one. It became popular in England in the seventeenth and eighteenth centuries and came to the United States in the early part of the nineteenth century. During the Mexican War there was much talk among expansionists of the duty of the United States, as an Anglo-Saxon nation, to "enlarge the area of freedom" on the North American continent. After the Civil War, the Anglo-Saxon tradition gained in influence among scholars and intellectuals with northern European backgrounds as well as in old-stock upper-class circles, expecially in New England, which looked to Great Britain for cultural cues. In an essay on "Manifest Destiny" for *Harper's Magazine* in 1885, John Fiske (who regarded himself as a lineal descendant of King Alfred) emphasized the superiority of Anglo-Saxon institutions and predicted that Anglo-Saxons would expand peacefully throughout the world until "every land on the earth's surface that is not already the seat of an old civilization shall become English in its language, in its religion, in its political habits and traditions, and to a predominant extent in the blood of its people."

In the same year that Fiske made the Anglo-Saxon's destiny manifest, Josiah Strong, zealous worker for the Congregational Home Missionary Society, published a pamphlet, later expanded into an enormously popular book, entitled *Our Country: Its Possible Future and Its Present Crisis,* which was even more ecstatic about the future of the Anglo-Saxons. Strong was severely critical of immigrants, Roman Catholicism, Mormonism, big cities, and Mammonism in his book, but for the Anglo-Saxon he had only kind words. In a chapter on "The Anglo-Saxon and the World's Future," Strong announced that the Anglo-Saxon race represented two great ideas—civil liberty and a "pure spiritual Christianity"—and that it was destined to spread these ideas around the globe. "Does it not look," he asked,

> as if God were not only preparing in our Anglo-Saxon civilization the die with which to stamp the peoples of the earth, but as if he were massing behind that die the mighty power with which to press it? My confidence that this race is eventually to give its civilization to mankind is not based on mere numbers—China forbid! I look forward to what the world has never yet seen united in the same race, viz., the greatest numbers *and* the highest civilization.

Strong had no doubt that the United States was to be the "great home of the Anglo-Saxon," with the greatest numbers, wealth, and influence, and with "the highest type of Anglo-Saxon civilization." Strong thought that God was preparing the Anglo-Saxon race, particularly the American branch, for world domination. When the pressure of population on the means of subsistence became severe, he said, the world would "enter upon a new stage of its history—*the final competition of race, for which the Anglo-Saxon is being schooled.*" Strong was confident of the outcome:

> Then this race of unequaled energy, with all the majesty of numbers and the might of wealth behind it—the representative, let us hope, of the largest liberty, the purest Christianity, the highest civilization—having developed peculiarly aggressive traits calculated to impress its institutions upon mankind, will spread itself over the earth. If I read not amiss, this powerful race will move down upon Mexico, down upon Central and South America, out upon the islands of the sea, over upon Africa and beyond. And can any one doubt that the result of this competition of races will be the "survival of the fittest"?

The Teutonic Germ Theory

Strong, whose book had a profound influence on American thought in the late nineteenth century, preferred Anglo-Saxons to Germans (too militaristic) and to French (too fickle). There were some Americans, however, who thought that Teutons and Normans, rather than Anglo-Saxons, were the source of all that was good in American (and modern) civilization. The upshot was the same in all three cases, however, since both Normans and Anglo-Saxons were branches of the Teutonic "race" and the Teutons were regarded by American racists as superior to Greeks, Slavs, Celts, and Romans. All three, moreover, could be comfortably accommodated by the Teutonic germ theory of institutional development, which had a great vogue among American scholars in the late nineteenth century.

The Teutonic theory, developed by British historians and taken over by American scholars, held that British and American political and legal institutions had evolved from primitive "germs" originating among the ancient Teutons. According to Johns Hopkins University historian Herbert Baxter Adams, foremost exponent of the Teutonist theory in the United States, the representative institutions of modern Britain and America could be traced back to the "seeds of self-government" planted by the ancient Teutons in their councils and village moots. Most American historians—Fiske, for example—emphasized the Anglo-Saxon or English aspect of the Teutonist theory. A few, like Henry Cabot Lodge, stressed the Norman contribution to American civilization. A third group, the Germanists, placed major emphasis upon the original Teuton stock.

John Burgess, political scientist at Columbia University who had studied history and political science in Germany, regarded the United States as "a Teutonic national state." The Teutonic character of the English, he thought, had been diluted by the French infusion following the Norman Conquest; but life in the American wilderness had sloughed off the "Norman-French veneer" from the seventeenth-century English immigrants and brought "the German element in the English character again to the front." Germany, thus, was the true—and Teutonic—motherland of the United States. Burgess was a devout believer in the mission of the Teutonic people. In *Political Science and Comparative Constitutional Law* (1890) he insisted that the Teutons had greater political and organizing ability than anyone else, that they had created the modern national state, and that the

Teutonic nations were "called to carry the political civilization of the modern world into those parts of the world inhabited by unpolitical and barbaric races, *i.e., they must have a colonial policy.*" Though Burgess opposed the Spanish-American War because he feared it would result in "mongrel races" overseas becoming American citizens, he concluded, after the war, that the Teutons had a civilizing mission to fulfill not only in the Philippines, but in China as well.

Germanists like Burgess tended to pass over the fact that the Saxon yeomen of England had been conquered by the Norman French in 1066. But Massachusetts Senator Henry Cabot Lodge did not forget; he was eager to emphasize the role of the Normans in shaping the American character. His own great-grandfather, George Cabot, whom he admired greatly, was of "pure Norman extraction," and, according to Lodge, he had descended from a man who accompanied William the Conqueror to England. Since Lodge believed that ancestry determined character, he was proud that his own ancestors were "of that Norman race which did so much for the making of England. . . ." But he denied that the Normans who invaded England were Frenchmen; they were "Saxons who spoke French . . . the most remarkable of all people who poured out of the Germanic forests. . . ." He could therefore eulogize Anglo-Saxons as well as Normans at the expense of other groups; and in his campaign for immigration restriction in the 1890's he filled the pages of the *Congressional Record* with a good deal of flagrant racialism.

An Anglo-Saxon Foreign Policy

By the time of the Spanish-American War, the idea that the Anglo-Saxons had a special civilizing and governing mission to perform in the world had become firmly embedded in American thought and it affected profoundly the attitudes of many prominent Americans toward America's relations with other nations. Senator Lodge, for one, favored an aggressive foreign policy as well as restriction of immigration from non-Teutonic nations. In an article on "Our Blundering Foreign Policy" for *Forum* in March, 1895, he criticized prevailing American policy as one of "retreat and surrender" and called for more ambitious objectives. "The great nations," he pointed out,

are rapidly absorbing for their future expansion and their present defense all the waste places of the earth. It is a movement which makes for civilization and the advancement of the race. As one of the great nations of the world, the United States must not fall out of the line of march.

Theodore Roosevelt, who thought English-speaking people belonged to the "highest races," joined his friend Lodge in seeking what they called a "large policy" for the United States; and both of them made extensive use of the expansionist ideas of Captain Alfred T. Mahan in their efforts to rouse the American people out of their sluggish "isolationism."

Captain Mahan probably reflected as well as encouraged the revival of Western imperialism that began agitating the world in the last part of the nineteenth century. He also played a major role in stimulating the growth of expansionist sentiment in the United States in the 1890's. His most celebrated book, *The Influence of Sea Power upon History,* published in 1890, was based on lectures on naval history and tactics which he had prepared for the Naval War College in Newport, Rhode Island, four years earlier. A study of the rise of British sea power between 1660 and 1783, Mahan's book has been compared to both *Wealth of Nations* and *Origin of Species* in its impact on the world. Not only was it cited time and again by Lodge, Roosevelt, and other American expansionists, in and out of Congress, in the 1890's; it was also promptly translated into other languages, and read with enthusiasm and studied with care in Germany and Japan as well as in Great Britain. Mahan's second major book, *The Influence of Sea Power upon the French Revolution and Empire, 1793–1812* (1892), was equally esteemed here and abroad; and the articles he wrote on sea power for the *Atlantic Monthly, Harper's Magazine,* and other periodicals helped disseminate his naval and expansionist philosophy to a wide audience in the United States. Mahan was undoubtedly one of the most successful propagandists ever produced in the United States; few writers have had as wide an influence on his times as he did.

Mahan's thesis was simple enough. A nation's strength and well-being, he declared, rests primarily upon sea power; without it, no nation has ever risen to first rank in the world of nations. Travel and traffic have always been easier and cheaper by water than by land, and this means that the sea must be regarded as a great highway made up of lines of travel or trade routes. To achieve prosperity and greatness, according to Mahan, a nation must develop a flourishing merchant marine of its own so that its foreign trade need not be carried in alien vessels; it should also develop a navy capable of keeping trade routes open and defending its shipping in time of war; and, in addition, it must develop colonies in various parts of the world to provide the merchant marine and the navy with stations for refuge and supplies, with commercial ports, and with naval bases. Mahan noted regretfully that of the three links in the chain that makes sea power—production of exportable goods, shipping, and colonies—the United States possessed only the first. "Having therefore no foreign establishments, either colonial or military," he said, "the ships of war of the United States, in war, will be like land birds, unable to fly far from their own shores." But in time of war the enemy must "be kept not only out of our ports, but far away from our coasts," and this necessitates a navy strong enough to engage in "offensive defense."

Mahan was anxious for the United States to develop its own merchant shipping, build up its navy, and obtain bases and colonies overseas. This was not only necessary, he said, for American security in a turbulent world; it was also essential if the American people were to fulfill their responsibilities as the upholders, with the British, of civilization around the world. Mahan wanted the United States to build an isthmian canal, gain control of the Caribbean, and acquire the Hawaiian Islands and other outposts in the Pacific; he also wanted the United States to assume a Christianizing and civilizing role among the ancient lands of eastern Asia. ". . . I am frankly an imperialist," he acknowledged in his memoirs, "in the sense that I believe that no nation, certainly no great nation, should henceforth maintain the policy of isolation which fitted our early history; above all, should not on that overlived plea refuse to intervene in events obviously thrust upon its conscience." Mahan's conscience was shaped by Anglo-Saxon imperatives as much as Josiah Strong's was. But since his father was admittedly "of pure Irish blood," Mahan was not precisely an Anglo-Saxon himself. "One-half Irish, one-fourth English, and a good deal more than 'a trace' of French," he confessed, "would appear to be the showing of a quantitative analysis." Still, he added stoutly, "as far as I understand my personality, I think to see in the result the predominance which the English strain has usually asserted for itself over others."

The Case for American Imperialism

Mahan, Lodge, and Roosevelt were overjoyed when the United States went to war with Spain in 1898, and they hoped that it would

produce a "large policy" for the nation. During the debate over annexing the Philippines which followed the war, they took the lead
in marshaling arguments in favor of an American overseas empire.
In this task they were aided enormously by Republican Senator Albert Beveridge of Indiana, who toured the Philippines in order to
gather information to support his annexationist views. Most of what
these men—and others—said about American foreign policy after
the Spanish War was a repetition of what exponents of America's
imperial world mission had been saying since the 1880's.

The arguments in favor of an imperial policy for America ranged
from the hardheaded to the softhearted. Priding themselves on their
realism, the imperialists placed special emphasis on what they regarded as a hard-boiled, no-nonsense view of international relations.
The world, they said, is a kind of Darwinian jungle in which a vigorous struggle for existence leading to the survival of the fittest nations
is forever raging. Universal warfare, according to journalist Thomson
Jay Hudson, is a law of history as well as of nature. The "slaughter
of the unfit," he insisted, in an article on "Evolution and the Spanish-
American War" for the *National Magazine* in February, 1899, is necessary in order to make room for "the existence and development of
the higher orders." Mahan held similar views. "All around us now is
strife," he said; " 'the struggle of life,' 'the race of life,' are phrases so
familiar that we do not feel their significance till we stop to think
about them. Everywhere nation is arrayed against nation; our own no
less than others." If the United States was to survive in such a world,
according to the imperialists, it must develop its military strength
and pursue its national interests aggressively on the international
scene. "Self-interest," Mahan reminded Americans, "is not only a
legitimate, but a fundamental cause for national policy; one which
needs no cloak of hypocrisy. . . . It is vain to expect nations to act
consistently from any other motive than that of interest." Acquisition
by war, he added, is "a legitimate international transaction." Mahan
did not deprecate peace as an ideal; but he continually warned
against the illusion that war is only a passing phase in human history.
"Let us worship peace, indeed, as the great goal at which humanity
must hope to arrive," he said; "but let us not fancy that peace is to be
had as a boy wrenches an unripe fruit from a tree." It was dangerous,
he thought, to exaggerate either "the charms of quiet, of prosperity,
of ease" or "the alarms and horrors of war."

Charles A. Conant, popular economist, emphasized the economic rather than the *Realpolitik* argument for imperialism. In an article on "The Economic Basis of Imperialism," appearing in the *North American Review* in September, 1898, Conant put the case bluntly: a congestion of capital (excess savings and surplus goods) had reached a critical point in capitalistic nations like the United States and imperialism was the only solution. If the "entire fabric of the present economic order is not be shaken by a social revolution," he warned, it was necessary for the United States to push investments in Asia, Africa, and the former Spanish islands, and also to enter into vigorous competition for an increased share in the world's markets. Whether the United States acquired colonies in the process was a matter of mere detail for Conant; his point was that finding overseas outlets for savings and goods that could not be absorbed at home was a matter of economic salvation. Senator Beveridge, who was cheered by the thought of Manila as a center of trade and as a key to the "illimitable markets" of China, put the economic case for imperialism more dramatically. "American factories," he told an audience of businessmen in Boston,

are making more than the American people can use; American soil is producing more than they can consume. Fate has written our policy for us; the trade of the world must and shall be ours. And we will get it as our mother [England] has told us how. We will establish trading posts throughout the world as distributing points for American products. We will cover the ocean with our merchant marine. We will build a navy to the measure of our greatness. Great colonies governing themselves, flying our flag, and trading with us, will grow about our posts of trade. Our institutions will follow our flag on the wings of our commerce. And American law, American order, American civilization, and the American flag will plant themselves on shores hitherto bloody and benighted, but by these agencies of God henceforth to be made beautiful and bright.

In addition to stressing the profits in imperialism, Beveridge liked to ring the changes on Anglo-Saxon destiny. The Filipinos, he said, were a "barbarous race," utterly incapable of self-government "in the Anglo-Saxon sense"; dull and stupid, for the most part, they have no comprehension of what "Anglo-Saxon self-government" means. "Savage blood, oriental blood, Malay blood, Spanish example—are these the elements of self-government?" he asked scornfully. "God," he said,

> has not been preparing the English-speaking and Teutonic peoples for a thousand years for nothing but vain and idle self-contemplation and self-admiration. No! He has made us the master organizers of the world to establish system where chaos reigns. He has given us the spirit of progress to overwhelm the forces of reaction throughout the earth. He has made us adepts in government that we may administer government among savages and senile peoples. Were it not for such a force as this the world would relapse into barbarism and night. And of all our race He has marked the American people as His chosen nation to finally lead in the regeneration of the world. This is the divine mission of America, and it holds for us all the profit, all the glory, all the happiness possible to man. We are trustees of the world's progress, guardians of its righteous peace.

The case for imperialism was invariably bolstered by ethical and religious imperatives. The Anglo-Saxon, it was said, was destined to serve as well as supervise; his duty was to uplift and civilize and Christianize the backward peoples of the earth. On the occasion of the presentation of the sword to Admiral George Dewey on October 3, 1899, Secretary of the Navy John D. Long hailed

> the dawn of a glorious new day—a day not of any mere selfish imperial dominion of one people over another, but of the imperial moral and physical growth and expansion of all the peoples, whatever their race or language or color, who are under the shelter of the broad shield of the United States of America.

James W. Bashford, Methodist minister and president of Ohio Wesleyan University, announced that God had called the Anglo-Saxons

> to bridle intemperance and lust, ambition and greed, at home and abroad. He sends us, as He sent His well-loved Son, to serve the world, and thus to rule the world. Anglo-Saxons in the twentieth century must say to all races—to red men, black men, brown men, yellow men—"We are brethren," and lift them up to our higher plane of opportunity. . . . Unselfishness and brotherliness are growing forces in the United States. Let us serve the world as Christ

saved the world, and we can no more fail in our providential tasks than Christ himself could fail.

President McKinley, a Methodist layman, was motivated by equally exalted conceptions of American destiny when he decided that the United States must annex the Philippines. "I didn't want the Philippines," he told a Methodist group in 1899, "and when they came to us as a gift from the gods, I did not know what to do with them." To give them back to Spain, however, would be "cowardly and dishonorable"; to turn them over to France and Germany, "our commercial rivals in the Orient," would be "bad business"; and to leave them to themselves was unthinkable, for "they were unfit for self-government." His conclusion: ". . . there was nothing left for us to do but to take them all, and to educate the Filipinos, and uplift and civilize and Christianize them, and by God's grace do the very best we could by them, as our fellow-men for whom Christ also died."

The Anti-imperialists

William James was repelled by the arrogant self-righteousness underlying the civilizing argument for American imperialism. "Could there be a more damning indictment of that whole bloated idolatered 'modern civilization' than this amounts to?" he exclaimed. "Civilization is, then, the big, hollow resounding, corrupting, sophisticating, confusing torrent of mere brutal momentum and irrationality that brings forth fruits like this." James, an outspoken anti-imperialist, was shocked by the brutal means employed by the United States to suppress the Filipino independence movement after annexing the Philippines.

Mark Twain was equally shocked by what was going on in the Philippines. Twain had supported the Spanish-American War because he thought the effort to free the Cubans from Spanish rule a worthy one. But annexing the Philippines and waging a bloody war to subdue the Filipinos produced scorn and bitterness in Twain. He became not only a vehement critic of American policy in the Philippines; he also became a passionate foe of Western imperialism in China, Africa, and other parts of the world. In an ironic piece entitled "To the Person Sitting in Darkness," Twain asked mockingly:

Shall we go on conferring our Civilization upon the peoples that sit in darkness, or shall we give those poor things a rest? Shall we bang right ahead in our old-time, loud, pious way, and commit the new century to the game; or shall we sober up and sit down and think it over first? Would it not be prudent to get our Civilization tools together, and see how much stock is left on hand in the way of Glass Beads and Theology, and Maxim guns and Hymn Books, and Trade Gin and Torches of Progress and Enlightenment (patent, adjustable ones, good to fire villages with upon occasion) and balance the books, and arrive at the profit and loss, so that we may intelligently decide whether to continue the business or sell out the property and start a new Civilization on the proceeds?

Twain admitted that the "Blessings-of-Civilization Trust" had been profitable in some respects and that there was still "more money in it, more territory, more sovereignty, and other kinds of emolument, than there is in any other game that is played." But he warned that Christendom

> has been playing it badly of late years, and must certainly suffer by it, in my opinion. She has been so eager to get every stake that appeared on the green cloth, that the People who Sit in Darkness have noticed it—they have noticed it and have begun to show alarm. They have become suspicious of the Blessing of Civilization. More—they have begun to examine us.

Andrew Carnegie was as indignant about American actions in the Philippines as Twain and James. To Whitelaw Reid, editor of the *New York Tribune* and a warm imperialist, Carnegie wrote sarcastically: "It is a matter of congratulation that you seem to have about finished your work of civilizing the Filipinos. It is thought that about eight thousand of them have been completely civilized and sent to Heaven." Imperialism, said Carnegie, was based on brute physical strength; civilization rested on moral force and education and could not be forcibly exported. Christian Socialist George D. Herron agreed with Carnegie, though his reasoning was somewhat different. To Herron the idea of exporting American civilization to other peoples seemed preposterous:

> . . . Shall we send to them the blessed condition of the thousands who spend their lives in mines for $200 a year? Shall we send to them the blessings of the men and women who toil in the 900

sweat-shops of this city of Chicago? Shall we send to them the blessings of a civilization which enables private corporations to openly and insolently govern 70 millions of people for private profit? May God deliver the islanders of the sea from our civilization!

James, Twain, Carnegie, and Herron were joined by other distinguished Americans—men like William Dean Howells, Samuel Gompers, E. L. Godkin, W. E. B. Du Bois, Henry D. Lloyd, Hamlin Garland, Charles Eliot Norton—in denouncing America's new role as imperial world civilizer. In addition to puncturing the pretensions of the civilizers and uplifters, the anti-imperialists (who organized an Anti-imperialist League, with headquarters in Chicago, to disseminate their views) found the democratic argument against imperialism especially compelling. To conquer and rule native peoples like the Filipinos, they insisted, ran contrary to the American democratic tradition; it was a flagrant violation of the principles enshrined in the Declaration of Independence and the Gettysburg Address. "Imperialism and republicanism are essentially hostile," declared W. Bourke Cockran, prominent New York lawyer. "The same government cannot be autocratic and representative. Two such hostile principles cannot dwell in the same system. One must inevitably seek to destroy the other." Massachusetts Senator George F. Hoar warned that democracy "cannot rule over vassal states or subject peoples without bringing in the elements of death into its own constitution." William Jennings Bryan declared that if the United States adopted a colonial policy, it would "muffle the tones of the old Liberty Bell," destroy the Declaration of Independence, and erase the Bill of Rights from the Constitution; ". . . this nation," he said, "cannot endure half-republic and half-colony—half-free and half-vassal." In Chicago, lawyer Clarence Darrow told a mass meeting that he did not want to see "the republic of Jefferson" replaced by "the empire of McKinley."

Some of those opposed to America's policy in the Philippines utilized a racial argument against the imperialists. It was impossible, they warned, for the United States to assimilate alien peoples like the Filipinos into its national structure. To Senator G. C. Vest of Missouri the thought of annexing islands containing "half-civilized, piratical, muck-running inhabitants" was too preposterous to be taken seriously. When the *Galveston* (Texas) *News*, an enthusiastic advocate of annexation, insisted that the U.S. government's experi-

ence in handling "inferior races" like the Indians and Negroes made
it probable that it would deal successfully with the Filipinos, the
Nation retorted indignantly: "We should consider it very deplorable
to have the inhabitants of the Philippine Islands treated as our
Indians have been treated, to have the people of Cuba ruled as the
negroes in the Southern States are ruled." But the *Nation* did not
question the idea of Anglo-Saxon superiority; time and again it
warned against taking over lands containing people "of various races,
that are for the most part either savages or but half-civilized." Some
anti-imperialists, however, rejected the very idea of Anglo-Saxon
destiny. The Reverend A. A. Berle, who shared William James's
revulsion over "sniveling cant" about Anglo-Saxons, characterized the
idea that the Anglo-Saxons were to rule the world in the interest of
civilization and Christianity as "racial blasphemy." In an address at
Oberlin College on February 22, 1900, Berle made fun of the notion
that "the world is merely to stand by, with open mouthed wonder to
see itself swallowed up in the Anglo-Saxon heaven or be shot to
pieces by the Christianizing Maxim guns" of Anglo-Saxons. "I protest against it," he declared, "in the name of the vast masses of that
humanity whose total interest is so much larger and profounder in
import and meaning, than the whole of Anglo-Saxondom with all its
commercial, material or intellectual and social pre-eminence at this
present hour." Berle found the identification of Anglo-Saxondom and
Christianity particularly shocking. The Christian message, he declared, was one of "human democracy"; and he could think of "no
more monstrous invasion of the ideal humanity of the New Testament" than that of "Anglo-Saxon dominion or mission in the world."

Opponents of American imperialism found the economic as well
as the racial case for overseas colonies unconvincing, though they had
no objection, of course, to the peaceful expansion of American foreign
trade. Bryan denied that there would be any "pecuniary profit" in a
colonial policy. "The advantages which may come to a few individuals who hold the offices or who secure valuable franchises," he said,
"cannot properly be weighed against the money expended in governing the Philippines, because the money expended will be paid by
those who pay the taxes." Senator Benjamin Tillman calculated that
the expense of holding the Philippines would be tenfold the amount
that the United States would earn as revenue from them; and he
thought that whatever economic benefits there were would go to rich
investors, not to the average American taxpayer. Like Bryan and

Tillman, Carl Schurz believed that possession of the Philippines would benefit "a speculative syndicate of wealthy capitalists, without at the same time paying the American people at large." In a hard-hitting "Philippine Catechism" printed on September 8, 1898, the *Nation* proved to its own satisfaction that the economic case for annexation was completely fallacious. But the favorite argument of the anti-imperialists was the democratic one. Imperial expansion, they said, would not only undermine the American tradition of self-government; it would also produce a militarism and bureaucratism hostile to the basic ideals of American civilization.

Perhaps the most powerful of all the indictments of America's end-of-the-century foreign policy came from the pen of that stout conservative, William Graham Sumner. In an essay on "The Conquest of the United States by Spain" for the *Yale Law Journal* in 1898, Sumner took the line that although the United States had defeated Spain in war, it was itself being conquered by the very imperialism that had produced the decline of Spain. Sumner urged the American people to resist firmly the impassioned appeals of the imperialists to their "national vanity and cupidity" and to ignore their solemn but delusive slogans about "the terrors of 'isolation.' " It was important, said Sumner, for Americans to take a hardheaded view of *"the inevitable effect of imperialism on democracy."* Imperialism, according to Sumner, meant "war, debt, taxation, diplomacy, a grand governmental system, pomp, glory, a big army and navy, lavish expenditures, political jobbery," all of which were inimical to democracy. It also meant militarism; and it was "the essence of militarism that under it military men learn to despise constitutions, to sneer at parliaments, and to look with contempt on civilians."

For the racial paternalism proclaimed by the world savers, Sumner, like Lewis H. Douglass, had only scorn:

> When the negro postmaster's house was set on fire in the night in South Carolina, and not only he, but his wife and children, were murdered as they came out, and when, moreover, this incident passed without legal investigation or punishment, it was a bad omen for the extension of liberty, etc., to Malays and Tagals by simply setting over them the American flag.

As for the economic effects of imperialism, Sumner had no doubt that imperialism would give a tremendous boost to plutocracy and thus an injurious blow to democracy in the United States. "The great foe of democracy now and in the near future," he said,

> is plutocracy. Every year that passes brings out this antagonism more distinctly. It is to be the social war of the twentieth century. In that war militarism, expansionism and imperialism will all favor jobbery, both in the dependencies and at home. In the second place, they will take away the attention of the people from what the plutocrats are doing. In the third place, they will cause large expenditures of the people's money, the return for which will not go into the treasury, but into the hands of a few schemers. In the fourth place, they will call for a large public debt and taxes, and these things especially tend to make men unequal, because any social burdens bear more heavily on the weak than on the strong, and so make the weak weaker and the strong stronger. Therefore expansion and imperialism are a grand onslaught on democracy.

In every respect, then, Sumner found imperialism wanting as a policy for the United States. As to the glory of victory over Spain:

> My patriotism is of the kind which is outraged by the notion that the United States never was a great nation until in a petty three months' campaign it knocked to pieces a poor, decrepit, bankrupt old state like Spain. To hold such an opinion as that is to abandon all American standards, to put shame and scorn on all that our ancestors tried to build up here, and to go over to the standards of which Spain is a representative.

Sumner regarded the year 1898 as "a great landmark" in the history of the United States. Though he acknowledged that good, as well as bad, might flow from the Spanish War, he was increasingly impressed with the evil consequences. He found himself, in fact, looking forward to the twentieth century with the gravest misgivings.

Chapter 10

Things to Come

"It is a new century," Henry Adams wrote John Hay from Paris on November 7, 1900,

> and what we used to call electricity is its God. . . . The period from 1870 to 1900 is closed. . . . The period from 1900 to 1930 is in full swing, and, gee-whacky! how it is going! It will break its damned neck long before it gets through, if it tries to keep up the speed. You are free to deride my sentimentality, if you like, but I assure you that I . . . go down to the Champ de Mars and sit by the hours over the great dynamos, watching them run as noiselessly and as smoothly as the planets, and asking them—with infinite courtesy—where in Hell they are going.

Henry Adams wasn't the only American who looked upon the dawn of the twentieth century as an occasion for retrospect and prospect. The approach of the new century inspired a flood of articles and editorials in the 1890's on the achievements of the nineteenth century and the possibilities of the twentieth. There was, inevitably, some dispute over the precise birth date of the new century. One man wrote the *Nation* in December, 1900, criticizing the magazine for totally ignoring the birth of the new century, only to be told that the old century still lacked completion. The *Nation* accepted January 1, 1901, rather than January 1, 1900, as the proper date; and most Americans did so likewise. Lord Hobhouse explained at length in the *Contemporary Review* for March, 1900, why the former date was correct; but he also predicted that a similar dispute would break out again in the year 2000.

Some writers acknowledged the artificiality of the occasion: "No one," said the *Century* in January, 1901, "expects the figures on the dial of the centuries to work any immediate changes. . . ." Still, the imagination was touched, the *Century* insisted, by the thought that one century was closing and another opening. "There is solemnity in the sounding of the fateful hour," said the editor. "The world looks 'before and after'; it broods 'on things to come'. And where the imagination is touched, there may well be, in some subtle way, an effect on human action." Writing in the *North American Review* in December, 1895, Harvard geologist Nathaniel S. Shaler noted that the civilized world was

> rapidly entering upon a state of sympathetic exaltation, the like of which has not been known since the end of the first thousand years, when all Europe awaited the millennium as the time when the earth was to pass away. In that old day it was despair; in this it is an inspiring desire to achieve. Such psychological moments are the rarest things of the world; they afford to the true philanthropist the precious occasions to contrive for the effective advance of man.

Looking Backward: The Wonderful Century

Most Americans agreed with Alfred R. Wallace in regarding the nineteenth century as "The Wonderful Century." "The Golden Age of the World, in all good senses," said a writer in *Popular Science Monthly* in May, 1901, "had its origin with the birth of the nineteenth century. . . ." According to B. O. Flower, writing in the *Arena* for February, 1901, the nineteenth century was the "most luminous period in the ages, when considered from the standpoint of material progress." No one could gainsay the material progress. "To-day, the United States is by far the richest country in the world," proclaimed Massachusetts Senator George Hoar when the hundredth anniversary of the city of Washington (as well as the close of the century) was being celebrated in 1900. In articles appraising the old century, its technological advances (especially in the United States) were listed with almost monotonous regularity: railroads, steamships, telegraphs, telephones, gas lighting, electric motors, automobiles, photography, and phonographs, as well as the development of such industries as textiles, oil, and iron and steel. But the nineteenth century, to retrospective writers, meant unprecedented advances in science as well as in technology. Discussing "A Century's Progress in Science" for the *Atlantic Monthly* in July, 1896, John Fiske summarized the achievements made in chemistry, astronomy, geology, physics, and other fields during the preceding hundred years and concluded that the scientific progress of the nineteenth century presented "a marvelous story without any parallel in the history of achievement." For Fiske, of course, the heroes of the century were Darwin and Spencer; and the old century's most momentous achievement was the replacement of the old static concept of the world by the "dynamical conception of a world in a perpetual process of evolution from one state into another." The *New York Post,* which ran a series of articles on the old century in January, 1901, also regarded the century as the "age of Darwin."

Not all writers casting a backward glance on the passing era emphasized science and technology. Some of them singled out the abolition of slavery, the advance in women's rights, the development of consolidations in business and labor, and the growth of personal liberty as of equal importance. When a group of writers surveyed the field for the *Outlook* at the end of 1900, they all agreed that the advance in freedom, in all realms of life, was the most noteworthy accomplishment of the nineteenth century. Only Mark Twain refused to join in the general chorus of praise being bestowed on the closing century. Though not denying its mechanical progress, he could not bring himself to overlook man's continuing moral failures, especially in international affairs; and in a sardonic greeting from the old century to the new he declared:

> I bring you the stately matron named Christendom, returning bedraggled, besmirched and dishonored from the pirate-raids in Kiao-Chou, Manchuria, South Africa and the Philippines, with her soul full of meanness, her pocket full of boodle and her mouth full of pious hypocrisies. Give her soap and a towel, but hide the looking-glass.

Looking Forward: Progress toward Utopia

Twain was apprehensive about the future as well as critical of the past, but most Americans appeared not to share his fears. When they turned from assessing the past to speculating about the future, they saw mostly good in store for mankind, especially for the American people. There was every reason to believe, they thought, that the scientific and technological progress of the nineteenth century would continue unabated into the twentieth century and beyond. "There can be no question," said a writer for *The Living Age* on February 26, 1901, "that the progress of science and of the applications of science to industry will go on in a geometrical ratio, and that eventually every country will benefit by this advance. . . ." "With the opening of the Twentieth Century," wrote engineer Robert H. Thurston in *Popular Science Monthly* for May, 1901, "we are indeed arrived at a Day of Great Things. . . ." Thurston thought the twentieth century promised near utopia when it came to mechanical achievement; it would, he said, "carry the world a long way toward that ideal which has been but feebly described in Plato's Republic and More's Utopia, and has been the aspiration of all good men." Edward W. Byrn, author of a history of invention, agreed. "Modern history . . ." he told readers of *Scientific American* on December 29, 1900, "marks the approaching millennium of happiness, good will and material prosperity which men have always longed for." In a poem entitled "The Nineteenth Century," appearing in the *Arena* for June, 1899, Kansas writer Richard J. Hinton expressed the general feeling:

> Mighty thy days, but grander still by far
> The days to be—built on the days that are!

Not all prognostications about the dawning century focused on material progress. The *Outlook* (December 20, 1900) forecast a steady movement in the direction of liberty, equality, and fraternity during the new century. The *Century* (January, 1901) foresaw improved conditions for working people, a stronger sense of social responsibility by capitalists, higher standards in public life, and possibly, even, a decline in man's love of war. For the *Atlantic Monthly* in January, 1902, John Bates Clark summed up the achievements of the twentieth century from the vantage point of the twenty-first. Pretending to look back on the twentieth century during turn-of-century festivities on

January 1, 2001, Clark saw enormous social as well as material gains. The material gains included tremendous advances in the use of electrical energy and automatic machinery ("We touch the buttons, and they do the rest"), as well as the achievement of a level of comfort for 200 million Americans "that was dreamed of, but not expected as a reality at a date much short of the millennium." The social gains included eradication of city slums, the achievement of municipal self-government, the breaking of the power of bosses and machines in American politics, tariff reform, and the development of "unusually fraternal" relations between capital and labor. "In individual morality," Clark admitted, "we are not yet at the portal of the millennium; for prosperity has brought its sore temptations." Still: "A certain manly quality in our people gives assurance that we have the personal material out of which a millennium may grow. Fraternity abounds where once it was rare."

The *Independent* was even more sanguine, if anything, than Clark in its hopes for the future. In an editorial greeting the new century on January 3, 1901, the New York weekly exclaimed: "All hail the Twentieth Century! On its threshold are the footprints of Divine Love! Its banner is the Golden Rule. Its leader is the Prince of Peace." The *Independent* went on to predict not only the building of a society of security and abundance for all in twentieth-century America, but also the development of peaceful and fraternal relations among the nations of the world. "It is not a claim of prophecy," said the editor confidently, "that anticipates the complete vindication of arbitration, the abolition of standing armies, and the peaceful co-operation of all the nations of the globe."

The *Independent's* belief that an end to war lay in the immediate future was not shared by all end-of-century observers. Alfred Mahan decried all such talk as sentimental and isolationist. Alarmed by the clamor for peace and disarmament in the 1890's, he wrote a piece for *Harper's* in September, 1897, reminding Americans that conflict was the law of life and warning them against becoming too peace-loving. Mahan's anxieties for his country were somewhat appeased when the United States went to war with Spain. For some Americans, however, the Spanish War and the embroilment in the Philippines cast a long shadow over their otherwise rosy vision of the century-to-be. As long as the United States and other nations see fit to engage in "imperial wars," wrote Elizabeth Bisland sadly in the *Atlantic Monthly* in January, 1901, the "millennium still remains a mirage upon the horizon of hope." William Graham Sumner was more blunt. "What will come of the mixture of sentimental social philosophy and warlike policy?" he snorted. "There is only one thing rationally to be expected, and that is a frightful effusion of blood in revolution and war in the century now opening."

B. O. Flower, editor of the *Arena,* was more hopeful than Sumner. He proposed, as America's first task in the twentieth century, the disbanding of its "army of destruction" in the Philippines and the creation of an "army of creators" to improve conditions in the United States. Frank Parsons, professor of law at Boston University, heartily endorsed Flower's proposal; he, too, saw the elimination of war as man's major task in the twentieth century. "We must climb the mountain a step at a time," he wrote in the *Arena* for May, 1901, "and every step away from war and barbarism, conflict, mastery, greed, and oppression toward peace and liberty and justice . . . is a step toward the grand brotherhood of man the twentieth century ought to evolve. . . ." Nathaniel Shaler also singled out war as the major piece of unfinished business facing the United States in the new century; he was convinced that the American people were "of all people the best fitted to undertake a movement to free the world from the evils of war." In an article for the *North American Review* in December, 1895, discussing the problems facing the world at the turn of the century, Shaler urged the United States to take the lead in establishing an international organization to promote arms limitation and mediate disputes among nations. Peace, he thought, could be the "last gift'" of the nineteenth century to the twentieth.

Brooks Adams' Law of Civilization and Decay

It was, then, mainly voices of hope that one heard in the popular press in the United States near the close of the nineteenth century; the new century, most Americans seemed to think, was to be one of unprecedented achievement. (The prognosticators ignored the race question completely; but Booker T. Washington, in *The Future of the American Negro* [1900], looked forward to the steady advance of the Negro by means of industrial education and to his eventual achievement of political and civil rights.) And yet the United States was not without its Cassandras. Here and there, amid the general chorus of approval, could be heard the still, small voice of despair. The Adams brothers, Brooks and Henry, in particular, stood apart from the applauding multitude and cried havoc. While the majority of Americans were congratulating the past and hailing the future, Brooks and Henry Adams were formulating quite bleak theories about the nature and destiny of man and looking forward to the new century with apprehension.

In the same year that Nathaniel Shaler made his plea for universal peace in the *North American Review*, Brooks Adams published a book whose very title called in question all the hopes and dreams of the end-of-century millennialists: *The Law of Civilization and Decay* (1895). Theodore Roosevelt, who reviewed the book at length for the *Forum*, called it "decidedly gloomy"; and even Mrs. Adams thought it should have been entitled "The Path to Hell: A Story Book." "I rather like the title," Brooks said to Henry of his wife's suggestion, "only I think it promises too much. How can I assure my readers that I will show them anything so good as a path to 'Hell'?" Instead of a kindly view of human nature and its possibilities, Adams took a quite melancholy view; for the linear, progressive view of social movement held by most Americans he substituted a cyclical theory of historical development; and where most American writers took it for granted that man possesses freedom and has some control over his fate, Adams insisted that man is governed by laws as binding as those governing the physical world.

In the preface to *The Law of Civilization and Decay*, Adams defined civilization as a condition of "concentration" and barbarism as one of "dispersion," and he proposed the hypothesis that human society forever oscillates between the two. To explain why societies move from barbarism (in which human energies are scattered and loosely organized) to civilization (in which they are consolidated and highly centralized) and back to barbarism again, he linked history with physics. Human societies, he said, are forms of animal life (differing among themselves in the amount of energy they possess), and animal life itself is one of the outlets through which solar energy is dissipated. Since the "law of force and energy" obtains in history as well as in nature, it is possible to explain social development as a phase of "cosmic dynamics," and Adams did so as follows: "Probably the velocity of the social movement of any community is proportionate to its energy and mass, and its centralization is proportionate to its velocity; therefore, as human movement is accelerated, societies centralize." In the case of man, thought is one of the major manifestations of energy; and Adams singled out two phases of thought which he believed had been predominant in history: fear and greed. Fear of the unknown, according to Adams, stimulates the imagination and produces religious, military, and artistic types of people; when greed is dominant, economic and scientific types rather than imaginative types prevail. "In the earlier stages of concentration," he said,

> fear appears to be the channel through which energy finds the readiest outlet; accordingly, in primitive and scattered communities, the imagination is vivid, and the mental types produced are religious, military, and artistic. As consolidation advances, fear yields to greed, and the economic organism tends to supersede the emotional and martial.

In advanced stages of centralization, the religious, martial, and artistic types of manhood decay and the capitalist, especially the moneylender, becomes autocratic in his control of things. At length a point is reached at which consolidation can proceed no further. Then, according to Adams, one of two things may happen:

> A stationary period may supervene, which may last until ended by war, by exhaustion, or by both combined, as seems to have been the case with the Eastern Empire (Byzantium); or, as in the Western, disintegration may set in, the civilized population may perish, and a reversion may take place to a primitive form of organism.

Adams attempted to explain the rise and fall of the Roman Empire by means of his formula; he also traced the history of Western civilization from the Middle Ages to the nineteenth century in terms of the movement from dispersion to concentration of social energies, the transition from fear to greed as the prime motivator of man, and the gradual replacement of the priest, soldier, and artist by the capitalist and banker as the chief expressions of human energy. In passing, Adams showed how the Crusades, begun as purely religious phenomena, ended by reviving trade between West and East and thus ushering in the modern economic age; and he also interpreted the Protestant Reformation as "eminently an economic phenomenon."

If there was any "villain" in Adams' thinking, it was the banker. Throughout the book, the banker is referred to as "the monied type," "the usurious mind," and the "most redoubtable variety of the economic intellect"; and at one point Adams asserted: "The instinct of the usurer has, however, never been to ruin suddenly the community in which he has lived; only by degrees does he exhaust human vitality." The family fortunes of the Adamses had been threatened by the financial crash of 1893 and Adams made no secret of his loathing for financial capitalism. It was the usurious moneylender, according to his theory, who gave the death blow to the Roman Empire; it was the emergence of the modern banker, with his insistence on a policy of monometallism and currency contraction at the expense of the producing classes, which signalized the imminent decay of the West. Adams found modern culture, with its commercial spirit, appalling. "No poetry can bloom in the arid modern soil," he declared,

> the drama has died, and the patrons of art are no longer even conscious of shame at profaning the most sacred of ideals. The ecstatic dream, which some twelfth-century monk cut into the stones of the sanctuary hallowed by the presence of his God, is reproduced to bedizen a warehouse; or the plan of an abbey, which Saint Hugh may have consecrated, is adapted to a railway station.
> Decade by decade, for some four hundred years, these phenomena have grown more sharply marked in Europe, and, as consolidation apparently nears its climax, art seems to presage approaching disintegration.

But though Adams abhorred the commercialism of modern times and looked with nostalgia back on the artistic endeavors (and chivalric enterprises) of the medieval period, he thought the movement of history was directed by impersonal forces, not by personal choices. The cyclical process, after all, was ineluctable: "Thus religions are preached and are forgotten, empires rise and fall, philosophies are born and die, art and poetry bloom and fade, as societies pass from the disintegration wherein the imagination kindles, to the consolidation whose pressure ends in death." Adams made no special predictions for the United States (which is scarcely mentioned in the book), but the direction of his thought was unmistakable: decay, not advance, faced Western civilization, including the United States, in the years to come. Though it was an open question as to what form the future would take, it was clear to Adams that the West had reached a stage of development similar to that of the later Roman Empire and that the historical cycle was about to swing downward again.

The *Fin-de-Siècle* Forebodings of Henry Adams

Henry Adams was enormously impressed by his brother's analysis. A distinguished historian himself, with a keen interest in penetrating the surface of events to underlying social forces, Henry found Brooks's speculations about the grand sweep of history immensely stimulating. When Brooks showed him the first draft of his book, somewhat diffidently, in 1893, he pronounced it "good and worth printing," and he regarded the completed volume as "a very great book." The two brothers had many long and exciting discussions about Brooks's law of civilization and decay during the summer of 1893 and Henry was soon led to strike off on his own. In December, 1894, he sent the American Historical Association (of which he was president) a letter on "The Tendency of History," which was to take the place of an address in person before the organization's meeting in Washington. In it he proposed that American historians begin thinking seriously about developing a science of history. "Any science," he told them, "assumes a necessary sequence of cause and effect, a force resulting in motion which cannot be other than what it is. Any science of history must be absolute, like other sciences, and must fix with mathematical certainty the path which human society has got to follow." Such a science, Adams said, might take several forms: it might reflect the pessimism of Paris, Berlin, London, and St. Petersburg; it might point to the triumph of socialism; it might conclude that the present evils of the world—huge armaments, vast accumulations of capital, advancing materialism, and declining arts—will continue and increase over the next thousand years; and it might forecast a return to the church and absolute faith in personal providence and the end of scientific inquiry. Adams carefully refrained from expressing any opinion as to which of the alternatives he considered most convincing, but he did warn that whatever form a science of history took, it was likely to threaten some powerful social interest—the church, the state, property, labor—and would face suppression.

For himself, though, Adams unquestionably shared the *fin-de-siècle* pessimism of the great European capitals. "I am seriously considering," he wrote John Hay in September, 1893, "whether I shall have a better view of the *fin-de-siècle* circus in England, Germany, France, or India, and whether I should engage seats to view the debacle in London, Paris, Berlin, or Calcutta." During the 1890's Adams followed domestic and foreign events with almost feverish interest and he tried continually to extrapolate from these events into the near and the distant future. Where Shaler, Fiske, Clark, and most other American prognosticators were filled with hope, Adams, like his brother, was filled with foreboding; where they looked forward to the new century with anticipation, he looked forward to it with loathing; where they forecast progress, he predicted degradation. "I expect troubled times for many years to come," he told Elizabeth Cameron in 1893. "On all sides, especially in Europe and Asia, the world is getting awful rickety." "Of late," he told Charles Milnes Gaskell a year later, "the century has amused me. It has become so rotten and so bankrupt that I am quite curious to see what the next one will do about it." He did not expect it would do much. In 1898 he told his brother Brooks Adams that the world had "entered on a new phase of most far-reaching revolution," and a little later he said that he gave it only "two more generations before it goes to pieces, or begins to go to pieces." Throughout the decade he observed domestic events—the panic of 1893, the industrial depression, Populism, the fight over silver, the growth of trusts, the social unrest, and the labor upheavals—as well as the foreign scene—the arms race and the intensification of imperialist rivalries among the Great Powers all over the globe—with mingled fear and fascination.

"My country in 1900 is something totally different from my own country of 1860. I am wholly a stranger in it," Adams confessed to Gaskell on March 29, 1900.

> Neither I, nor anyone else, understands it. The turning of a nebula into a star may somewhat resemble the change. All I can see is that it is one of compression, concentration, and consequent development of terrific energy, represented not by souls, but by coal and iron and steam. What I cannot see is the last term of the equation.

But Adams had no doubt that the last term of the equation represented disaster for mankind. The dawn of the new century intensified his anxieties. In May, 1901, he told his brother that

> at the rate of increase of speed and momentum, as calculated on the last fifty years, the present society must break its damned neck in a definite, but remote, time not exceeding fifty years more. This is an arithmetical calculation from given data, as, for example, from explosives, or electric energy, or control of cosmic power.

In August, 1902, he was still pursuing this line of thought. "I apprehend for the next hundred years," he wrote Brooks,

> an ultimate colossal, cosmic collapse . . . My belief is that science is to wreck us, and that we are like monkeys monkeying with a loaded shell; we don't in the least know or care where our practically infinite energies come from or will bring us to. . . . It is mathematically certain that another thirty years of energy development at the rate of the last century must reach an *impasse.*

Adams did not deny that his *fin-de-siècle* forebodings were at least in part temperamental. "Thank God, I was never cheerful," he once said jubilantly. "I come from the happy stock of the Mathers, who, you remember, passed sweet mornings reflecting on the goodness of God and the damnation of infants." To Elizabeth Cameron he confessed: "I am a pessimist—dark and deep—who always expects the worst, and is never surprised when it comes."

Henry Adams and American Democracy

Adams had not always expected the worst. When he settled in Washington as a young man after the Civil War, his objective was reform and his hopes were high. "We want a national set of young men like ourselves or better," he said, "to start new influences not only in politics, but in literature, in law, in society, and throughout the whole social organism of the country. . . ." In the national capital young Adams joined a group of "working practical reformers" (as the *Nation* called them), made up of journalists and economists, which attempted to exert its influence on Congress through men like James A. Garfield. While lobbying for reform, Adams also engaged in critical journalism of a high order. For the *Nation* and the *North American Review* he wrote carefully researched articles on American finances, civil service reform, and the conspiracy of Jay Gould to corner the gold market in 1869; he also examined the Congressional sessions of 1869 and 1870 in some detail and with an extremely cold eye.

Adams' views were those of an aristocratic conservative reformer. He disliked radical Reconstruction, was appalled by the spoils system, favored lowering the tariff, feared the growing concentration of wealth and power in the hands of big industrial and financial corporations, was a zealous sponsor of civil service reform, and made high standards of private morality his chief remedy for social ills. "As I belong to the class of people who have great faith in this country," he told Charles Gaskell in November, 1877, "and who believe that in another century it will be saying in its turn the last word of civilization, I enjoy the expectation of the coming day, and try to imagine that I am myself, with my fellow *gelehrte* here, the first faint rays of that great light which is to dazzle and set the world on fire hereafter." Even after the assassination of Garfield, on whose administration he had placed such high hopes, Adams was undaunted. "Luckily we are a democracy," he reassured Attorney General Wayne MacVeagh. "Nothing can shake society with us, now that slavery is gone."

Adams was one of the liberal Republicans who fought against "Grantism" in the Republican Party and in 1884 he joined the Mugwumps in bolting the party to support Cleveland rather than Blaine for president. James G. Blaine was Adams' personal devil; to Adams Blaine symbolized everything that was wrong with American politics in the Gilded Age. For the hard-pressed farmer and the oppressed workingman in the new industrial age (as well as for the mass of immigrants huddled together in the slums of the big cities) Adams had little sympathy and no comprehension. The elimination of political and commercial fraud, the elevation of high-minded gentlemen with lofty ideals of public service to high office, and the removal of obstacles to the operation of the laws of laissez-faire economics were for him the main roads to social salvation. The impossibility of fitting the increasingly complex and recalcitrant social realities of the age neatly into the aristocratic patterns that Adams had inherited from his ancestors left him puzzled and angry and drove him, finally, to despair.

In 1870 Adams left Washington to teach medieval history at Harvard. He also served as editor of the *North American Review* and attempted to carry on the cause of patrician reform in the pages of that distinguished monthly. History led him to the Teutonic theory, which he accepted with reservations, and to the publication, in 1876, of *Essays in Anglo-Saxon Law*, a collection of studies by Adams and his graduate students (including Henry Cabot Lodge) tracing English democracy to its origins in ancient Teutonic institutions. Shortly before leaving Harvard in 1877 to settle in Washington again as an independent writer and scholar, Adams shifted to American history, and during the next few years he published a *Collection of Documents Relating to New England Federalism, 1800–1815* and biographies of Albert Gallatin (1879) and John Randolph (1882) and began working on his masterpiece, a nine-volume history of the United States during the administrations of Jefferson and Madison. Adams' work in history was shaped by his desire to write "scientific history," that is, historical accounts based on extensive and impartial use of primary sources, with emphasis on the development of broad concepts like nationalism and democracy and a concern for the relevance of his findings to other periods and places. In the case of Gallatin, Adams thought the problems facing Jefferson's Secretary of the Treasury—currency and finances, tariff revision, the spoils system, and the like—were similar to those facing the United States after the Civil War; he also regarded Gallatin as an ideal statesman worthy of emulation by American public officials in any age. "To do justice to Gallatin was a labor of love," he confessed. "After long study of the prominent figures in our history, I am more than ever convinced that for combination of ability, integrity, knowledge, unselfishness, and social fitness, Mr. Gallatin has no equal."

Adams saw no Gallatins in places of power during the Gilded Age and his vexation with American politics mounted steadily. "Politics have ceased to interest me . . ." he told Lodge discouragedly in June, 1876. "The caucus and the machine will outlive me, and that being the case, I prefer to leave this greatest of American problems to shrewder heads than mine." Politics continued, in fact, to fascinate Adams to the end of his life, but there is no denying his increasing disillusion. In a novel entitled *Democracy*, which he published anonymously in 1880, Adams voiced his growing doubts about the practical workings of American political democracy. In the novel, Madeleine Lee, a wealthy, sophisticated widow, with high standards of morality, comes to Washington, "bent on getting to the heart of the great American mystery of democracy and government" and discovering "whether America is right or wrong" in its democratic faith. What she discovers, chiefly in the person of Senator Silas P. Ratcliffe (who represents Blaine), a corrupt party dictator who aspires to the presidency, leaves her quite shaken and at the end of the novel she leaves for Europe in disgust. Ratcliffe admits frankly that the old standards of public service exemplified by George Washington are gone forever in the United States. "Washington" he says,

> was no politician at all, as we understand the word. He stood outside of politics. The thing couldn't be done today. . . . If Wash-

ington were President now, he would have to learn our ways or lose his next election. Only fools and theorists imagine that our society can be handled with gloves and long poles. One must make one's self a part of it. If virtue won't answer our purpose, we must use vice . . .

Adams' indictment of American democracy is expressed even more forcefully by Baron Jacobi, a foreign diplomat who attends Mrs. Lee's salons. "You Americans believe yourselves to be excepted from the operation of general laws," he says.

You care not for experience. . . . Well, I declare to you that in all my experience I have found no society which has had elements of corruption like the United States. The children in the street are corrupt, and know how to cheat me. The cities are all corrupt, and also the towns and the counties and the States' legislatures and the judges. Everywhere men betray trusts both public and private, steal money, run away with public funds. . . . I do much regret that I have not yet one hundred years to live. . . . The United States will then be more corrupt than Rome under Caligula; more corrupt than the Church under Leo X; more corrupt than France under the regent.

Yet another of Madeleine's guests, Nathan Gore, poet-historian from Massachusetts, keeps the faith. "I believe in democracy," he says simply at one point in the novel.

I accept it. I will faithfully serve and defend it. I believe in it because it appears to me the inevitable consequence of what has gone before it. Democracy asserts the fact that masses are now raised to a higher intelligence than formerly. All our civilization aims at this mark. We want to do what we can to help it. I myself want to see the result. I grant it is an experiment, but it is the only direction society can take that is worth its taking; the only conception of its duty large enough to satisfy its instincts; the only result that is worth an effort or a risk. Every other step is backward and I do not care to repeat the past. . . .

Though English reviewers were impressed chiefly by the "hideous system of corruption" revealed in *Democracy*, there is every reason to believe that Adams himself, for all his revulsion against American machine politics, actually shared the hopes for American democracy which he put in the mouth of Nathan Gore. Even Madeleine, he is careful to tell us, felt that "underneath the scum floating on the surface of politics," there was "a healthy current of honest principle, which swept the scum before it and kept the mass pure."

When *Democracy* appeared, Adams was already at work on his historical masterpiece, *History of the United States of America during the Administrations of Thomas Jefferson and James Madison* (1889–91). In his *History*, which he looked upon as "a fixed and documented starting-point" for future historians seeking to evaluate the American democratic experiment, Adams continued to have mingled hopes and doubts for his country. His *History* is filled with irony: an emphasis on the tendency of events to resolve themselves into outcomes quite the reverse of those intended by the participants. It is also permeated with an intense awareness of the overwhelming pressure of circumstances on individuals and a feeling (as Adams once confessed) that Jefferson and Madison were "mere grasshoppers kicking and gesticulating on the middle of the Mississippi River" and "carried along on a stream which floated them, after a fashion, without much regard to themselves." Still, Adams' hopes for his country, though muted, were real enough when he wrote his *History*. The "experiment of embracing half a continent in one republican system," he declared early in the first volume, put the United States "in advance of the Old World." "Stripped for the hardest work," he continued, "every muscle firm and elastic, every ounce of brain ready for use, and not a trace of superfluous flesh on his nervous and supple body, the American stood in the world a new order of men." Compared to "this lithe young figure," said Adams, Europe, with its artificial class distinctions, endless wars, huge debts, and social anomalies, was "actually in decrepitude" and was as little prepared to compete with America as a medieval knight was to run a modern cotton mill. Adams' pride in his nation was unmistakable; in describing instances of American valor during the War of 1812, in fact, he reached such heights of eloquence at times that his brother Charles wrote in the margin of the manuscript: "In writing history suppress the patriotic glow."

At the end of the *History*, in a final chapter entitled "American Character," Adams came to some tentative conclusions about the quality of the American people as it revealed itself in the years with which he was concerned. One of their outstanding traits, he thought, was antipathy to war; at the same time, when war came, he insisted, they displayed a surprising degree of skill in naval affairs, a superior skill, in certain respects, on land, and a gift for scientific engineering. Adams thought that the United States, because of its democratic nature, offered fewer opportunities for the development of unusual individuals than older and smaller societies; the chief function of the American Union, he said, was "to raise the average standard of popular intelligence and well-being." Adams concluded that the United States had succeeded in this function; the "superior average intelligence of Americans," he said, was an established fact in 1817. American morality, moreover, was also high, "when compared with the morality of many older societies," though, like American intelligence, it "discouraged excess." Two other American traits caught Adams' attention: an "un-English rapidity in movement" which led Americans to accept swift changes in politics and religion and a mildness of outlook which disposed them to "relax severity" in religious matters. "The traits of intelligence, rapidity, and mildness," according to Adams,

> seemed fixed in the national character as early as 1817, and were likely to become more marked as time should pass. A vast amount of conservatism still lingered among the people; but the future spirit of society could hardly fail to be intelligent, rapid in movement, and mild in method. Only in the distant future could serious change occur, and even then no return to European characteristics seemed likely. The American continent was happier in its conditions and easier in its resources than the regions of Europe and Asia, where Nature revelled in diversity and conflict.

Despite the cautious optimism expressed in this passage, Adams preferred to end his *History* with a series of questions about the future. The American people, he said,

> were intelligent, but what paths would their intelligence select? They were quick, but what solution of insoluble problems would quickness hurry? They were scientific, and what control would their science exercise over their destiny? They were mild, but what corruptions would their relaxations bring? They were peaceful, but by what machinery were their corruptions to be purged? What

interests were to vivify a society so vast and uniform? What ideals were to ennoble it? What object, besides physical content, must a democratic continent aspire to attain? For the treatment of such questions, history required another century of experience.

Adams was still living in 1917 (he died the following year), a century after the period he had described in his *History*, but there was no longer any hope in him. The questions he had posed at the end of his *History* by then seemed to him to be totally irrelevant to what was going on in the world.

Adams' Loss of Faith

While Adams was working on his *History*, a terrible tragedy struck him: his wife killed herself in a fit of depression in December, 1885. Adams never really recovered from this blow; after this, he once said, he had no more interest in life "except as a bystander." Religion could provide him with no consolation; he had long since given up the mild Unitarian faith of his boyhood. In a novel entitled *Esther*, published under a pseudonym in 1884, Adams had explored the theme of religious faith with sympathy but with negative conclusions. In it, Esther, a talented young painter who is an agnostic, is wooed by an Episcopalian clergyman. Esther loves the clergyman but in the end she turns him down because she cannot accept his religion. At the same time she also rejects a geologist who becomes her suitor because, although she can share his intellectual outlook, she does not love him. Toward the end of the novel Esther asks the geologist:

"It science true?"
"No!"
"Then why do you believe in it?"
"I don't believe in it."
"Then why do you belong to it?"
"Because I want to help in making it truer."

But the pragmatic view of science—and of religion—had no real appeal for Adams, for it lacked absolutes. It was certitude that Adams sought; he needed some kind of ultimate and absolutely trustworthy guideline—religious, scientific, psychological—to make life seem worth living. When the death of his wife removed the one secure anchor he had come to count on, Adams began to feel with increasing poignancy the breakdown in certainties wherever else he looked.

Religious reassurance was no longer compelling for Western intellectuals like Adams; and, in science, the mechanistic view (which provided intellectual security for many nineteenth-century agnostics) was crumbling as the implications of the evolutionary outlook became clearer and the notion of scientific law as a kind of conceptual shorthand, only provisionally and approximately true, gained force. For Adams the quest for certainty ended in failure in both religion and science; he felt the failure keenly and was able to compensate for it only partially in art. The financial crash of 1893, moreover, shattered Adams' faith in the immutabilities of economic truth and the terrible depression that ensued filled him with gnawing doubts about the future of the West as a whole. Meanwhile, the stability of an assured social position, which Adams held as a New England Brahmin, was being threatened, so he thought, by the masses of immigrants flocking to the United States in the late nineteenth century, and he occasionally sought scapegoats, especially among the Jews, for his status anxieties. With his wife no longer beside him, Adams came to feel more and more deeply the frailty of human life and the precariousness of human existence, and it seemed to him as he grew older that the world as a whole was moving rapidly toward the kind of disintegration and chaos that he felt within himself. Something unanalyzable, deep down inside of him, remained as firm as a rock and enabled him to go on living after his wife's suicide and the collapse of the world of his ancestors; but his view of things, never rosy at best, became steadily more bitter, mocking, and sardonic.

In his last years, Adams found satisfaction only in predicting doom for Western civilization, and he eventually worked out an elaborate theory of historical degradation in order to show that man was precipitously headed for hell and beyond. Subjective need (the desire to historicize his pessimism) and objective inquiry (the effort to think seriously about long history) combined in Adams to produce a grand but melancholy theory of history. Henry's theory was more pessimistic, in a way, than Brooks's; where history, for Brooks, ran around in circles, so to speak, in Henry's view history moved steadily downward toward chaos and death. Adams spent his later years working on his theory partly for diversion; but he was also serious about what he was doing. If what he had to say about great history was not literally true, Adams said in effect, then American historians had an obligation to come forward with alternative theories grounded in the most advanced scientific thinking of the day.

A Pessimistic View of History

Like his brother, Henry Adams turned to physics for clues to the nature of history, but he was far more thoroughgoing in his "scientizing" of history than Brooks was. Henry was enormously impressed by two formulations of the new physics of his day and he thought they had momentous consequences for thinking about the movement of history: (1) Lord Kelvin's second law of thermodynamics, which states that entropy, that is, dissipation of energy, tends to a maximum in the universe; and (2) Yale physicist Willard Gibbs's rule of phase, a mathematical formula for determining under what conditions of temperature and pressure different substances exist together in equilibrium in a closed system and how changes in these conditions transform substances from one phase of equilibrium into another. (Water, for example, exists in three phases—vapor, liquid, and ice—depending on what the temperature and pressure are.) The second law of thermodynamics suggested to Adams the possibility that history, like nature, was the story of the gradual dispersion of energy on earth, leading (as the sun gradually cools) to the extinction of life. Gibbs's phase rule inspired Adams with the notion that human thought, like a chemical substance, passes through different phases in which man's knowledge leads him to use up energy on earth in different ways. From this point of view, man was fundamentally a "thermodynamic mechanism"; he progressively untaps the energies latent in nature for his own use (and abuse) and thus acts thoroughly in accord with Kelvin's law and helps speed the day when energy in the solar system will be at too low a level to sustain life or to perform work of any kind. For Gibbs's three phases (solid, liquid, gaseous) Adams substituted historical stages (religious, mechanical, electrical) based on the kind and amount of energy being used up by man.

Assuming the role of physicist-historian, Adams calculated that the religious phase of man's existence on earth, the first and longest phase, had lasted about 90,000 years. During this period, religion was the most powerful force directing the energies of mankind, and it reached its climax in medieval Europe with the worship of the Virgin Mary. The religious phase ended around 1600, when Galileo and Newton introduced the notion of mechanical causation and thus enabled man, through the use of the steam engine and other mechanical devices, to release tremendous new energies in nature. The mechanical age lasted until about 1900, according to Adams' calculations, and it was then succeeded by an even more intense phase, the electrical age, which was symbolized for Adams by the dynamo. The discovery of radium around the turn of the century convinced Adams that a new period of energy dissipation was about to commence (he tentatively called it the "ethereal" phase), and that in it man would let loose new and even more potent natural forces than ever before. Each phase, it was clear to Adams, was not only shorter than the previous phase, but also more violent; in each new phase the dissipation of energy was taking place at an increasingly rapid and breathtaking rate. "From the physicist's point of view," wrote Adams,

> Man, as a conscious and constant, single, natural force, seems to have no function except that of dissipating or degrading energy . . . man does more to dissipate and waste nature's economies than all the rest of animal or vegetable life has ever done to save them. . . . He startles and shocks even himself, in his rational moments, by his extravagance, as in his armies and armaments which are made avowedly for no other purpose than to dissipate or degrade energy, or annihilate it as in the destruction of life, on a scale that rivals the operations of nature.

Where it would all end Adams did not predict with certainty. The electrical age he thought would terminate in 1917 and the ethereal age in 1921, but he was not sure what would happen after that. He was convinced, however, that the twentieth century would be one of unprecedented violence, and he once picked "1950 as the year when the world must go smash." He did not predict the atom bomb; but he did foresee that bombs, in some form, would play a major part in the life of twentieth-century man. In his last years Adams amused himself by collecting material from newspapers and magazines about alcoholism, mental illness, suicide, and disease in order to support his feeling that the human race was rapidly heading downhill.

A Melioristic View

William James refused to be impressed by Adams' morose speculating about things to come. "To tell the truth," he told Adams, it doesn't impress me at all, save by its wit and erudition; and I ask you whether an old man soon about to meet his Maker can hope to save himself from the consequences of his life by pointing to the wit and learning he has shown in treating a tragic subject. No, sir, you can't do it, can't impress God that way.

James acknowledged that, according to Kelvin's law (which scientists must accept until "someone hits on a newer revolutionary concept"), the universe started with a certain amount of energy, that everything happening thereafter was a result of parts of that energy falling to lower levels, and that ultimately there would be a "cessation of perceptible happening and the end of human history." But he insisted that the second law of thermodynamics was really irrelevant to history; it set a terminus to man's life on earth, but it said nothing about what actually went on in history. Within history, the amount of cosmic energy utilized by man was far less important than what man did with his energy. "Physically," James pointed out,

a dinosaur's brain may show as much intensity of energy-exchange as a man's, but it can do infinitely fewer things, because . . . it can only unlock the dinosaur's muscles, while the man's brains, by unlocking far feebler muscles, indirectly can by their means, issue proclamations, write books, describe Chartres Cathedral, etc., and guide the energies of the shrinking sun into channels which never would have been entered otherwise—in short, *make* history.

Dissipation of solar energy, in short, by no means necessitated a degradation of human energies. "Though the *ultimate* state of the universe may be its vital and psychical extinction," said James,

there is nothing in physics to interfere with the hypotheses that the penultimate state might be the millennium—in other words a state in which a minimum of difference of energy-level might have its exchanges so skillfully canalisés that a maximum of happy and virtuous consciousness would be the only result. In short, the last expiring pulsation of the universe's life might be, "I am so happy and perfect that I can stand it no longer." You don't believe this and I don't say I do. But I can find nothing in "Energetik" to conflict with its possibility.

James did not of course believe in the possibility of a millennium any more than he believed that man was headed for inevitable disaster. He was attracted by neither the exuberant optimism of John Fiske nor the querulous pessimism of Henry Adams. The collapse of absolutes—in science, in religion, and in all forms of thought—following from the evolutionary world view did not mean confusion and chaos for James as it did for Adams; it meant challenge and adventure in a dynamic universe. In a world that is forever changing and never completed, man's future, James thought, depended to a large extent upon himself. "The world, it thinks," said James of his own melioristic philosophy, "may be saved, on condition that its parts shall do their best." But he also warned: ". . . shipwreck in detail, or even on the whole is among the open possibilities."

Bibliographical Essay

This book has been based chiefly on primary printed sources: books, articles, and letters written by James, Holmes, Veblen, the Adamses, and other outstanding thinkers of the Gilded Age, and on essays and books published in the late nineteenth century dealing with the major issues discussed in these pages. There is, obviously, no substitute for reading the major intellectual documents of the period—James's *Principles of Psychology,* Holmes's *Common Law,* and the like—and the student's ultimate objective should be to master these works. References to the great books of the period are clear in the text and there is no need to repeat them here; most of them are now available in relatively inexpensive paperbound editions. As for essays, there are several excellent anthologies, also in paper, among which the best are: Perry Miller, *American Thought: Civil War to World War I* (1945), containing a long introductory section by Miller and excellent selections from Wright, George, Sumner, Ward, James, Holmes, Veblen, Brooks and Henry Adams, and others; and R. J. Wilson, *Darwinism and the American Intellectual* (1967), a collection of essays written by American scientists, theologians, philosophers, and social thinkers of the Gilded Age exploring the implications of Darwinism for their respective fields. If the student is fortunate enough to have access to libraries containing back issues of the *Nation, Popu-*

lar Science Monthly, the *Independent,* and some of the other magazines quoted in the text, he can re-create the climate of opinion of the age for himself by riffling through their pages and scanning whatever catches his eye. He will be endlessly fascinated, impressed, amused, and instructed.

Secondary sources have also shaped this book: biographies and intellectual portraits of individual thinkers as well as studies of the major currents of thought of the period by specialists. In deciding what to include and what to omit in the text (because of limitations of space), the author has been guided by what authorities in the field have considered important as well as by personal preferences. He has also familiarized himself with various interpretations of the thinkers and issues treated in the book, if only to thrust them aside and make his own presentation. What follows are suggestions for further reading, mainly from secondary sources, selected from the vast historical literature dealing with the Gilded Age. As in the text itself, the emphasis here is on intellectual rather than on social and cultural history.

For general interpretations of the American mind in the Gilded Age, Parrington and Beard are still eminently worth reading: Vernon L. Parrington's *The Beginnings of Critical Realism in America,* Volume 3 of *Main Currents in American Thought* (1927, 1930), and Charles and Mary Beard, *The American Spirit* (1942), an analysis of the idea of civilization in the United States. Ralph Henry Gabriel's *The Course of American Democratic Thought* (1940, 1956) is indispensable; a superb pioneer effort in American intellectual history, it examines the impact of modern science and industrialism on American religious, political, economic, and social thought, and it is filled with valuable information and imaginative insights. Merle Curti's *The Growth of American Thought* (1943, 1964) is also valuable; it is a treasure trove of data about almost every field of intellectual endeavor, popular and professional, of the period, and a point of departure for further study of a host of topics. Stow Persons, *American Minds* (1958), stresses ideas (and has a particularly fine chapter on racism) and Harvey Wish, *Society and Thought in America,* Volume 2 (1962), stresses the social and institutional setting of ideas. For a more philosophic approach, Joseph L. Blau, *Men and Movements in American Philosophy* (1952), has excellent chapters on Wright, Fiske, Peirce, Royce, and James; and Morton G. White, *Social Thought in America* (1949), links Holmes and Veblen with Beard, Dewey, and James Harvey Robinson in a revolt against formalism in thinking.

Morris R. Cohen, *American Thought* (1954), contains interesting comments on the economic, political, legal, religious, and philosophical thought of the period; and Henry Steele Commager, *The American Mind* (1950), an interpretation of American thought and character from the 1880's to the 1940's, has sections on Fiske, James, Ward (especially good), Veblen, Holmes, and the Social Gospel. Arthur M. Schlesinger, Jr., and Morton White, *Paths of American Thought* (1963), is a collection of interpretative essays by various scholars and it contains discussions of such topics as Social Darwinism, laissez-faire individualism, nineteenth-century science, and pragmatism. But it is not nearly so useful as Robert E. Spiller *et al.*, *Literary History of the United States* (3rd ed., 1963), which Schlesinger blasted when it first appeared because he insisted that the "team" approach to historical problems was hopeless. There are especially informative essays on Mark Twain and Henry Adams in *Literary History*.

To get some idea of the impact that Darwin had on his contemporaries (Chapter 1), the student is urged to read that marvelous product of scientific imagination and empirical investigation: *On the Origin of Species by Means of Natural Selection, or the Preservation of Favored Races in the Struggle for Life*. For the background and genesis of Darwinism, Loren Eiseley, *Darwin's Century: Evolution and the Men Who Discovered It* (1958), and Gertrude Himmelfarb, *Darwin and the Darwinian Revolution* (1959), are particularly stimulating. For an overview of the influence of Darwinism on American thought as a whole down to World War I, Richard Hofstadter, *Social Darwinism in American Thought* (1944), is outstanding. Some of the essays in Stow Persons, ed., *Evolutionary Thought in America* (1956), are also useful. For the reception of Darwinism in the United States, three essays by Bert J. Loewenberg are standard: "The Controversy over Evolution in New England, 1859–1873," *New England Quarterly*, 8 (June 1935): 323–57; "Darwinism Comes to America, 1859–1900," *Mississippi Valley Historical Review*, 28 (December 1941): 339–68; and "The Reaction of American Scientists to Darwinism," *American Historical Review*, 38 (July 1933): 687–701. W. M. Smallwood, "How Darwinism Came to the United States," *Scientific Monthly*, 52 (April 1941): 342–49, covers some of the same ground. For individual scientists, see Bernard Jaffe, *Men of Science in America* (1944), David Starr Jordan, *Leading American Men of Science* (1910), and Henry Fairfield Osborn, *Impressions of Great Naturalists* (1928). A. Hunter Dupree's *Asa Gray, 1810–1888* (1959) is a splendid biography and it examines the controversy over Darwinism in America in some detail. Gray's *Darwiniana*, a collection of essays and reviews first published in 1876, is now available in paper with an introduction by Dupree (1963). For Gray's exchanges with Darwin, see Jane Loring, ed., *Letters of Asa Gray* (2 vols., 1893), and Francis Darwin, ed., *The Life and Letters of Charles Darwin* (2 vols., 1959). Among the better biographical studies of scientists other than Gray discussed in Chapter 1 are Edward Lurie, *Louis Agassiz, A Life in Science* (1960), Henry F. Osborn, *Cope: Master Naturalist* (1931), and Charles and Clara Mae Levine, *O. C. Marsh, Pioneer in Paleontology* (1940).

The impact of Darwinism on American religious thought (Chapter 2) has been examined by Frank Hugh Foster in *The Modern Movement in American Theology* (1939). Arthur M. Schlesinger's "A Critical Period in American Religion, 1875–1900," *Proceedings of the Massachusetts Historical Society*, 24 (June 1933): 523–48, deals with Biblical criticism, comparative religion, and the Social Gospel, as well as with evolution, and it is crammed with useful information and bibliographical leads for further exploring. James Ward Smith and A. Leland Jamison, *Religion in American Life* (4 vols., 1961), has chapters on similar topics and an excellent bibliography. Chapter 16 in the third volume of the *Cambridge History of American Literature* (4 vols., 1917–21) deals with the religious reaction to evolution; and Herbert Schneider, "The Influence of Darwin and Spencer on American Philosophical Theology," *Journal of the History of Ideas*, 6 (January 1945): 3–18, examines the problem from a philosophical point of view. Andrew D. White, *A History of the Warfare of Science and Theology in Christendom* (1895), now available in soft cover, contains material on the heresy cases of the period. There is no full-scale study of Beecher's thought, but Paxton Hibben's *Henry Ward Beecher* (1927) is a stimulating biography. In *Lyman Abbott, Christian Evolutionist* (1953), Ira V. Brown has done for Abbott what needs to be done for Beecher. On the Protestant resistance to Darwinism, there are sections in Steward G. Cole, *The History of Fundamentalism* (1931), and Maynard Shipey, *The War on Modern Science* (1927), dealing with the Gilded Age, but the emphasis is on the twentieth century. John Rickards Betts has examined the Catholic response to evolution in "Darwinism, Evolution, and American Catholic Thought," *Catholic Historical Review*, 45 (July 1959): 161–85. No study of American Jewish thought about evolution has been made as yet, but some information can be found in Beryl Harold Levy, *Reform Judaism in America* (1933), and in Israel Knox, *Rabbi in America: The Story of Isaac M. Wise* (1957). Two studies of John Fiske are good on both Fiske's thought and the evolutionary controversy: Milton Berman, *John Fiske, the Evolution of a Popularizer* (1961), and H. Burnell Pannill, *The Religious Faith of John Fiske* (1957). Edward H. Madden, *Chauncey Wright* (1964), is a fine contribution to the excellent Great American Thinkers Series published in paper cover by the Washington Square Press. For American freethinkers and their organizations in the Gilded Age, see Stow Persons, *Free Religion, an American Faith* (1947), and Sidney Warren, *American Free Thought, 1860–1914* (1943). Edward A. White, *Science and Religion in American Thought: The Impact of Naturalism*, deals with both religion and philosophy. For Ingersoll, see Clarence H. Cramer, *Royal Bob; The Life of Robert G. Ingersoll* (1952); Eva Ingersoll Wakefield, ed., *The Letters of Robert G. Ingersoll;* and, of course, Ingersoll's *Works* (12 vols., 1900), edited by C. P. Farrell.

When it comes to the influence of evolution on American social thinking (Chapter 3), Hofstadter's *Social Darwinism* is standard. There is also information about Spencerism in America in Sidney Fine's *Laissez Faire and the General-Welfare State, A Study of Conflict in American Thought, 1865–1901* (1956). In *Dream and Thought in the Business Community, 1860–1900* (1956), Edward C. Kirkland questions the popularity of Social Darwinism in the American business community; so do Irvin G. Wyllie, in "Social Darwinism and the Businessman," *Proceedings of the American Philosophical Society*, 103 (October 1959): 629–35, and Edward A. Purcell, Jr., "Ideas and Interests: Businessmen and the Interstate Commerce Act," *Journal of American History*, 54 (December 1967): 561–78. For the gospel of wealth, see Gabriel's *Course of Democratic Thought* and Edward Kirkland's edition of Andrew Carnegie's *Gospel of Wealth and Other Timely Essays* (1962). There are chapters on William Graham Sumner and Lester Ward in Hofstadter, Gabriel, and Fine, as well as in William T. O'Connor, *Naturalism and the Pioneers of American Sociology* (1940), and Fay Berger Karpf, *American Social Psychology* (1932). Robert G. McCloskey has critical essays on Sumner, Stephen J. Field, and Carnegie in *American Conservatism in the Age of Enterprise* (1951). For Sumner's writings, there are two little soft-cover collections: Maurice R. Davie, ed., *William Graham Sumner, An Essay of Commentary and Selections* (1963), and Stow Persons, ed.,

Social Darwinism, Selected Essays of William Graham Sumner (1963). Harris E. Starr's biography, *William Graham Sumner* (1925), is a good one, and A. G. Keller's *Reminiscences (Mainly Personal) of William Graham Sumner* (1933) gives insights into Sumner's personality that also illuminate his thought. For Lewis H. Morgan, Leslie A. White's introduction to the latest edition of *Ancient Society* (1964) is extremely rewarding, and there is a good chapter in Gabriel. Bernhard Stern's *Lewis Henry Morgan, Social Evolutionist* is worth examining, but a fuller and more careful biographical and critical study is badly needed. Gabriel, Hofstadter, and Fine have material on Lester Ward and there is a good chapter on Ward in James P. Lichtenberger, *Development of Social Theory* (1938). Samuel Chugerman, *Lester F. Ward, the American Aristotle* (1939), is a full-scale study of Ward's life and thought. Henry S. Commager, *Lester Frank Ward and the Welfare State* (1967), is a paperbound collection of Ward selections.

For economic thought (Chapter 4), Joseph Dorfman, *The Economic Mind in American Civilization* (4 vols., 1946–51), Volume 3, is comprehensive, detailed, and masterly. Sidney Fine's *Laissez Faire and the General-Welfare State* is also excellent and it concentrates less on the technical side of economic theory than Dorfman. J. F. Normano, *The Spirit of American Economics* (1943), has a long section on economic thought in the Gilded Age. For the "old" political economy, see Alan Grimes, *The Political Liberalism of the New York Nation, 1865–1932* (1953), as well as E. L. Godkin's *Problems of Modern Democracy* (1966) in an up-to-date edition with an introduction by Morton Keller. Among the older economists, Perry, Wells, and Atkinson have had their biographies: Carroll Perry, *A Professor of Life, A Sketch of Arthur Latham Perry of Williams College* (1923), Fred Bunyan Joyner, *David A. Wells, Champion of Free Trade* (1939), and Harold F. Williamson, *Edward Atkinson, the Biography of an American Liberal* (1934). James Phinney Monroe's *Life of Francis Amasa Walker* (1923) is uncritical but contains many useful quotations from Walker's writings. John R. Everett, *Religion in Economics* (1946), a study of John Bates Clark, Richard T. Ely, and Simon Patten, is a good introduction to the "new" political economists. For Ely, there is a recent study by Benjamin Rader, *The Academic Mind and Reform: The Influence of Richard T. Ely in American Life* (1967), and Ely's autobiography, *Ground under Our Feet* (1938). There is no detailed study of the life and thought of John Bates Clark, but there are chapters on Clark in H. W. Spiegel, ed., *The Development of Economic Thought* (1952), and in Paul T. Homan, *Contemporary Economic Thought* (1928), and several essays on his ideas in Jacob H. Hollander, ed., *Economic Essays, Contributed in Honor of John Bates Clark* (1927). James L. Boswell has studied *The Economics of Simon Nelson Patten* (1934) and Rexford G. Tugwell has edited Patten's *Essays in Economic Theory* (1924).

The literature on complaint and reform in the late nineteenth century (Chapter 5) is extensive, but most of it does not emphasize ideas. Two comprehensive studies with a concern for ideas as well as institutions are Eric F. Goldman's *Rendezvous with Destiny* (1952), a lively history of reform from Grant to F. D. R., and Richard Hofstadter, *The Age of Reform from Bryan to F. D. R.* (1955), a thoughtful study of Populism, Progressivism, and the New Deal and their interrelations. Goldman and Hofstadter are critical of parochial elements in Populism, but Norman Pollack vigorously champions the Populists in both *The Populist Response to Industrial America: Midwestern Populist Thought* (1962) and *The Populist Mind* (1967), a superb anthology of Populist writings. C. Vann Woodward, "The Populist Heritage and the Intellectual," *American Scholar*, 29 (Winter 1959–60): 55–72, Martin Ridge, *Ignatius Donnelly, The Portrait of a Politician* (1962), and Walter T. K. Nugent, *The Tolerant Populists: Kansas Populism and Nativism* (1963), join Pollack in defending the Populists against charges of bigotry and anti-intellectualism. Walter B. Rideout's introduction to the latest edition of Donnelly's *Caesar's Column* (1960) is good on Donnelly's outlook and George B. Tindall's *A Populist Reader* (1966) is a useful short anthology. Historians have done much less with labor philosophies in the Gilded Age than with Populist thought, but Paul K. Crosser, *Ideologies and American Labor* (1941), is suggestive, and Gerald N. Grob, *Workers and Utopia: A Study of the Ideological Conflict in the American Labor Movement, 1865–1900* (1961), is excellent on the thought of the N.L.U., K. of L., and A.F.L. and of their leaders. Grob makes a distinction between "reform unionism" and "trade unionism" which has been utilized in this book. Charles Madison, *American Labor Leaders* (1950), has material on Sylvis, Stephens, Powderly, and Gompers. Louis S. Reed has made a good study of *The Labor Philosophy of Samuel Gompers* (1930), and Dan A. Levine, *Varieties of Reform Thought* (1964), has a chapter on Gompers. Leon Litwack, *The American Labor Movement* (1962), is a collection of documents.

For the rest, students will need to consult comprehensive histories of American labor by John R. Commons, Norman Ware, and Philip Foner, as well as biographies like Jonathan Grossman's *William Sylvis: Pioneer of American Labor* (1945) and autobiographies like Powderly's *The Path I Trod* (1940) and Gompers' *Seventy Years of Life and Labor* (1924).

On individual reformers, two books are especially good: Daniel Aaron's *Men of Good Hope* (1951), which analyzes the thought of George, Bellamy, and Lloyd, among others; and Charles Madison, *Critics and Crusaders* (1947), which has chapters on George and Bellamy. Charles A. Barker has written the most detailed biography of *Henry George* (1955) and George R. Geiger presents *The Philosophy of Henry George* (1933) at some length. For Lloyd, Caro Lloyd's *Henry Demarest Lloyd, 1847–1903* (2 vols., 1912) is a popular biography and Chester M. Destler's *Henry Demarest Lloyd and the Empire of Reform* (1963) is a scholarly study. Destler's *American Radicalism, 1865–1901* (1946) has a good defense of Lloyd (as well as sections on Populism, labor, socialism, and anarchism) and Thomas C. Cochran has prepared an abridged paperbound edition of *Wealth against Commonwealth* (1963). For Bellamy, Arthur E. Morgan has written both a biography, *Edward Bellamy* (1944), and an analysis of his thought, *The Philosophy of Edward Bellamy* (1945). Sylvia E. Bowman has also done two studies: *The Year 2000: A Critical Biography of Edward Bellamy* (1958) and *Edward Bellamy Abroad: An American Prophet's Influence* (1962).

Howard Quint has made an authoritative study of *The Forging of American Socialism* (1953) and Donald D. Egbert and Stow Persons have put together a collection of essays on *Socialism and American Life* (1952) which contains Daniel Bell's brilliant study of the American socialist movement. Madison's *Critics and Crusaders* discusses anarchism as well as socialism and Max Nomad's *Apostles of Revolution* (1939) tells us about John Most. On the Social Gospel, Henry F. May, *Protestant Churches and Industrial America* (1949), is first-rate, and Charles H. Hopkins, *The Rise of the Social Gospel in American Protestantism, 1865–1915* (1940), and Aaron I. Abell, *The Urban Impact upon American Protestantism, 1865–1900* (1943), are also useful. For the famous pioneer Social Gospeler, see Jacob H. Dorn's *Washington Gladden, Prophet of the Social Gospel* (1967), and Gladden's own *Recollections* (1909). As for the Social Gospel in American Catholicism and Judaism, Aaron Abell, *American Catholicism and*

Social Action; A Search for Social Justice, 1865–1950 (1960), David Philipson, *The Reform Movement in Judaism* (1907), and Beryl H. Levy, *Reform Judaism in America* (1933), are informative.

For William James (Chapter 6), the Modern Library edition of *The Writings of William James* (1968) has a good selection of essays, and several of James's books—*Principles of Psychology, Varieties of Religious Experience, The Will to Believe and Other Essays, Pragmatism and Four Essays from The Meaning of Truth*—are now available in paperbound editions. James was a superb letter writer as well as essayist, and the student will want to do some reading in Henry James, ed., *Letters of William James* (2 vols., 1920). Gay Wilson Allen has done a recent full-scale biography of *William James* (1967), but Ralph Barton Perry, *The Thought and Character of William James* (2 vols., 1935), remains unsurpassed both for insight into James's personality and for critical discussions of his philosophy. Lloyd Morris, *William James* (1950), is a good brief introduction to James, and George Santayana, *Character and Opinion in the United States* (1955), makes interesting observations about the man. Edward C. Moore's *William James* (1965), in the Great American Thinkers Series, contains an excellent exposition of James's thought. Bernard P. Brennan has examined *The Ethics of William James* (1961) and Julius S. Bixler has studied *Religion in the Philosophy of William James* (1926). In *American Pragmatism* (1961), Edward Moore links James with Peirce and Dewey, and in *Evolution and the Founders of Pragmatism* (1965), Philip Wiener links him with Wright, Fiske, Holmes, and others.

For Oliver Wendell Holmes, Jr. (Chapter 7), Mark De Wolfe Howe's introduction to the John Harvard edition of Holmes's *Common Law* (1963) is a good guide for the beginner, and Max Lerner's *The Mind and Faith of Justice Holmes* (1943), an anthology of selections from Holmes's speeches, essays, and letters, as well as from the *Common Law*, contains a running commentary on Holmes's writings that will be helpful for the student. Julius J. Marke, *The Holmes Reader* (1955), is a good paperbound collection, but the student will also want to consult *Speeches by Oliver Wendell Holmes* (1913) and some of the essays in Holmes's *Collected Legal Papers* (1920). Mark De Wolfe Howe lived to complete two volumes of his definitive study of Holmes's life and thought: *Justice Oliver Wendell Holmes: The Shaping Years, 1841–1870* (1957) and *Justice Oliver Wendell Holmes: The Providing Years, 1870–1882* (1963). Shorter biographies are

Catherine Drinker Bowen, *Yankee from Olympus* (1943), Silas Bent, *Justice Oliver Wendell Holmes* (1932), and Francis Biddle, Jr., *Justice Holmes* (1942). For analyses of Holmes's thought, see Dorsey Richardson, *Constitutional Doctrines of Justice Oliver Wendell Holmes* (1924), Samuel J. Konefsky, *The Legacy of Holmes and Brandeis, A Study in the Influence of Ideas* (1956), and Max Fisch, "Justice Holmes, The Prediction Theory of Law, and Pragmatism," *Journal of Philosophy,* 39 (1942): 85–97. Gabriel and Fine have chapters on laissez-faire and the law, and so do Edward R. Lewis, *A History of American Political Thought* (1937), and Charles E. Merriam, *American Political Ideas* (1920). The following examine the subject at length: Charles G. Haines, *The Revival of Natural Law Concepts* (1930), Benjamin R. Twiss, *Lawyers and the Constitution: How Laissez Faire Came to the Supreme Court* (1942), and Arnold M. Paul, *Conservative Crisis and the Rule of Law* (1960). Carl B. Swisher's *Stephen J. Field, Craftsman of the Law* (1930) is a standard biography.

In tackling Thorstein Veblen (Chapter 8), one begins with *Theory of the Leisure Class;* the Mentor paperbound edition (1953) is worth examining for C. Wright Mills's introductory essay. Most of Veblen's other books are also in soft-cover editions and Max Lerner's *The Portable Veblen* (1948), one of the Viking anthologies, is also now in paper. The student will find Joseph Dorfman, *Thorstein Veblen and His America* (1934), heavy going at times, but it is absolutely essential for Veblen's life, personality, and thought. Aaron, Madison, and White all have informative chapters on Veblen, but there have also been a number of detailed studies of his thought: Richard V. Teggert, *Thorstein Veblen, A Chapter in American Economic Thought* (1932), Wesley C. Mitchell, *What Veblen Taught* (1936), Stanley M. Daugert, *The Philosophy of Thorstein Veblen* (1950), David Riesman, *Thorstein Veblen, A Critical Interpretation* (1953), Bernard Rosenberg, *The Values of Veblen* (1956), Lev E. Dobriansky, *Veblenism: A New Critique* (1957), and Douglas Dowd, *Thorstein Veblen* (1964), one of the Great American Thinker Series.

Thomas F. Gossett, *Race, The History of An Idea in America* (1963), is a broad-scale study of racialism in American thought (Chapter 9) and deals with white attitudes toward Indians, Chinese, and immigrants as well as toward Negroes. W. J. Cash, *The Mind of the South* (1941), is a classic study of the Southern outlook, and Rayford W. Logan, *The Betrayal of the Negro* (1965), formerly entitled *The*

Negro in American Life and Thought: The Nadir, 1877–1901 (1954), presents a mine of information about white attitudes in all sections of the country. Kenneth Stampp, *The Era of Reconstruction, 1865–1877* (1966), is excellent on attitudes during Reconstruction, and C. Vann Woodward, *The Strange Career of Jim Crow* (rev. ed., 1966), is a fine book on the South and the Negro after Reconstruction. In an anthology entitled *Forgotten Voices: Dissenting Southerners in an Age of Conformity* (1967), Charles E. Wynes has assembled selections from Cable, Dudley, Watson, Blair, and other Southern whites concerned with the Negroes after the Civil War. August Meier, *Negro Thought in America, 1880–1915, Racial Ideologies in the Age of Booker T. Washington* (1963), is a detailed study of Negro views and Howard Brotz, ed., *Negro Social and Political Thought, 1850–1920* (1966), is a good collection of the writings of Douglass, Washington, Du Bois, and other Negro leaders. For attitudes toward immigrants, both John Higham, *Strangers in the Land: Patterns of American Nativism, 1860–1925* (1955), and Barbara M. Solomon, *Ancestors and Immigrants, A Changing New England Tradition* (1956), are of a high quality. Edward N. Saveth, *American Historians and European Immigrants* (1948), contains, *inter alia*, a good discussion of the Teutonic germ theory, and E. Digby Baltzell, *The Protestant Establishment, Aristocracy and Caste in America* (1964), has much to say about Anglo-Saxonism. For the thinking of American imperialists, the following should be examined: Julius Pratt, *The Expansionists of 1898* (1936), Albert K. Weinberg, *Manifest Destiny* (1936), Edward M. Burns, *The American Ideal of Mission* (1951), Frederick Merk, *Manifest Destiny and Mission in American History* (1963), Ernest R. May, *Imperial Democracy* (1961), and Richard Hofstadter, "Manifest Destiny and the Philippines," in Daniel Aaron, ed., *America in Crisis* (1952). Walter La Feber, *The New Empire, An Interpretation of American Expansion, 1860–1898* (1963), makes a convincing case for the economic basis of American foreign policy. For anti-imperialist thought, see William M. Armstrong, *E. L. Godkin and American Foreign Policy, 1865–1900* (1957), Robert L. Beisner, *Twelve against Empire: The Anti-Imperialists, 1898–1900* (1968), and two articles by Fred H. Harrington: "The Anti-Imperialist Movement in the United States," *Mississippi Valley Historical Review*, 22 (September 1935): 211–30, and "Literary Aspects of American Anti-Imperialism," *New England Quarterly*, 10 (December 1937): 650–67.

There is a superb study, as yet unpublished, of American religious and scientific thought at the turn of the century by Barbara L. McClung, "Science and Certainty at the Turn of the Century," master's thesis at Tulane University, 1965. For Henry Adams' outlook, *The Degradation of Democratic Dogma* (1911), with a long introduction by Brooks Adams, and *The Education of Henry Adams* (1918), as well as the Adams writings mentioned in Chapter 10, require careful study. Adams' letters should also be examined: W. C. Ford, ed., *Letters of Henry Adams* (2 vols., 1930–38), and Harold Dean Cater, *Henry Adams and His Friends, A Collection of His Unpublished Letters* (1947). Elizabeth Stevenson has compiled *A Henry Adams Reader* (1959) and written a good biography, *Henry Adams* (1955), but the definitive biographical study is by Ernest Samuels: *The Young Henry Adams* (1948), *Henry Adams, The Middle Years* (1958), and *Henry Adams, The Major Phase* (1964). Robert A. Hume, *Runaway Star, An Appreciation of Henry Adams* (1951), is an interesting short analysis, and William H. Jordy, *Henry Adams, Scientific Historian* (1952), and J. C. Levenson, *The Mind and Art of Henry Adams* (1957), are excellent studies of Adams' thought. Both Frederic C. Jaher, *Doubters and Dissenters: Cataclysmic Thought in America, 1885–1918* (1964), and Timothy Paul Donovan, *Henry Adams and Brooks Adams* (1961), analyze the historical philosophy of the two Adamses. For Brooks Adams, there are two good biographies: Thornton Anderson, *Brooks Adams, Constructive Conservative* (1959), and Arthur F. Beringause, *Brooks Adams* (1955).

Index

PRINTED IN U.S.A.

VERMONT COLLEGE
MONTPELIER, VERMONT

DATE DUE

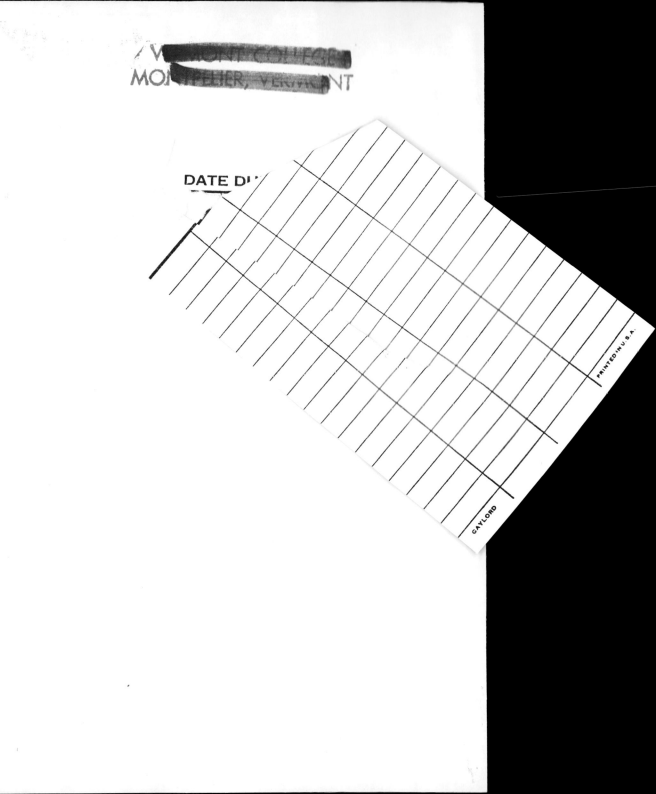

GAYLORD

PRINTED IN U.S.A.